ANCIENT
BIBLE
CONTEXT

ANDREW LEE SULLIVAN

The Purpose of the Book

I believe that Jesus Christ has anointed this little book. Soon, He shall return to slay the Antichrist. Learn how to wait upon the Lord and trust. Meanwhile, He prepares souls for the renewal of His Church. After Christ's indispensable intervention, a purified Church shall emerge. It shall irresistibly draw the world to the splendor of His truth and love. This humble book reflects God's provision to help bring a renewed Church back to the ancient Gospel. This hidden treasure in your hands beckons you to fall in love with the historical yet ever-present Jesus Christ. "Thy kingdom come. Thy will be done on earth as it is in heaven." (Matthew 6:10)

Perhaps Jesus may inspire you to help make this book known far and wide. If so, please contact me:

Andrew Lee Sullivan
P.O. Box 43012
Phoenix, Arizona 85080

CONTENTS

The Bible and Church Endure: After the Antichrist

After the waters receded and the ark settled in the mud, Noah and his family re-birthed humanity. Salvaging the fundamentals of their educational inheritance, with God's grace, they re-started human knowledge and culture. Noah's family rejected the bad and kept the good. We race toward a similar destiny. This book is meant for after a storm. Today, a battered Church and depraved world scramble to survive Satan's climactic confrontation against God. After that storm passes, this book shall come to light.

Our global flood, however will be different: not predominately water, but fire shall rage from the heavens. The earth shall groan with upheavals. Fear shall paralyze the whole world. An ocean of unrepentant souls shall perish and fall into hell forever. We are the prophesied generation that faces the False Prophet and the Antichrist of Saint John's Apocalypse. Most of the Church shall apostatize and worship Lucifer. A remnant shall take cover underground, be hunted down, and martyred. Purified saints shall emerge triumphant.

After its bloody ecclesial crucifixion and the victorious return of Jesus, the one Church founded by Christ, the Catholic Church, shall gloriously resurrect. Satan's veil of illusion shall be ripped away. Protestants, Muslims, Buddhists, Hindus, and every other kind of religion shall abandon their errors and flock to the Catholic Church. Baptisms shall wash over the world, and a period of peace shall be granted. At that time, Christ's ancient revelation shall be earnestly sought.

In the wake of that end-time hurricane, a re-generated Catholic world will hunger for the truth of ancient Christianity. After the catastrophic failure of fake history and demonically guided "Biblical scholarship," the one Church packed with billions of fresh converts shall yearn to rediscover the authentic origins of the Bible and Church. Consider this book in hand, a beginner's orientation for that purpose.

The following pages then journey back to ancient times to witness the birth of the Bible and the Catholic Church, and their inseparable, complementary relationship. This book is a primer on how the Bible and Church grew up together from the times when Jesus and the Apostles walked the earth. It's an introduction or an ABC book on the cultivation of the Bible by the Catholic Church.

In these pages, you will discover the basics of seeing scripture through the eyes of historical context. After diffusing the oral Gospel far and wide, six Apostles and two disciples, all Catholic bishops, wrote the New Testament. In AD 325, the Council of Nicaea combatted Arianism and had nothing to do with the canon of scripture nor the founding of the Catholic Church, at that time, already 292 years old. The context of Biblical development substantiates that Jesus Christ founded His one and only Church upon Saint Peter, the first Catholic Bishop of the City of Rome. The Catholic Church authoritatively set the seventy-three-book content of the complete Bible in AD 382.

Further, you will learn about the honored place of the Alexandrian Septuagint in the early Church, the sifting of ancient apocrypha, and the value and limits of Saint Jerome's scriptural translation into Latin. You'll discover the indispensable ancient liturgical context of scripture, the unbroken succession of papal authority, and its impact on the canon of scripture. Besides, the dubious nature of the Muratorian Fragment and the mistaken scriptural premises of Father Martin Luther both find a place in this book. From a historical and theological perspective, the imminent Great Apostasy of the Catholic Church is included.

From multiple perspectives, I am not qualified to write this book. From an educational viewpoint, I'm not a professor's likely choice to venture forth as I did. Academically, I have standard BA degrees in philosophy and theology from the University of the Santa Croce in Rome, Italy, without specializations in scripture or ecclesiology. Although I am familiar with scripture as a believer, I lacked the robust habit of studying it. I knew just enough to be ordained a Catholic priest and set aside for the unrelated purpose of fundraising. I never received a pastoral assignment. During my seven years as a priest, I baptized one baby.

My fleeting priesthood left me unprepared to teach about the Bible. In summary, I survived as an emotionally retarded person in a rogue religious community that functioned as a cult. For years, this plunged me into despair, with suicidal tendencies. Jesus then rescued me and gave me the gift of intimate prayer, causing me to grow beyond my burdensome emotional immaturity. This prayer also opened my eyes to the toxic environment where I lived. Having grown courageous in Christ, I fled to the Vatican with eighty-nine pages of sworn testimony to report my situation. Having been recruited into the group by deceit, and advanced in commitments by ignorance and coercion, I voluntarily requested a laicization from Pope Benedict XVI, which was speedily granted in AD 2008. I subsequently moved on and wrote my memoir: *Vatican Intervention.*

I had been profoundly traumatized in the Catholic Church. Many who suffer from similar calamities leave the Church and lose their faith. But Jesus's mercy fell upon me! The gift of prayer healed me and filled my soul with love. I then married, welcomed two baby boys, and accepted a job as a hospice chaplain. There's nothing like suffering to grace the heart with compassion. So, this was God's job for me, filling my days and on-call nights with comforting the dying and the recently bereaved. These last three paragraphs demonstrate my inaptness to author a scholarly exposition of the Bible.

Yet, the treasure of this book flows neither from my average education nor my broken life experience. I don't deny that these parts of me had an influence, but prayer made this book appear above all else. I only dared to write because Jesus asked. There's no way on earth that I'd disobey. I'm in love with Jesus, and he wanted this book for his own purposes. He cares little if the instrument is not suitable. Such judgments make little difference to God.

After thirteen years of hospice work, during my morning prayer, I casually turned to Jesus and asked if I should finally leave hospice. I saw his familiar face and glistening eyes and felt the warmth of his presence. Shockingly, he turned to me and said, "Yes, Andy, it is time to leave. I have a mission for you." He knew my disposition. I was ready to stay or leave. It made no difference. I was willing to do anything for him, with him. That happened a year ago as I write this introduction.

I was so sure of his word that morning that I resigned that day. He reassured me that if I abandoned myself to his interests, affairs, and service, he would take care of my family. In faith, I accepted the invitation and sent in my notice with no provision for the future. I had little idea what I was called to do, but I knew he wanted me to walk by faith. My wife believed in my relationship with Jesus.

Shortly thereafter, with my wife out of work, I lost a decent salary, the company car, and our family health insurance. Life became very different. I was not certain what Jesus wanted, except for my trust. Without income, we lived on our quickly dwindling life savings. We learned how to do without. We only bought the absolute essentials. Haircuts took place at home. We learned how to pick up donated food at city pantries. When our television broke, we had no money to fix it. I missed the nice little extras we used to buy. No more eating out. We figured out how to drive less and save on gas. Our diet changed, dropping down a notch in quality. There would be a human cost to bring about what God had in mind.

Jesus then spoke to me again during my prayer one morning. He said, "Write. Andy, I want you to write." I was certainly willing, but about what? So, I asked. He responded, "Write about the Bible." I said, "Really? What do I know about the Bible?" We both laughed. But he insisted.

The absolute awareness of his desire filled me. So, after prayers that morning, I sat before a newly created Word Document on the screen and asked Jesus to write what he wanted. With his hand resting upon me, I felt his presence behind my right shoulder. I wrote the first urge I felt: "God is the primary author of scripture." I didn't know what I was doing or where I was going.

This suggests a methodology that guided my writing. Without intricate planning or outlining, I simply rose every morning around 3:00 a.m. and prayed for an hour. Inspirations emerged from conversations between Jesus and me. The themes, titles, chapters, sections, and content appeared as spontaneous intuitions of prayer. Whenever I got stuck, I prayed more: twenty minutes, forty minutes, or another hour. New direction or insight would blossom. These intuitions and insights often pulled me into research, pushed forward by prayer. I often knew that God was producing exactly what he wanted, as the ideas often seemed so foreign to me that they didn't originate in my head. I'd read them and cry, knowing that Jesus was leading.

I suggest that the reader advance chapter by chapter in the order presented. Each chapter builds on the prior. May prayer be part of your learning. As Jesus Christ gifted the book through faith and prayer, it seems that by faith and prayer, you are meant to receive the Master's giving.

CHAPTER ONE

New Testament Beginnings

Divine Authorship

The Bible is a collection of little books and letters written by God's inspiration through human writers. As such, God is the primary author of the Bible, while devout men are secondary, instrumental authors.

Consider when a person writes a letter. It's the person who writes, not the pen in hand. Similarly, God wrote the Bible, but through freely cooperating human instruments. These holy men wrote by the inspiration and urging of the Holy Spirit, even though their distinct personalities reflected in diverse ways of expression.

A bit more can be gleaned from this author and pen analogy. When an author writes, it's his ideas that are communicated, not the ideas of the instrument of the writing process. The pen does not independently write, nor does the quill, nor the typewriter, nor Microsoft Word. Regarding the Bible, the divine author was God himself. He inspired the truth to be written.

But he left it to the different authors to write, each in his personal style. It's noticeable that Matthew's manner of expression differs from John's or Paul's. But above all else, all three wrote what God inspired to be written.

For instance, when Matthew wrote his Gospel, God stirred up and impelled him to write. God moved him interiorly to conceive in his mind exactly what He intended to reveal.

Working through Matthew's inner faculties, God assured that His infallible, revealed truth was recorded, with neither the slightest subtraction nor addition apart from the divine will. Accordingly, when you read the Bible, you read what is revealed from God's mind, yet through the help of an "instrumental human author."

When a writer is employed as an instrumental cause by God, human imperfections and frailties are not miraculously suspended. The message and meaning placed in the mind are not the author's, but God's. Then the writer is allowed to exercise his unique writing modality. As such, divinely inspired writing is not divine dictation.

Whenever instrumental causality is at work, there are effects from both the primary and instrumental causes. As the Bible is inspired, God's written revealed truth is the primary effect. The human author's way of writing is the secondary effect.

Modern scriptural scholars sometimes forget these most basic points about the Bible. Like weak-believing scientists, many scholars launch into great amounts of human analysis of this or that sacred page and end up questioning and doubting everything. A childlike faith is needed to believe in God's authorship of the Bible. Personal surrender was part of writing the Bible; personal surrender is part of reading it.

Human Writers

Focusing on the New Testament, everything was likely written during the window of time between Pentecost and AD 70. The writing didn't start until around AD 40, seven years after Jesus ascended to heaven and the Holy Spirit descended at Pentecost. Imagine that: seven years of an infant Church without even the first word of the New Testament etched on papyrus.

Reflect on the three thousand persons Peter converted in AD 33, on Pentecost. (Acts 2:14-47) If each convert averaged thirty years of age, and the Gospels were likely written between AD 40 and AD 62, most of these converts would have experienced a written Gospel, perhaps within seven to twenty-seven years following Pentecost. The written Gospels grew out of the oral Gospels.

(Note: The approximated completion dates of the Gospels are: Matthew, AD 40 – AD 60; John, AD 40 – AD 65; Mark AD 45 – AD 60; Luke, AD 57 – AD 62. (See Chapter Fourteen for further details.) That chapter is dedicated to the dating of the New Testament.)

These early converts neither owned nor read a New Testament. They received the Gospel orally, in its primitive and raw form. They were not even called "Christians" yet. That would come roughly seven years down the road, as a pejorative term. (Acts 11:26) So, without the New Testament in hand, what set apart these converts as Christ's own? We're talking of the pure, pre-denominational days of Christianity. Today there are forty thousand denominations. That day, there was just one newborn Church. Peter's appeal was to repent, be baptized, and receive the Holy Spirit. The converts devoted themselves to the Breaking of the Bread, prayer, learning from the Apostles, and communal life –without the New Testament yet written.

Eight human authors contributed to writing the New Testament. Six were Apostles: Matthew, John, Peter, James, Jude, and Paul. The two others were Mark and Luke, immediate disciples of Jesus and close colleagues of the Apostles. Except for Matthew, they originally wrote in Greek, the common language of the ancient world at that time. Yet, some argue that the original language of the New Testament was Aramaic, Jesus's and his Apostles' native tongue. However, the arguments favor Greek originals. They preached in Greek, so wrote in Greek.

The New Testament consists of twenty-seven thin booklets. There are the four Gospels of Matthew, Mark, Luke, and John; the Acts of the Apostles recounting the early life of the Church; various letters oriented toward teaching the faith to new Christian communities mostly authored by Paul, the most educated of the Apostles; and John's book of the *Apokalypsis*, Greek for "revelation."

According to the day's custom, the New Testament books were written by hand on papyrus, a material like thick paper made from the pith of the papyrus plant. The "ink" was a mixture of charcoal, oil, and plant gum. This substance adhered well to the matted and dried fibrous papyrus.

Throughout the writing process, a finely split reed or bone was repeatedly dipped into the "ink" and employed like a pen. The papyrus and "ink" produced a durable product that might last a few decades. If attached to a scroll and stored in a jar in a consistently dry atmosphere, the written product could last much longer. (Note: The Dead Sea scrolls discovered in AD 1946 in protective jars in the dry Qumran Caves date back to the time of Christ and even earlier.)

Technically speaking, writing a manuscript at that time was a considerable effort. The task required an education in writing, a steady and artful hand, and great patience and focus. There was no room for errors, no possibility of erasing or deleting. We cheat in our modern way of writing: cutting, pasting, editing, deleting, replacing words, adding, and re-editing until we settle upon the perfect printout. Not so, back then.

Above all else, God required holy men for this task, souls attuned to the ways of his inner promptings. The writing of the New Testament was a special work of God's. He called and gifted chosen men for this monumental divine work that would impress upon mankind forever.

The Primacy of Christ's Oral Gospel

Underlining the vocation of the New Testament writers, consider that Jesus did not bequeath anything written by His hand. He preached, leaving the writing for others years later. Neither did he instruct his Apostles nor Disciples to write. These were sent to preach. Jesus did not say: "Go forth and write."

He decidedly chose not to be memorialized as a great author. He could have, but it would have distracted Him from His paramount mission to save the world from sin by his death and resurrection. Others could teach and write; only the divine person of the Son of God could redeem! He had something more important to accomplish. Our salvation! He left the design and authority of written memories and commentaries in the hands of His Church. He lived the story. The Church would tell it.

A little context goes a long way here. The Apostles and Disciples spread throughout a world that hovered at a 3% literacy rate. It was less in rural areas, more in cities, perhaps up to 20% in places like Antioch, Alexandria, and Rome. Most early converts could not read; only a fraction could write. The emphasis on the oral preaching of the Gospel made perfect sense. It was practically human.

But the oral Gospel was more so, thunderously divine! The oral Gospel was not merely a practical matter, either then or now. By its pronounced words into the world, it empowers with divine efficacy. Vocalized words have energy behind them to effect change. God's spoken words more so. The oral Gospel, repeating the words of Jesus Christ, penetrates souls and bodies and brings about new realities. Repentance. Healing. Miracles of all kinds! "Then God said, 'Let there be light,' and there was light." (Genesis 1:3) What God says, happens!

Scriptural instances abound: "'Lord, if it is you, command me to come to you on the water.' He said, 'Come.' Peter got out of the boat and began to walk on the water toward Jesus." Just a single word pronounced by God!

Back to practical considerations. In sober terms, imagine you're an Apostle arriving at a village to preach. Further, imagine it's a rural area with a 3% literacy rate. You remember how Jesus connected with such listeners with simplicity, authority, and parables. Perhaps five hundred people in a village square gather to listen. A 3% literacy rate would mean that fifteen people could read. Half of the fifteen could write. Most educated people probably were Pharisees, cynically hovering in the back. Consequentially, written materials would be memorized and spoken, or read out loud. The Apostles preached accordingly.

"Go into all the world and preach…." (Mark 16:15) "And he ordered us to preach to the people…." (Acts 10:42) "…How are they to believe in him of whom they have never heard? And how are they to hear without someone preaching?" (Romans 10:14-15) "Faith comes from hearing, and hearing through the word of Christ." (Romans 10:17) Through the seal of Pentecost, Jesus commissioned ferocious preachers on fire with God's love and embodied with divine wisdom to fearlessly persuade conversions.

Village by village, the primitive Christian communities lacked properties and buildings. They could barely find acceptance at the synagogues. So, they congregated in their own houses to listen to the oral Gospel and pray. They did not meet for "Bible studies," yet certainly pondered ancient Old Testament texts read to them or partially memorized at synagogues. They listened to preachers who came with perhaps a few written resources to share orally. Maybe a group of households could make a copy of a letter from Paul, for instance, before the traveling preacher would move on with his cherished personal copy still in hand.

The early pieces (books) of the New Testament then were employed as pastoral tools in the hands of the preachers (Apostles or Disciples) moving from town to town. The Church rapidly expanded, and the preachers were few to tackle a vast terrain.

In this Christian environment of growth and expansion, the early writings filled an exceedingly practical purpose: the message of Christ could either be left behind or sent ahead where the preachers targeted. More so, the Gospels and letters filled the need to nurture a unified belief and address the issues characteristic of each developing community, especially at the weekly gathering of "Breaking Bread."

The pieces of the New Testament appeared progressively. One community might receive a copy of the Gospel of Luke, while another might cherish its own copy of Paul's letter to the Romans. As such, the parts of the gradually forming New Testament were scattered far and wide according to needs and preaching opportunities. But copies somehow got around.

Then, communities copied what they had, and a circular sharing of writings ensued. Or, Paul would simply write a letter and have it delivered to a church community. Surely, a few Christians there were educated enough to read it to the group.

Apocrypha

As the "manuscript pillars" of the New Testament were progressively written and spread, a fresh flow of apocryphal writings emerged throughout the Christian communities. ("Apocrypha" derives from the Greek plural noun: *apokrypha,* meaning "things that are hidden or secret.") Such writings came to be widely circulated, valued, and used by preachers. Along with the Gospels and Paul's letters, for instance, these other writings were frequently initially assumed to be authentic, especially at the beginning of their circulation.

As time advanced, numerous Gospels flourished far and wide, besides those of Matthew, Mark, Luke, and John. There were the Gospels of Philip, Thomas, Egerton, James, Nicodemus, Thaddaeus, and Peter. A Gospel, according to the Hebrews, appeared. There was also the Gospel of the Twelve and a Gospel that told the story of Jesus's infancy.

There were plenty more Acts and epistles, too. There were the Acts of Andrew, Paul, and Peter. There were additional letters from Paul to the Laodiceans and Alexandrians. There was even a letter from the Corinthians back to Paul. Then, there were the epistles of Barnabas, Clement, Ignatius, Polycarp, Abgar, and more.

Besides John's Apocalypse, there were also the Apocalypses of Adam and Peter. A Christian vision by a former slave circulated, too, called "The Shepherd of Hermas." There was also the famous Didache, entitled: "The Lord's Instruction to the Gentiles through the Twelve Apostles." This was a wonderful, simple summary with a spelled-out moral code of how a Christian should live. It was written at the same time the New Testament was written, probably around AD 40 – 60. Christians held it in high esteem, but the specific author remained unclear.

This surge of Christian writings was a mixed blessing. It provided many occasions for learning and spiritual growth. But the gradual swell of shared writings soon beckoned for scrutiny. Indeed, not everything in writing could possibly be valued with the same degree of usefulness, authority, and validity.

As years advanced, the need to sift through a vast variety of early writings and identify God's genuine inspiration became indispensable for a universal belief, practice, moral code, and way of prayer. The genuinely divine writings had to be separated from the respected, useful, or dubious.

Consider that "non-scriptural" writings came to be viewed as such after many years of discussions among wise and spiritually mature shepherds of souls seeking to feed their flocks with the true word of God. Less worthy writings came to be known as apocrypha after hindsight, prayer, the judging of origins and fruits, and discernment.

Whenever Paul signed his name to a pastoral letter, for instance, no miraculous sign distinguished the letter as scripture, old or new. There were plenty of holy and beautiful letters whirling about. Yet, this does not mean that Paul's letters were not extraordinarily valued as treasures in hand.

His letters were immediately guarded as something special for the Christian communities that cherished them. At that time, Paul's letters were not yet authoritatively and universally categorized as divine writings equal to the Old Testament scriptures.

The Twenty-seven Book New Testament

After many years of discernment, the Twenty-seven books of the divinely inspired writings finally settled and listed together. Athanasius was the first prominent pastor of a great flock (the Bishop of Alexandria, Egypt) to pronounce the twenty-seven-book canon precisely as we know it today.

(Note: The term "canon" connotes a "list." The term "canonization" refers to a "formal listing." These terms are frequently used when describing the official, collective list of books that comprise scripture, either the Old Testament or New Testament.)

Athanasius built upon a historic string of men who almost had it right, most immediately referencing Origen, a prominent Christian scholar. After considerable travels and research, Origen's list included the four Gospels, the Pauline letters, Acts, the Apocalypse, I Peter, and I John.

Additionally, Origen asserted his personal belief that some contested writings were, certainly, divinely inspired, too. These included Hebrews, II Peter, II and III John, James, Jude, Barnabas, the Shepherd of Hermas, and the Didache.

Athanasius removed Barnabas, the Shepherd of Hermas, and the Didache. Even so, he held that the "Shepherd of Hermas" may be read along with the Didache but added that these writings were distinctly not part of his list of inspired writings. All other writings, he held, should henceforth be considered apocrypha and no longer formally used by church communities. Athanasius's list included John's Apocalypse, often excluded in many prior lists.

At last, Athanasius's list included the following: The Gospels of Matthew, Mark, Luke, and John; The Acts of the Apostles; The Letter to the Romans; The First and Second Letters to the Corinthians; The Letter to the Galatians; The Letter to the Ephesians; The Letter to the Philippians; The Letter to the Colossians; The First and Second Letters to the Thessalonians; The First and Second Letters to Timothy; The Letter to Titus; the Letter to Philemon; Hebrews; The Letter of James; The First and Second Letters of Peter; The First, Second, and Third Letters of John; The Letter of Jude; and The Book of Apocalypse by John.

This first-time, definitive list was asserted with strength in AD 367. Today, 1,656 years later, the Catholic and Christian world of Two and a half billion believers (with a few exceptions) continues to embrace this same twenty-seven-book list as the official New Testament.

Canonization: A Gradual Process

Noting AD 70 to AD 382 (the time frame when the canonization of the New Testament was completed), why did it take three hundred and twelve years to arrive at the universally proclaimed twenty-seven-book list that delineated the New Testament?

A humble acknowledgment of history is the first step to illuminate this brainteasing question. Today, we feel that finalizing the official canon of scripture was too important to have taken so long to formalize universally. I agree. I feel the same way!

But it's neither theology nor prejudicial presumptions of history that offer an answer. Critical, historical context explains the arduous nature of the long journey.

Four widespread historical overlays of the post-Apostolic era caused the canonization of the New Testament to creep along like a turtle. The first overlay was the culture of a neophyte Church oriented toward expansion and local problem-solving. The second was the ever-flowing avalanche of apocryphal writings: the inspired, good, useful, faulty, and dubious circulating together. The third overlay was, of course, the intermittent Roman persecutions of the Christians. The fourth was the cancerous spread of heresies that demanded the immediate time and attention of the early Church.

These four challenges of early Christian life progressively crept side by side. They soon dynamically intertwined and characterized a complex superimposition of various issues that competed for Christianity's focus.

For instance, if one Christian community had difficulties with questionable customs and writings, another focused on surviving persecutions, and still another concentrated on rooting out heretical tendencies. An awful lot was happening throughout the entire Mediterranean and beyond, where Christians mushroomed everywhere. These were Church growing pains.

CHAPTER TWO

Ancient Church Discernment

The Rapid Proliferation of Christianity

Let's consider the first of these four unavoidable obstacles to a speedy, universal formalization of the New Testament canon. History shows an aggressive proliferation of Christian communities. Resolutely obeying the commission of Christ, the Apostles, and Disciples burst upon the world with great expansive power. Keenly aware of their mission, they ventured to modern-day Syria, Armenia, Lebanon, Iran, Turkey, Iraq, Egypt, Ethiopia, Tunisia, Afghanistan, India, Greece, Italy, India, Spain, Romania, Ukraine, Britain, and Ireland.

Nothing held them back —except martyrdom, where each Apostle welcomed his glorious appointment of perfect testimony. These were real men, filled to the brim with the explosive fire of the Holy Spirit!

(Note: John's end is an exception to martyrdom. Yet, the Romans did place him in a vat of boiling oil as a punishment for preaching the Gospel. Having failed to harm him, they exiled him to Patmos, a rocky island off the western coast of modern-day Turkey. Jesus, no doubt, had destined John for the extraordinary task of creating the *Apokalypsis*.)

The whirlwind of ventures to the frontiers of the known world bequeathed a fast-moving, pervasive spread of Christianity. Simultaneously, the far-reaching diffusion of the faith left scattered communities of believers primitively structured, isolated, diverse in needs and customs, and self-reliant to resolve faith-related issues locally.

Paul's letters and John's addressing of various churches in his Apocalypse hint at the diverse needs of Christian communities. The letters very much focused on the particularities of local churches, yet once shared from region to region, everyone benefited.

After baptizing a fresh, local church of converts, time was devoted to teaching the doctrines and morals of the Christian way of life. Perhaps a newly founded region might have hundreds of scattered households of believers from village to village. Everyone met at a home every Sunday for the "Breaking of Bread."

Like the structure of the Passover celebration, this custom included recounting Old Testament scriptures before the sacred meal ensued. Eventually, various Gospels and Paul's letters were shared, too, as they trickled throughout the Roman empire. Powerful preaching tied everything together. At times, baptisms were included. An orientation to further spread the Gospel was infused –an integral part of the revelation of Jesus Christ.

Early Church Organizational Structure

When the founder of a particular community finally moved on, mature believers were sensibly appointed to carry on –as replacement leaders for the local church. The New Testament sketches a few passing references that touch upon this provisional, organizational Church development.

The Greek New Testament mentions the role of an appointed *presbuteros* (the Greek term for "elder." The term connotes more than age but a seasoned man of mature judgment.) Such were the assigned spiritual leaders that belonged to any new local church community. (James 5:14; I Peter 5:1; I Timothy 5:17) By way of the later Latin translation of *presbyter,* the English term "priest" derives.

The Greek New Testament also indicates the role of the *episkopos*: (I Timothy 3:2; Acts 20:28; Philippians 1:1; Titus 1:5-7; I Peter 2:25). The Greek meaning of *episkopos* was a superintendent who exercised a supervising function, overseeing those under his care. It was a commonly used Greek word, not exclusively employed in a religious context.

In its scriptural context, however, this Greek word connoted an assigned "regional supervisor" who looked intently over an entire local church community. Further, this *episkopos* (singular) assigned his own *presbuteroi* (plural) and kept an eye on their ministries, an aspect of his many responsibilities.

(Note: In the New Testament, the Apostles and Disciples sometimes introduce these positions and terms in an overlapping manner, differentiating while still lacking precision. However, during the Apostolic age, the period immediately following the Apostles, the terms settled and were soon comfortably handled in a strict and exact manner within the Church.

This should not be surprising, as any developing, governing structure refines its titles, positions, and roles, especially at the initial stages of growth. Nurturing a fresh term, notice the initial care of the Apostles not to equate the *presbuteroi* with the priests of the Old Covenant, who were exclusively from the tribe of Levi. Christ initiated a brand-new priesthood rooted in himself.)

As the Apostles or Disciples either died or moved to another pagan horizon, a local *episkopos* was typically placed in charge. Through the later Latin translation of *episcopus*, the English term "bishop" derives.

Some concrete history may help: After leaving Israel, Peter went to Antioch, where he lived for seven years and became the first *episkopos* there. Antioch became the hub of Christianity, where the followers of Jesus Christ were first called Christians. (Acts: 11:26) When Peter moved to Rome, a replacement *episkopos* was left in charge at Antioch. His name was Evodius. The next *episkopos* was Ignatius of Antioch, and so forth.

Once in Rome, Peter became the first *episkopos* there, later replaced by Linus after Peter's martyrdom in Nero's Circus (an ancient race track once situated near present-day St. Peter's Square in Rome). A historic line of "replacement" *episkopi* (plural) continued. Cletus followed Linus, then Clement, then Evaristus. This latter *episkopos* assumed his responsibilities in AD 97, one year before John the Apostle died in AD 98.

Another example: Sometime before AD 57, the Apostle Paul made the Greek, Titus, the *episkopos* of the island of Crete. Titus then appointed *presbuteroi* beneath his supervision. The succession of bishops paved the way for an authoritative Church structure directly linked to the Apostles. Some describe this continuous replacement of bishops as the "Apostolic line of Succession."

In AD 110, Bishop Ignatius of Antioch reminds believers of the ancient Church structure of bishops, priests, and deacons. While captive and en route to Rome to be executed, he jotted a letter to the Christians of Smyrna, a Greek city on the eastern end of Turkey, on the Aegean coast. His reference highlights God's design in the Church structure itself, set in place by the Apostles: "Flee from schism as the source of mischief. You should all follow the bishop as Jesus Christ did the Father. Follow, too, the presbytery as you would the Apostles, and respect the deacons, as you would God's law." (Ignatius of Antioch, Letter to the Smyrnaeans, chapter VIII)

Not long after this letter, part of the glorious testimony of his life, Ignatius stood in chains before Emperor Trajan in Rome. Ignatius was condemned on the spot for defiantly declaring the Roman gods to be evil spirits and demons. During his trial, Ignatius testified too that Jesus Christ truly lived within him. Emperor Trajan promptly sent the man to his death, mockingly quipping to a nearby scribe: "These Christians are insane! He's going to be torn to pieces by a lion, and he's happy." In his 70's, Ignatius was soon attacked and eaten by lions in Rome's Colosseum, where eighty-seven thousand Romans applauded.

Bishops' Discernment of Christian Writings

The rapid and vast diffusion of the oral Gospel and the role of the *episkopos* are vital to understanding how ancient believers approached the use of early Christian writings. With Christian communities extended far and wide, each with its appointed *episkopos*, the available writings for local church use were primarily subject to the discernment of the local *episkopos*.

He was ultimately responsible for feeding his flock with the true revelation of Christ. Undoubtedly, the Old Testament Septuagint was publicly read as a standard practice. Regarding newer writings, he exercised his judgment, but not independent of advice and instructions from highly respected Church leaders, whenever opportunities for consultation allowed. A letter from Paul, however, would have been an immediate no-brainer to share and promote, assuming it manifested authenticity.

As time advanced, the standard Gospels and Paul's letters came to be readily perceived as divinely inspired and freely used in home-church services. From locality to locality throughout the Roman Empire, there were often other acceptable writings esteemed and used here or there. Some writings seemed authentic but were less useful. Other writings felt suspicious.

Although this manner of discerning Christian writings sometimes fell short of certainty, it adequately fit the spontaneous needs of the local communities during those early years of Church growth. The diffusion of Christian communities and accompaniment of Christian writings advanced so fast that the appointment of discerning "overseers" made plenty of practical sense.

At this moment in history, the Church was shepherded by holy men. They genuinely cared for their flocks and would readily die for them if needed. Many of them did. They bravely fought errors and announced the truth, regardless of the consequences. They were in love with Jesus Christ, who worked through them in full force. Rules were carved in hearts, less so scribbled on papyrus.

CHAPTER THREE

Marcion

Marcion the Heretic

The earliest attempt to make a universal list of the inspired books of the Bible was a veritable disaster. This is because it was done by an industrious heretic. Marcion was the son of an *episkopos,* and a well-off shipowner. He had a persuasive personality and sharpened organizational skills. Hence, Marcion was able to attract and manage a decent number of followers.

Marcion was a heretic. What's that? A heretic is someone who obstinately denies or rejects a divinely revealed truth of the faith. For instance, a baptized Christian who defiantly affirms that Jesus Christ never resurrected, or who teaches there's no such thing as the Blessed Trinity, or who holds firm that adultery is not a sin but a virtue –is a heretic.

In the summer of AD 144, Marcion was brought before a gathering of *presbuteroi* in Rome and asked to explain his beliefs and teachings. Representatives of the Church wanted to hear for themselves what Marcion taught and offer him a chance to humbly correct himself. After hearing what he firmly held, Marcion was promptly declared a heretic and removed from the Church.

Marcion could not comprehend how Yahweh of the Old Covenant could be the same God of the New Testament. The tyrannical, creator-god of the Jews who approved the stoning of adulterous women and commanded the complete wiping out of nations by the sword could not possibly be the same loving and merciful God revealed in Jesus Christ. Finding a reconciliation of the two very different Gods impossible, Marcion abandoned monotheism (belief in one God) and embraced dualism (belief in two gods).

Marcion accordingly maintained that Christianity's break with the old covenant had to be absolute. The Old Testament's cruel and vengeful God, the Mosaic law, and every element of Judaism had to be entirely rejected. Christianity should not be tainted and corrupted by anything Jewish. The Gospel of Christ completely superseded the Torah, and the break with the old had to be uncompromising.

Marcion's Canon

Such conclusive beliefs impelled Marcion to shape a list of divinely inspired writings that complemented his convictions. Delimiting his "Bible," Marcion threw out the entire Old Testament. Nothing was divinely inspired there! After looking closely at the newer writings used in churches, he only kept the bare minimum.

Marcion's "New Testament" included only ten clearly authored letters from Paul and the Gospel of Paul's trusted companion, Luke. Even so, this Gospel was purged of content that referred to Jesus as Jewish. For example, Luke's infancy narrative had to be thrown out because of its explicit Jewishness. Marcion's canon of scripture then included eleven books: Ten Pauline letters and one radically edited Gospel. That's a disaster of a Bible!

Yet, God typically draws good out of evil. The Church reacted to Marcion's radicality. Marcion's canon unexpectedly influenced local churches to confirm a core canon of the four standard Gospels and the totality of Paul's letters. Of course, this was already the trend, but Marcion's canon fiasco helped cement the common practice more firmly.

In hindsight, Marcion's canon does highlight an important theological principle. The inclusion, exclusion, or editing of the Bible should not be according to subjective, personal beliefs. God's objective revelation comes first. Our role is to humbly receive his revelation, not shape it to suit our feelings.

CHAPTER FOUR

Discussions and Canons:
AD 200 – AD 367

Historical Stages of Canonization

The long Church journey to delimit a Twenty-seven-book New Testament could be divided into three historic periods:

The first would be a writing period from AD 40 to AD 70. During this period, the monumental-inspired writings were produced. Overlapping this same period and extending to AD 200, apocryphal writings appeared. Alongside the inspired writings, the apocryphal writings circulated far and wide. Each local church developed a straightforward and *ad hoc* manner of distinguishing between the good and bad. During these years, the primary focus of each bishop was to ensure that his flock only followed the true revelation of Jesus Christ passed on through the Apostles.

The second period can be reduced to a long stretch of "next level" discussions that progressively envisioned a confirmed, authoritative, and universal list of declared inspired writings. This took place between AD 200 and AD 367. Organically growing beyond single bishops discerning locally, bishops and scholars proceeded toward a comprehensive examination and sifting of all known Christian writings. The hunt for a universal list had begun. As heresies spread everywhere, the value of an authoritative and universal list became more vital.

Following Athanasius's climactic list in AD 367, a brief third historic period finally solidified the twenty-seven-book New Testament. Although the list had been authoritatively resolved in the preeminently Christian city of Alexandria by Bishop Athanasius, it still needed time to take on an absolute, universal, and immovable character.

Nonetheless, the proclamation of Athanasius was significant because his thundering voice represented great orthodox influence. He was a chief *episkopos,* a veritable "intellectual warrior" against the pervasive heresy of Arianism. This heresy, hatched by a *presbuteros* in his diocese in Alexandria, claimed that Jesus Christ was not divine. Athanasius shouldered the responsibility to beat down this error that invaded the body of Christ like an aggressive cancer.

Taking place from AD 367 to AD 419, some describe this completion period as a historical moment of "fixation." During these fifty-two years, multiple groups of bishops in a council and several synods authoritatively confirmed and re-confirmed the twenty-seven-book list of the New Testament, establishing its "institutionalized" place in Christianity.

(Note: The terms "council" and "synod" are used here. Both are large gatherings of bishops at a single location to hash through matters of importance and urgency for the Church. Usually, a doctrinal matter is discussed at length, with subsequent documents of clarification ensuing. A council has an international character focused on a global concern; a synod has a regional character limited in scope.)

Criteria for Setting the Canon

Now, we'll take a step back from this timeline overview and focus on the discussion period of AD 200-AD 367. During this time, the books and loose scraps of Christian writings were gathered, compared, and sifted. A search was made to identify only the divinely inspired writings the Church could rely upon as God's revealed word. Various canons (lists) were proposed throughout these years.

But what criteria were used to decide which books to include or exclude? Eventually, the following three criteria emerged:

First, the book or letter must be either from an Apostle or a close associate of an Apostle. Matthew and John met this criterion. Luke was a Disciple and colleague of Paul's. He had received his Christian education from Apostles and Disciples who knew Jesus intimately and were personal eyewitnesses of him. Mark was a close colleague of Peter's. As a Disciple, Mark's Gospel reflected a type of memoir from Peter.

Second, the writing in question must have a history of universal usage back to apostolic times. This would include a universal character not only back to apostolic days but also in widespread use. For example, it would be enough for a written source to be excluded that only circulated in Syria or Africa or to have been known only from AD 120 onwards. Further, if a writing lacked any history of liturgical use, this would be enough to fall short of this criterion for inclusion.

Third, the theology in the writing must consist of what Jesus taught and the ancient Church's beliefs and practices. In particular, the Book of Hebrews so strongly represented this criterion that it was eventually included in the canon. But it had appeared excluded or included in various canons for a while. Hebrews was either written by Paul or a colleague of Paul's. Its orthodoxy represented an ancient, clear, profound, and precise body of teachings of Jesus and the Apostles.

Categories of Early Christian Writings

As the sifting years advanced, the various writings eventually settled into three distinct categories. The first was commonly held inspired writings. The core of these was represented by the standard Gospels of Matthew, Mark, Luke, John, and Paul's letters. Some fluctuations existed beyond that, for instance, in the letters of Peter, John, James, and Jude. Some canons included or excluded Acts, Hebrews, or John's Apocalypse.

The second category was acceptable and even encouraged apocrypha that fell short of the strict criteria of ancient, divine inspiration. Careful discernment separated apocrypha. Not all apocryphon was considered equal.

The "good apocrypha" was recognized as useful, instructive, valuable, and trusted but separated from divinely inspired writings. As such, it fell short of canonical inclusion for liturgical use. At the same time, familiarity with such writings was recognized as offering value outside of liturgical use.

Examples of this second category of Christian writings include I Clement, the Letter of Barnabas, the letters of Bishop Ignatius of Antioch, the Letters of Polycarp, the Shepherd of Hermas, and the Didache.

The third category was dubious apocrypha, which should be held at a distance and not used at all. This was the batch of phony stuff. There were too many doubts and questions regarding true authorship and genuine content. Examples might be the Gospels of Mary, Thomas, and Philip; the Gospel According to the Hebrews; the Acts of Paul; and many other lesser-known writings.

Up front, it might seem that anything that had an Apostle's name attached should be included in the official New Testament canon. But various Gospels had the hallmarks of doubt. Some simply abbreviated and resembled the canonical Gospels; others told pious stories that were entirely unverifiable; others merely lifted the name of an Apostle to promulgate questionable doctrines.

For instance, the Gospel of Thomas did not circulate until far past the death of Thomas. Somebody just used the name to gain reading traction, it seemed. It was simply a list of one hundred and four quotes out of context, surrounding the life of Christ. Many sayings were clearly "borrowed" from the canonical Gospels. Many more were rehashed episodes found in the canonical Gospels but freely embellished with stretched details. Some entries included gnostic philosophy implied or inferred in the texts.

CHAPTER FIVE

Origen: AD 185 – AD 254

Origen: A Christian Speculative Theologian

Origen was a devoted Christian, even if his theology was not consistently perfect. He took his faith seriously. When he was a young man, he discerned a personal call to follow Christ in a radical manner. Based on the words of Jesus Christ taken literally, Origen removed his testicles with his own hand. "There are those who have made themselves eunuchs for the kingdom of heaven's sake." (Matthew 19:12) He tried to conceal the fact, but it eventually became known. The man was determined to follow Jesus Christ, no matter the cost.

Although rash and mistaken, yet pious in his youth, Origen rocketed to the heights of intellectual adulthood. He was a prolific writer of six thousand works in theology, apologetics, and homiletics. Besides everything Christian, he studied the great philosophers, too. This served him well as the head of the great catechetical school in Alexandria, which welcomed pagans who inquired about Christianity. Origen knew every argument of the unbeliever and enjoyed a profound grasp of the Christian faith.

Origen tended toward orthodox teaching, adhering to the long-held truths of the faith. He insisted on following Christ, genuinely known by what the Apostles taught and practiced. As such, our ideas and beliefs should be subjected to the faith of apostolic times. Contemporaries had great respect for Origen, and his influence was vast.

Yet, he had speculated and said some things in such a way as to raise eyebrows. Especially after his death, some accused him of heresy. But he was never formally charged with heresy while alive. Perhaps he was given some space for academic freedom of some kind; I don't really know, and it's hard to determine. But Origen did live with a deferential disposition toward Church authority while teaching the faith. Significantly, he never fermented a heretical movement empowered by his personal speculations.

Some accused him of adulterating the Gospel with pagan philosophy. Others accused Origen of suggesting the inferiority of the Son to the Father, paving the road to Arianism. A few of his speculations entertained doubts about bodily resurrection and the existence of eternal hell. Somehow, he thought that perhaps after a great length of time in hell, all would be restituted, and the eternity of hell would not really happen.

Despite these erroneous teachings, Christian history tends to remember Origen more favorably than otherwise. Unfortunately, either an orthodox or unorthodox theologian today could cite Origen to support either genuine Christian doctrine or innovative heresy.

Origen's Canon

Although Origen was not a bishop and did not declare a Biblical canon for his own diocese, he was nonetheless the first great Christian scholar. Many subsequent pastors and intellectuals would look back to Origen as a significant theological reference. Future bishops would be influenced by Origen's canonical ideas. It's instructive then to glance at his distinctions regarding the scriptural canon.

Origen affirmed that the four standard Gospels, Acts, and Paul's fourteen letters were certainly divinely inspired, counting Hebrews as one of those letters. He held confidently that I John and I Peter were divinely inspired, too. Then, as a scholar might footnote, he listed other books attached with distinctions.

Origen personally believed that James, Jude, II John, III John, and II Peter were all divinely inspired but noted contestations or reservations by some. Along with these books, he added his personal view that Barnabas, the Didache, and the Shepherd of Hermas were divinely inspired just as well. The divine inspiration of John's Apocalypse was not entirely clear. At the end of his life, Origen reflected a bit and wrote that we really do not know who wrote the Book of Hebrews, but he believed that this would not alter its divine inspiration.

CHAPTER SIX

Eusebius: AD 260 – AD 341

Eusebius: Foremost Church Historian

Eusebius was the Bishop of Caesarea in Palestine. He was born, baptized, and instructed in the faith in Caesarea, Maritima ("by the sea"), an ancient Roman port on the Mediterranean coast of present-day Israel. This was the city where Pontius Pilate resided, and Peter baptized the first recorded gentile into Christianity. Early in life, Eusebius was ordained a priest here and pursued his interests, especially in scripture.

By the AD 290s, Eusebius dug into the hallmark academic work of his life, his *Ecclesiastical History*. It presented a comprehensive historical account of the Church from the apostolic age to his present day. Around the same time, he also produced the *Chronicle*. This laid out the major events of history from creation to his present day. These significant works were completed by AD 300.

There's an organic growth of the New Testament canon, preeminently traceable from Origen through Eusebius –to a culmination in the Festal Letter of Athanasius. Spanning a rough one hundred years, these three canons are developmentally linked to each other. It's not difficult to see the refined canon of Athanasius drawing from the works of Origen and Eusebius. Specifically, Athanasius inclusively drew from the canonical ideas contained in the *Ecclesiastical History* of Eusebius. Eusebius certainly gathered canonical ideas laid out by Origen.

His Four Categories of Christian Writings

Eusebius particularly contributed to the canon's development by a straightforward and clear categorization. He listed four kinds of works: accepted, disputed, rejected, and heretical. This elementary division further advanced the Church's finalization of the twenty-seven-book New Testament.

Eusebius's first category of written sources was those accepted by the Church: The Gospels of Matthew, Mark, Luke, and John; the Acts of the Apostles; Paul's letters, I John, I Peter, and the Apocalypse of John. However, this Apocalypse is listed with a note of reservation, as some accepted it and others did not.

The second category is disputed books. But Eusebius quickly adds that these disputed books are accepted by many. These are James, Jude, II Peter, II John, and III John. Then he notes regarding II John and III John "whether they belong to the Evangelist or another person of the same name."

The third category is the rejected books –but "not discarded." So, they're not in the canon but nonetheless offer value. These are the Acts of Paul, the so-called Shepherd and Didache, the Apocalypse of Peter, and the Letter of Barnabas. Again, he lists the Apocalypse of John's, adding the same note as before that some reject or accept this book. Eusebius also notes that some list the Gospel of the Hebrews as rejected but not discarded.

Finally, Eusebius's last category is heretical writings. These are the Gospel of Peter, the Gospel of Thomas, the Gospel of Matthias, the Acts of Andrew, and the Acts of John. Besides, he includes all other works at variance with apostolicity. Such are cast aside as absurd and impious.

Note that Eusebius didn't really declare a canon with his episcopal power as an act of governing his flock. Rather, as a historian, he attempted to record the commonly held positions on Christian writings. Accordingly, while refraining from asserting an immovable canon, Eusebius surely nudged the Church closer to an authoritatively declared, permanent canon.

CHAPTER SEVEN

The Council of Nicaea: AD 325

Nicaea Did Not Set the Canon of Scripture

Since a multitude of Christians believe that the Council of Nicaea resolved the content of the Bible and founded the Catholic Church, this sectional detour is necessary. These two unsubstantiated presuppositions are both incorrect. The Council of Nicaea had nothing to do with either. We're not talking theology –just history. "Fake news" exists. So does "fake history!"

Unfortunately, many innocent souls uncritically swallow hook, line, and sinker, the oftentimes fake narratives of movies. In his book *Da Vinci Code,* by Dan Brown, the Biblical canon is set by the Council of Nicaea. The movie actor, Tom Hanks, asserts it in the subsequent movie. It's the same entrenched mistruth, mindlessly circulated for many years.

An attentive glance at the past should further highlight the understanding of a gradual, organic process that led to the finalization of the twenty-seven-book New Testament. Patience! This detour through vital history will further enrich our yet incomplete journey to the canonization of the New Testament. But we must first put to rest the age-old misconception that the Council of Nicaea made the Biblical canon. Here are a few snapshots of what really happened at Nicaea:

Background: A Priest Named Arius

In AD 321, *Episkopos* Alexander gathered about one hundred bishops in Alexandria on the north shore of Egypt to expose Arius, a *presbuteros* under his care. There, in the most Christian intellectual hub of the day, Arius taught that Jesus Christ was the most unique, perfect being ever created, but a creature nonetheless, not equal to the Father. He explained that there was a time when this being did not exist, and therefore Christ was not God.

As Arius was stubborn in his persuasion, gathering followers, and unresponsive to attempts to help him change his mind and abandon his error, Bishop Alexander decided to condemn Arius's errors and strongly deal with the newborn and alluring heresy.

Alexander and one hundred visiting bishops denounced Arius's heresy —yet the unrelenting priest kept preaching the theological scandal as he pleased. The burdensome situation would soon split Christianity into two sizable factions: those with Arius and those against. Like metastatic cancer, the heresy quickly traveled and lodged throughout the body of Christianity.

Meanwhile, eleven years after permanently legalizing Christianity, Constantine became the sole Roman Emperor in AD 324. He soon sent an eloquent letter addressed to Arius and Bishop Alexander, respectfully urging them to amend their differences and let concord and harmony reign within the church of the East especially. The letter delivered by Constantine's religious counselor, Bishop Hosius, had little effect. The ongoing battle between Arius and Alexander raged fiercely. The heresy was now spilling over the borders of Alexandria.

Constantine's Governing Quandary

Although Constantine would not be baptized until AD 337 on his deathbed, he was a favorable "student" of Christian beliefs and practices for many years. His heart leaned toward Christianity, even though he fell short of a personal surrender to baptism until the end of his life.

But his positive impact on Christianity ought not to be underestimated. During his reign, Christians moved from the threat of persecution to a respectable practice of the faith publicly. No more coercion to sacrifice animals to Mars or Jupiter or face execution! Constantine had courageously settled that!

Upon assuming undivided power, Constantine faced a unique choice as the solitary emperor of the known civilized world. Four delicate circumstances weaved a complex problem that demanded scrutiny and decisive action.

These were the four circumstances: First, according to an ageless tradition, the emperor was the head of both state and religion. There was no such concept as the separation of church and state. The emperor typically ruled over both, and there was only one official religion of the state. A sole, official religion was seen as the chief unifying factor that facilitated secular governance. Indeed, in prior years, the waves of persecution against the Christians had rested on this immovable political premise. Everyone was expected to believe and practice the same religion, governed by the secular emperor.

Second, Constantine "inherited" an empire where this way of governing needed to be questioned. Polytheism was waning, and Christianity growing. The old Roman gods would no longer reign over society. But it was more complex than that. The newly allowed religion, Christianity, already lived by its own embedded traditions of belief and practice. It additionally had in place its own hierarchical governing structure for hundreds of years. That structure consisted of deacons, priests, and bishops on a grand scale throughout the entire known world. Constantine then had to find his place in it all and self-define his role in the religious realm. He was the emperor, but would he exert his sovereign rule over the vast Christian authoritative establishment? Would he place himself as the supreme ruler over Christianity? That was a monumental decision.

Third, because of the diffusion of the Arian heresy, Christian unity was now compromised. If the quickly growing split of Christianity continued, the very unity of the state was perceived as threatened. A divided Christianity was seen as integrally linked to a weaker state. A unified religion was always held as the cultural and political glue of society. Suddenly, the developing split of Christianity had to be checked at least for the harmony of the political order.

Fourth, the weighty political decision at hand was also profoundly personal. Even though Constantine was the emperor, he simultaneously journeyed on his own spiritual path toward an ultimate commitment to Jesus Christ.

By now, Constantine's military quests were mostly behind him. He had already granted a pluralistic accommodation for both pagan and Christian practices, allowing all to worship as they pleased. Yet, he walked a sure path that would increasingly favor Christianity.

While Constantine progressively devoted much energy to making a better secular society, he also grew spiritually. He befriended bishops, enacted just moral laws, became a catechumen, built his own chapel, and learned the habit of regular prayer. As time advanced, he granted many privileges to Christianity, such as immunity from taxation, exemption from military or governmental service, and freedom to own property. He even built the four major basilicas of Christianity in the city of Rome, Italy.

Two Months of Episcopal Discussions

Upon assuming unrestricted power, the above circumstances pressed upon Constantine to choose the best future for the Roman Empire. After carefully contemplating his possible choices, Constantine settled on the greatest urgency. He rolled up his sleeves, as it were, and vigorously organized a grand gathering of numerous bishops to meet in Nicaea in the spring of AD 325. He chose the unity of Christianity, the curbing of Arianism as a significant priority.

So, Constantine's letter summoned the bishops for a synod, saying, "I believe it is obvious to everyone that there is nothing more honorable in my sight than the fear of God." The emperor expressed his intention to be "present as a spectator and a participator." Note: At this moment in history, Constantine deferred from assuming the position of acting as a religious ruler over the bishops. He assumed a teamwork approach. His purpose was to promote the unity of the Christian faith. The invitation letter referred to the bishops as "beloved brothers."

Constantine coordinated his appeal for a synod, mostly of the eastern bishops where Arianism thrived, with Pope Sylvester in Rome. The Pope, old and failing in health, declined a burdensome trip to the east for the gathering. But he did appoint Bishop Hosius of Cordova to preside over the theological discussions and sent two priests as delegates to represent him. Crucially, all three were anti-Arians.

Taking advantage of the pleasant climate, three hundred and eighteen bishops came from Europe, Africa, and Asia and, for a couple of months, focused on the details of Arius's teachings. While residing in the summer imperial palace at Nicaea (not far from today's Istanbul, Turkey), they conducted daily sessions. Arius was often called upon to answer questions and explain his theology. His views and opposing opinions were carefully discussed.

Day by day, most bishops strongly declared themselves opposed to the unorthodox doctrines of Arius. Some got angry that the priest would cause such a mess by calling Christ's divinity into question. Bishop Nicholas of Myra (dressed in red and white) questioned Arius too. Nicholas was a saintly man known for his great charity, love of children and the poor, miraculous manifestations, and selflessness. Santa Claus is rooted in this real lover of Christ. Some claim Bishop Nicholas got so agitated and angry with Arius's insult against Jesus Christ that the saint slapped Arius in the face! There's considerably more to the story, but we must continue. Constantine sensibly left the direction of the theological discussions in the hands of Bishop Hosius and Pope Sylvester's legates, the presbyters Victor and Vincentius.

(Note: Sometimes modern comparisons clarify: The Jehovah's Witnesses' doctrine regarding Jesus Christ is a modern-day version of Arianism. They believe Jesus is a created spirit-son of the Father's. Their doctrinal position is that this "first creation" is not equal to the Father. Jesus is the "son of God," but not truly God. This special creation is Michael the Archangel, who took on flesh at the incarnation. The Mormons believe that Jesus's spirit was born from the Father and a wife in heaven before the creation of the earth. He was neither begotten *only* from the Father nor *eternally* from the Father. Jesus then is considered as a *god*, but not truly God –like the Father is God. As such, Mormon Christology reflects Arianism by denying the absolute, divine, eternal equality of the Father and the Son. None of this is to say that Jehovah's Witnesses and Mormons are bad people, only that their Christology is different from that of the early Church.)

The Nicene Creed

After about a month's time, after many discussions, both informal and formal, the body of bishops reached their conclusion. Arius's teachings were heretical and must be condemned. For clarity's sake, a statement of belief regarding the divine nature of the Son would be formalized in writing. This statement would be known as the "formulation of the symbol" or later as the "Nicene Creed."

Bishop Hosius and the young Deacon Athanasius from Alexandria shouldered a large part of the work drafting the statement. Only in his 20's, Athanasius was the competent secretary of Bishop Alexander. He'd later become the bishop of Alexandria and would suffer a large part of his life fighting against the Arian heresy. The "war horse" Athanasius would not proclaim his twenty-seven-book stance regarding the definitive canon of the New Testament until forty-two years later. Meanwhile, he battled, completely absorbed in a different world, defending the divinity of Jesus Christ. Soon, he'd write a book aimed at shattering the Arian errors.

The statement of faith concisely spelled out what Christians believe of the divinity of Jesus Christ. Throughout the ages, it has taken on the nature of a prayer, a profession of faith prayed until today. Here's the original document of profession written in Nicaea in AD 325:

We believe in one God the Father Almighty, Maker of all things visible and invisible; and in one Lord Jesus Christ, the only begotten of the Father, that is, of the substance of the Father, God of God, light of light, true God of true God, begotten not made, of the same substance with the Father through whom all things were made both in heaven and on earth; who for us men and for our salvation descended, was incarnate, and was made man, suffered and rose again the third day, ascended into heaven and cometh to judge the living and dead. And in the Holy Ghost.

Those who say: There was a time when He was not, and He was not before He was begotten; and that He was made out of nothing or who maintain that He is of another hypostasis or another substance than the Father, or that the Son of God is created, or mutable, or subject to change, them the Catholic Church anathematizes.

This profession of faith was well received by all the bishops except for two holdouts. The body of bishops agreed that this profession contained the ancient faith of the Church from apostolic times. The two opposing bishops, along with Arius, were anathematized and exiled. Lastly, Arius's writings were cast into a fire to prevent the spread of heresy. (No, Arius was not burned at the stake too!) The delegates from Rome took the profession of faith back to Pope Sylvester, who approved it and died within five months.

(Note: This was not the first time the Church composed and fostered a creed. There was already an established history of creed usage by the Church. Creeds were sometimes used to help teach and enrich prayers and beliefs with concise, sound doctrine. Creeds were relied upon to promote a clear grasp of the faith. Consider that the baptismal creed was used to assert our belief in the Blessed Trinity. The famous Apostle's Creed was used as a summary of what we believe as Christians. The Nicene Creed would now be used to assert our belief in the divinity of Christ. Soon, a Creed of Constantinople would help assert the divinity of the Holy Spirit. Various creeds often came about as simple means to battle heretical ideas. Every Creed is rooted in the revelation of Jesus Christ and the teachings of the Apostles.)

Baby-step of Universal Canon Law

Before the bishops broke up and headed back home, another matter seemed opportune. Acknowledging the convenience of the moment, they took the time to underline and list some internal organizational issues that evoked confirmation. These rules derived from long-practiced customs. Why not list them for the sake of clarity and universal observance?

So, they recorded twenty rules that should be practiced universally under the leadership of the bishops everywhere. This was the first rudimentary, disciplinary list of canon law. The bishops simply wanted everybody on the same page.

While sidestepping the comprehensive list, five excerpts adequately suggest the overall content: for instance, anyone who castrates himself can no longer remain a bishop or priest; preparation and experience should be required before being made a bishop or priest; a bishop or priest may not live with a female except for a mother, sister, aunt, or someone entirely beyond all suspicion (notwithstanding marriage); lending money with interest is enough to remove anyone from church leadership; Sunday worship should be done standing; because it's a day of celebration, fasting and kneeling should be prohibited.

(Note: this canon did not establish the Lord's Day as Sunday, replacing the Saturday Sabbath. That change reached way back to apostolic times, initiated by the Apostles themselves, as a day of celebration of the resurrection. The Apostles truly grasped the daring authority vested in them by Jesus Christ. They suspended the old laws of circumcision and restricted foods. They even moved the Lord's Day from Sabbath to Sunday; Acts 20:17; I Cor 16:2; Colossian 2:16; Apocalypse 1:10; Galatians 5:1-6. Early Christian writers echoed the same understanding: see the Didache in AD 40, the letter of Barnabas in AD 75, the letter of Ignatius of Antioch to the Smyrnaeans in AD 110, and Justin Martyr's Apology in AD 155. These details are given because some claim that Constantine, at the Council of Nicaea in AD 325, moved the day of worship from the Sabbath to Sunday. Obviously, not so.)

Once the meetings finished, Constantine hosted a grand banquet and handed out gifts to every participating bishop. The repression of Arianism now looked hopeful.

Yet, this was not the happy ending of the Arian story. It was merely a dramatic pause, the beginning resistance of a great war on the horizon. Arius would return; Arianism would strike back. Athanasius would be exiled from Alexandria five times during his fight against the Arians.

No less than two-thirds of all the bishops would end up subscribing to Arianism theology. Eventually, the famed Latin translator of the Bible, St. Jerome, would grieve. "The whole world woke up one morning, lamenting and marveling to find itself Arian." This story goes on, but at present, so must we.

The Ancient Term: Catholic

The above section set out to clarify that the Council of Nicaea had nothing to do with establishing the canon of the Bible. Of course, the fact could have been flatly stated without the drawn-out details. But the persistent mistruth is so prevailing and presumed, the above historical sketch is pertinent. Let it be etched in the reader's mind that the Council of Nicaea dealt with Arianism, not the Biblical canon.

Yet, there's another ubiquitous error that should be addressed. Multitudes hold that the Council of Nicaea in AD 325 founded the Catholic Church. This is too big of a misunderstanding to leave hanging. It seems fit to correct this popular misrepresentation of history before moving on.

Note the end of the profession of faith written by the Council of Nicaea. It concludes: "…the Catholic Church anathematizes." The unpacking of this phrase adequately demonstrates that the Council of Nicaea did not institute the Catholic Church.

Consider what this concise declaration implies: first, the Christian Church was also known as the Catholic Church; second, this Church preexisted the Council; third, the leaders of this Church presumed the authority to teach and discipline as needed; and fourth, this Church exercised the authority to remove any Church member who denied the divinity of Christ.

It was many *episkopi* of the Church whose appointments traced back to the Apostles, who attended the Council of Nicaea. There was no other Christian *Ekklesia* (assembly, congregation, or church) than this one, led by these bishops, and of course, including the bishops who couldn't attend.

This sole Church had shuffled through multiple name changes or additions for almost three hundred years. In early times, the "*Ekklesia*" had been identified as the "New Way," the "Brothers," the "Saints," the "Followers of the Way," and then "Christians" in Acts 11: 26 in Antioch. Consider that when something is called by different names, the nature of the thing itself remains constant. For instance, a "football" may be called a "pig skin," but the thing is constantly the same. In all these instances, a name change merely accentuates a different aspect of the same reality.

During the post-apostolic era, different terms applied to the *Ekklesia*. As "*Christianous*" it was the assembly of the followers of Christ. As "*katholikos*" (catholic), it was the same body of believers spread far and wide. The word "catholic" means "universal." We're speaking of the same reality here: the Christian Church present in the world in a universal way.

While on his way to Rome to be martyred around AD 110, Bishop Ignatius of Antioch wrote a letter to the Smyrnaeans. For the first time in the historical record, the *Ekklesia* is described as Catholic: "Wherever Jesus Christ is, there is the Catholic Church." *(St. Ignatius of Antioch's Letter to the Smyrnaeans, chapter 8:2).* This assertion is a short twelve years after the death of the last Apostle, John.

St. Ignatius's assertion of the Church as catholic was 218 years before the Council of Nicaea. The term "Catholic" grew into steady usage, especially from Ignatius onward. By the time the bishops at Nicaea used the term, it was common. Accordingly, Constantine had nothing to do with founding the Catholic Church. It already existed and functioned like a tiger throughout the entire Mediterranean and beyond hundreds of years before Constantine was even born.

The *episkopi* at the Council of Nicaea not only self-identified as "Catholic," they equally saw themselves as an authoritative body shepherding Christianity. They entertained no doubts regarding their mission to pasture Christ's Church.

Part of pastoring meant disciplining members of the Church when necessary. Besides, when an offense was substantial, stubborn, and gravely dangerous to the faith, harsh discipline was appropriate.

Theologically rooted in Matthew 18:15-18, Galatians 1:8-9, and Corinthians 16:22, these bishops properly used their authority as Jesus Christ intended. A person is anathematized who preaches a false gospel. This means that the person is cut off from the Christian community as a way of driving the false teacher to repentance. The anathematization of Arius and his two supporters then demonstrates the bishops at that time wielding their proper authority in an act of responsibly governing the Church.

CHAPTER EIGHT

Athanasius: Festal Letter of AD 367

A Man Prepared by God

Bishop Alexander died within six months following the Council of Nicaea. By popular demand, Athanasius was soon consecrated as the new Bishop of Alexandria. It was an enormous responsibility to inherit such a vast territory to govern. He became the foremost shepherd of hundreds of churches and outposts scattered throughout Egypt and present-day Libya. They needed an annual visit by the bishop who doggedly journeyed far and wide through scorching wastelands to care for his extensive flock.

Athanasius guided his spiritual flock for the next forty-eight years and died in AD 373 at 76 years old. Meanwhile, because of his fierce fight against the Arians, Athanasius was exiled from Alexandria five times by five different emperors, not including the six times he had to flee from the city to escape for his life. His whole life was marked by a perpetual war against the Arians. They had swept through the world and almost subdued the truth faith.

With his innately gifted intellect, after fighting so long and hard against the Arians, Athanasius earned a reputation as the "father of orthodoxy." Universally respected, he became the "teaching champion" of Christ's divinity and the Blessed Trinity.

It's worth saying that the city of Alexandria reigned supreme in the world at that time in history, not politically but culturally. It enjoyed a particular primacy as a sophisticated hub of ideas, greater than Rome, Constantinople, and Antioch. By comparison, today, those wanting a great education go to Harvard; back then, it was Alexandria. (Not that I commend Harvard; an anti-Christian rat hole.)

The great catechetical school of Alexandria was highly respected and known everywhere. It welcomed refined minds and offered a profound understanding of the Christian faith. This was Athanasius's prolific milieu, where he encouraged the depths of living Christianity with understanding. He swam in this environment with ease. The famous Sozomen testified that Athanasius was so intellectually gifted that "from his tenderest years, he practically taught himself." God had reserved the glorious task of the Biblical canon for such a holy and learned soul.

It so happens in history that God intervenes and destines an extraordinary man for an epic mission. Surely, this happened with Moses, the irreplaceable liberator. It happened too with Saul, a soul educated from his youth for a unique path God alone knew. Then there was Athanasius. The world still reverberates from the divine assignments he completed of defending the divinity of Christ and delineating the twenty-seven-book New Testament.

The Festal Letter

As far as we know, nobody told Athanasius to clarify the canon of the Bible. He just saw the need. God declared the time. While fulfilling his duties as the bishop, Athanasius wrote his 39th annual festal letter to the churches to share the dates of Lent and Easter.

Athanasius used this "ordinary" letter to identify the Biblical canon in his own diocese. He, once and for all, authoritatively tied all the loose ends together of an age-old discernment customarily done locally and everywhere. Precisely because his stature was so exalted, the whole world paid attention. His finely tuned list was immediately deemed special and quickly adopted by many bishops.

The following four paragraphs are excerpted from Athanasius's Festal Letter of AD 367. (Since we are focused on the New Testament, the Old Testament section is removed, for the most part. The canon of the Old Testament will be covered a bit later.) As he identifies the divinely inspired twenty-seven books, the context is to protect his flock from heretics and false writings. Notably, from a warrior who battled against heretics his whole life, Athanasius pursues the safety of clarity:

Since, however, we have spoken of the heretics as dead but of ourselves as possessors of the divine writings unto salvation, and since I am afraid that —as Paul has written to the Corinthians [II Cor.

11:3] –some guileless persons may be led astray from their purity and holiness by the craftiness of certain men and begin thereafter to pay attention to other books, the so-called apocryphal writings, being deceived by their possession of the same names as the genuine books, I, therefore, exhort you to patience when, out of regard to the Church's need and benefit, I mention in my letter matters with which you are acquainted. It being my intention to mention these matters, I shall, for the commendation of my venture, follow the example of the evangelist Luke and say [cf. Luke 1:1-4]: Since some have taken in hand to set in order for themselves the so-called apocrypha and to mingle them with the God-inspired scripture, concerning which we have attained to a sure persuasion, according to what the original eye-witness and ministers of the word have delivered unto our fathers, I also, having been urged by true brethren and having investigated the matter from the beginning, have decided to set forth in order the writings that have been put in the canon, that have been handed down and confirmed as divine, in order that everyone who has been led astray may condemn his seducers, and that everyone who has remained stainless may rejoice, being again reminded of that.

I must without hesitation mention the scriptures of the New Testament; they are the following: the four Gospels according to Matthew, Mark, Luke, and John, after them, the Act of the Apostles and the seven so-called catholic epistles of the Apostles –namely, one of James, two of Peter, then three of John and after these, one of Jude. In addition, there are fourteen epistles of the Apostle Paul written in the following order: the first to the Romans, then two to the Corinthians, and then after these, the one to the Galatians, following it, the one to the Ephesians, thereafter the one to the Philippians and the one to the Colossians, and two to the Thessalonians and the epistle to the Hebrews, and then immediately two to Timothy, one to Titus and lastly the one to Philemon. Yet further, the Revelation of John.

These are the springs of salvation, in order that he who is thirsty may fully refresh himself with the words contained therein. In them alone is the doctrine of piety proclaimed. Let no one add anything to them or take anything away from them.

But for the sake of greater accuracy, I add, being constrained to write, that there are also other books besides these, which have not indeed been part of the canon but have been appointed by the Fathers as reading matter for those who have just come forward and which to be instructed in the doctrine of piety: the Wisdom of Solomon, the Wisdom of Sirach, Esther, Judith, Tobias, the so-called Didache of the Apostles, and the Shepherd. And although, beloved, the former are in the canon and the latter serve as reading matter, yet mention is nowhere made of the apocrypha; rather, they are a fabrication of the heretics, who wrote them down when it pleases them and generously assign to them an early date of composition in order that they may be able to draw upon them as supposedly ancient writings and have in them occasion to deceive the guileless.

Notice that Athanasius didn't set out to write a book on the subject. He just fulfilled his duty by a letter, as bishops had been doing for hundreds of years. He simply grasped that the Christians of his diocese needed further clarity about the canon of divinely inspired books.

The ground-breaking value of his letter did not lie in the labor of a keen intellect, although he certainly possessed that, but in the enduring love of a saint for the flock entrusted to his care. God had his own intentions that would endure far past the time and place of Athanasius. As He's accustomed to do, God would use an ordinary task fulfilled to enrich eternity.

A Monumental Promulgation

Athanasius was the first significant bishop to authoritatively promulgate the twenty-seven-book New Testament canon. Some predecessors neared his distinguished list but continually fell short of precision; they characteristically noted doubts, uncertainties, and disputations of this or that book. But Athanasius tied up the loose ends and declared the canon in black-and-white terms with no reservations. Even more, he taught the precise canon as a prestigious bishop. His conclusive stance would echo through history. Many Church authorities would henceforth repeat it, making it progressively immovable.

Taking a step back and looking at the Bible as a whole, both the Old Testament and the New, Athanasius listed seventy-three books that he affirmed were divinely inspired. There were forty-six books in the Old Testament and twenty-seven in the New Testament. This seventy-three-book

Bible in AD 367 would continually be reasserted by significant Church authorities for the next 1,657 years (until today, AD 2024).

For example, the following authorities asserted the same seventy-three-book Bible, consisting of forty-six Old Testament books and twenty-seven New Testament books: Pope Damasus I and the Council of Rome in AD 382; the Synod of Hippo in AD 393; the Synod of Carthage in AD 397; Pope Innocent I and the Vulgate in AD 405; the Synod of Carthage in AD 419; the Council of Nicaea II in AD 797; the Council of Florence in AD 1442; the Council of Trent in AD 1546; the Council of Vatican I in AD 1870.

So, Athanasius's promulgation established a next-level, historic standard that has been repeatedly asserted by Church authorities. Of course, he arrived at his conclusion by closely following a long-standing discernment process of the Church and the gradual refinements of both scholars (notably Irenaeus, Origen, and Eusebius of Caesarea) and *episkopi* always seeking greater clarity stretching back to apostolic times.

CHAPTER NINE

Athanasius and the Septuagint

The Forty-six-book Septuagint

Looking now at the whole Bible, consider how Bishop Athanasius approached the canonization (listing of the divinely inspired books) of the Old Testament. Just as with the New Testament, he specified the accepted books of the Old Testament.

Note the forty-six divinely inspired books listed by Athanasius: Genesis, Exodus, Leviticus, Numbers, Deuteronomy, Joshua, Judges, Ruth, I Samuel, II Samuel, I Kings, II Kings, I Chronicles, II Chronicles, Ezra, Nehemiah, Tobit, Judith, Esther (full version), I Maccabees, II Maccabees, Job, Psalms, Proverbs, Ecclesiastes, Song of Songs, Wisdom of Solomon (or sometimes simply called Wisdom), Sirach (or at times called Wisdom of Sirach or Ecclesiasticus), Isaiah, Jeremiah, Lamentations, Baruch (including the letter of Jeremiah), Ezekiel, Daniel (full version: including the Prayer of Azariah and the Song of the Three Holy Children, Susanna, and Bel and the Dragon), Hosea, Joel, Amos, Obadiah, Jonah, Micah, Nahum, Habakkuk, Zephaniah, Haggai, Zachariah, and Malachi. That makes forty-six promulgated divinely inspired Old Testament books accepted into the Christian Bible in the year AD 367 by Athanasius in his diocese of Alexandria, Egypt.

During Jesus's public ministry, a provisional canon of the Old Testament still fluctuated. The Hebrew sacred texts fit into a threefold categorization: the Torah, the Prophets, and the Writings. There were variations of accepted Writings, inclusions, or exclusions, sometimes this or that book or part in question. The Sadducees only accepted the Torah as canonically, divinely inspired. The Pharisees accepted the books of all three categories as divinely inspired. There was an enormous gulf between the two viewpoints.

The canonization of the Hebrew texts moved slowly. During Jesus's public ministry, the Torah was universally accepted; the Prophets were, for the most part, universally accepted; the Writings were more subject to flux. Jesus appeared in the middle of the Old Testament canonization process. He would initiate its completion —along with his Apostles and succeeding *episkopi* and *Ekklesia*. The completion of the Old Testament canonization process would require the authoritative voice of God.

Yet, along with the varied Hebrew collections that circulated, there was also a forty-six-book Greek Old Testament collection called the Septuagint. Septuagint is the Greek word for "seventy," the number of Israelite translators involved in the work of translation.

The Septuagint came about during the third century BC, long before the dawn of Christianity. Precisely, the Pentateuch (also called the Torah: the first five books of the Old Testament) was translated from Hebrew into Greek by the middle of the third century BC. The translation of the rest of the Hebrew books trickled in time. By AD 130, the translated forty-six-book Old Testament was widely circulated and commonly used. So, by the time of Jesus, both the Hebrew and Greek Old Testament scriptures were familiar.

The Septuagint had resulted from a significant Jewish population in the city of Alexandria. The whole world spoke Greek at that time, and the Hebrews in Alexandria were progressively weaned from the Hebrew language and reared in Greek. Besides, Greek flourished everywhere among non-Hebrew-speaking gentile converts to Judaism. So, sensibly, Alexandrian Jews birthed the Septuagint. Eventually, the original Septuagint would sometimes be referenced as the Alexandrian Canon.

Christian Affinity for the Septuagint

Bishop Athanasius approached the canonization of the Old Testament with the same criteria for identifying the divinely inspired writings of the New Testament. He considered apostolicity, universal acceptance by *episkopi* and usage in liturgies, and the ancient role the Old Testament scriptures exercised in spreading the Gospel of Christ.

Accordingly, bypassing multiple versions of Hebrew-language canons, Athanasius identified the forty-six-book canon of the Septuagint as the divinely inspired word of God and declared it so —for continued Church usage.

Why was the Greek Septuagint recognized as divinely inspired? The scrutiny and deliberate choice of Athanasius boiled down to accepting the ancient choice of the *Ekklesia* during apostolic times. Athanasius plainly formalized what the Church had already nurtured for hundreds of years by practical usage.

The divinely inspired writers of the New Testament, mostly Apostles, characteristically referenced the Septuagint. Weaved into the inspired beauty of God's word in the New Testament, most Old Testament references and quotes (about 70%) are from the Septuagint. This was clearly the apostolic Old Testament of choice.

Another statistic underlines that the New Testament authors quoted the Septuagint around 300 times and the Hebrew scriptural versions about 50 times. Although the percentages and numerical stats don't perfectly match, they adequately convey the New Testament's ample reliance upon the Septuagint. This should be no surprise because the Apostles and early Church swam in a Greek world. The authors of the New Testament wrote in Greek and mostly quoted the Old Testament in Greek.

Missionizing in a Greek world, the Apostles and ancient Church relied upon the Septuagint to argue and prove the message of the Gospel. The earliest witnesses of Christ as the Messiah authenticated their teachings mostly from the pages of the Septuagint. The prophecies that proved the Messiah were taken from the Septuagint. As such, it immediately became a suitable apostolic teaching instrument.

The Septuagint's evangelistic instrumentality included the use of terminology and concepts relatable and easily understood by Greek-language listeners. This certainly facilitated the rapid propagation of Christianity. In God's design, the Septuagint appeared in history providentially in time for the dissemination of the Gospel.

From ancient times, the Apostles, Disciples, *episkopi*, and churches everywhere embraced the Septuagint, even at times when it strayed from Hebrew texts. Besides, the original Hebrew texts were supplanted by the Septuagint at the liturgical services of the Breaking of the Bread from apostolic days. In short, the Septuagint rocketed to become the standard Christian's Old Testament.

Yet, there's more that reveals just how meaningfully God intervened with the blessing of the Septuagint for Christians. Sometimes, the rabbi translators of the Septuagint chose terms that allowed a subtle insertion of oral tradition. In this way, Greek-speaking converts to Judaism would immediately grasp the ancient, enriched meaning of what was heard or read.

For example, prophesying the birth of the Messiah, the ancient Hebrew text of Isaiah 7:14 reads, "…the 'young woman' will be with child and will give birth to a son, and will call him Immanuel." However, the Septuagint translates this accordingly, "…the 'virgin' will be with child and will give birth to a son, and will call him Immanuel." (See Matthew 1:23.)

The Hebrew word for "young woman" was *"almah,"* which should have been translated as "young woman" or "maiden," not really "virgin." Most often in the Hebrew scriptures, it was not translated as "virgin," though grammatically speaking, that was a possible word choice, as a young, unmarried women may be a virgin. Aware of the oral tradition held by learned Hebrew rabbis surrounding this passage, the rabbi Septuagint translators chose the Greek word *"parthenos,"* deliberately meaning "virgin." They incorporated oral tradition to convey what was long believed about the passage in Isaiah. The Messiah would be born of a virgin.

In this way, with additional similar translation choices, the Septuagint towered as a powerful tool for apostolic purposes. Many years into the Christian era, some rabbis would later point to this example as a colossal translation error by the Septuagint translators who should have known better. But it wasn't a translation mistake. Those astute translation-rabbis were too smart for that.

It should be considered, too, that later Jews would have little interest in proving that Jesus Christ was the Messiah. The Messiah's virgin birth was a lofty and holy speculation about the future, only if it did not inconveniently infringe upon the present. But Another explanation is that the Spirit of the Most High divinely inspired conscientious and learned rabbi translators as they fulfilled the duties of their work. By God's design, they unknowingly destined the diffusion of Christianity. God has his own roundabout ways of bringing about his purposes.

The vigorous adoption of the Septuagint by early Christianity and its effective instrumentality in evangelization persuaded the Jews to abandon it eventually. Yes, of course, why hold on to a tool that labors against you? Some early Christian writers, notably St. Irenaeus, came to believe that the Septuagint, precisely as a sacred translation, had its own particular divine inspiration.

CHAPTER TEN

The Divine Inspiration of All Forty-six Books of the Septuagint

Jesus: Master of Scripture

It's hard to grasp how long it took to write the Old Testament. Beyond one thousand years! By the time Jesus Christ walked upon the earth, it was finally entire, in Greek, and ready to be cultivated with the blinding new revelation of God in the flesh.

Its completion (writing, not canonization) was less an ending than a fresh beginning. For a thousand years, the divine intellect had inspired humble minds and guided nimble fingers to record hidden truths in ancient scrolls that even human authors did not fully penetrate. The "manuscript" was finally set and dry for the Son of God to incarnate and fully explain.

The eager twelve-year-old Jesus could hardly wait: "After three days they found him in the temple, sitting in the midst of the teachers, listening to them and asking questions, and all who heard him were astounded at his understanding and his answers." (Luke 2:46-47) Yet, he still had to wait just a little more.

Finally, seizing the appointed time to lay bare the sacred texts, the full meaning of God's revelation rolled forth from his tongue: "…on the Sabbath, he entered the synagogue and taught. The people were astonished at his teaching, for he taught them as one having authority and not as the scribes." (Mark 1:21-22) Again: "When the Sabbath came, he began to teach in the synagogue, and many who heard him were astonished. They said, 'Where did this man get all this? What kind of wisdom has been given to him?'" (Mark 6:2)

He stood up to read and was handed a scroll of the prophet Isaiah. He unrolled the scroll and found the passage where it is written: 'The Spirit of the Lord is upon me, because he has anointed me to bring glad tidings to the poor. He has sent me to proclaim liberty to captives and recovery of sight to the blind, to let the oppressed go free, and to proclaim a year acceptable to the Lord.' Rolling up the scroll, he handed it back to the attendant and sat down, and the eyes of all in the synagogue looked intently at him. He said to them, 'Today this scripture passage is fulfilled in your hearing.' (Luke 4:16-21)

The resurrected Jesus taught again:

Then beginning with Moses and all the prophets, he interpreted to them what referred to him in all the scriptures. As they approached the village to which they were going, he gave the impression that he was going on further.… Then they said to each other, 'Were not our hearts burning [within us] while he spoke to us on the way and opened the scriptures to us?' (Luke 24:27-28; 32)

These passages hint at the divine light of Christ's mind. He was not a mere extraordinary scriptural scholar who might research and eloquently communicate discoveries. No! Jesus Christ was –is God. This eternal Son was the principal author of all that was written of him. He need not find the meaning of his own handiwork of inspirations divinely infused into minds ages past –by the effortless power of his will. He had written every single word of the Old Testament for his future usage and reference.

When the divine person of Jesus recalled and taught Old Testament scripture, he simply picked up what he had laid down in ancient days past. He had set words, concepts, phrases, and expressions in place for his own future provision. He was the master of those words, and they were recorded in the scrolls to conform to him. The words of the sacred texts were designed by Him to later unfurl their mature and perfect meanings through His tongue.

The divine person of Jesus was the master of every word He long ago inspired. Each word was equally inspired. Without superfluous waste, each word was purposeful. All the words of the sacred texts were appointed to obey Him, not Him to them. Before the eternal Son even assumed His human nature, with the Father and Holy Spirit, He infused every inspired thought into the human souls of every Old Testament writer. Then, each writer gave form to the revealed truth that Jesus would take up and bring to fruition in due time.

The conception of each word and the glory of each expression would flow through the lips of Jesus. No wonder, in multiple places, the scriptures warn never to change a thing!

Jesus Christ's Mysterious Presence to the Reader

Yet, God's living words in scripture are not only inspired in their origins, they are also inspired in their mode of reception. Jesus moves us to receive his word. As we read, Jesus moves within, unlocking inner doors, breaking down interior resistance, opening the eyes of understanding, and empowering the soul. The words are not isolated, earth-bound scribbles from thousands of years ago, disconnected from him. No, the reading of scripture occasions an encounter with Jesus very much alive –mysteriously present.

Consider his personal presence hidden in scripture –capable of converting a soul. In the year AD 386, at thirty-one years old, Augustine had been so bound by lust that he could barely go a night without the touch of a woman and sexual intercourse. Then, his heaven-sent moment of rescue came. Off in the distance, he heard the repeated phrase of children singing: "Take up and read! Take up and read!"

So, Augustine picked up the Bible and read a few lines in midstream, sentences that somehow randomly opened before him:

> Let us conduct ourselves properly as in the day, not in orgies and drunkenness, not in promiscuity and licentiousness, nor in rivalry and jealousy. But put on the Lord Jesus Christ, and make no provision for the desires of the flesh.

Augustine instantly received the power of conversion as Jesus's presence overshadowed him. It was exactly what he needed to hear. A sweet brush of grace conquered. Inner clarity, surrender, and spiritual power appeared. It was the pivotal moment of his life. Jesus emanated through the reading, penetrating his body and lodging in his soul.

The amazing conversion of Sergei Kourdakov also testifies to the power of the words of scripture. During the 1960s, Sergei was a KGB agent and naval officer in the Soviet military. He excelled as a member of a "Special Action Squad" dedicated to the "service" of violently breaking up underground Christian prayer gatherings. He was a revolutionary atheist with one hundred and fifty brutal raids behind his belt.

One bitter day in 1970, Sergei was instructed at a police station to burn confiscated Christian literature in a basement furnace to warm up the building. As he threw papers into the fire, curiosity took over. He thought, "What do young people see in this trash?" He grabbed a page and hid it in his pocket to read when he might find the time and privacy. His autobiography, *The Persecutor*, tells the story of the first time he read the Bible. It was a crumpled-up scrap from the Gospel of Luke:

At the first opportunity I had, lying in my bunk at the naval academy, I opened the pieces of paper and began to read them. Jesus was talking and teaching someone how to pray. I became more curious and read on. This certainly was no anti-state material. It was how to be a better person and how to forgive those who do you wrong.

Suddenly, the words leaped out of those pages and into my heart. I read on, engrossed in the kind words of Jesus. This was exactly the opposite of what I had expected. My lack of understanding, which had been like blinders on my eyes, left me right then, and the words bit into my being.

Through the days and weeks ahead, those words of Jesus stayed with me. I couldn't shake them, hard as I tried. I wished I hadn't read them. Everything had been so organized in my life, but those disturbing words had changed something. I had feelings I never had felt before. I couldn't explain or understand them.

Years later, madly in love with Jesus Christ, Sergei would die a glorious death as a martyr –loving God in return.

So, we've seen that scripture is written by the Son, for the Son. Jesus is the teacher of scripture *par excellence*, unrestricted in time or place. We've also noted that there is a two-fold inspiration of scripture. There's a divine inspiration when scripture is written, but another personal, inner kind of inspiration when scripture is read. Both the giving and the receiving of scripture are surrounded by the presence of the Son of God. No other book is alive like this. Its pages breathe an anointing.

The Removal of Seven Divinely Inspired Books

Yet, Jesus Christ's mastery and lordship over scripture extends still further. As the divine artisan, God's design of scripture is whole, complete, and perfect. Imagine a million-piece puzzle –locked harmoniously together. Similarly, the profound complementarity and interconnectedness of every word in scripture is overwhelming. Every chapter, phrase, and word are providentially related to hundreds of others within the same book, which all contribute to the eternal salvation of souls.

Jesus is the master of every word in scripture. He is also the master of every book in scripture. He inspired and placed all forty-six books of the Old Testament in the Septuagint and all twenty-seven books in the New Testament. He inspired everything, intending to use everything to foment personal relationships with him. Accordingly, just as each word demands respect, so does each book. Just as each word must remain in place, each book of the Bible must also remain intact. What God has joined, let no man separate. To subtract from God's united whole is to interfere with his divine design to save the world.

A scripture scholar might presume himself inspired or gifted enough to nonchalantly criticize, degrade, or even remove specific books from the scripture whole. So doing, such an ignorant scholar clings to his personal judgment over divine wisdom itself. It's like opening a new puzzle and throwing a handful of pieces away before setting out to construct the whole.

Mindful of the above theological context, we can now discuss the forty-six-book Septuagint –as an undividable whole. The completed "scriptural puzzle" was conceived in the mind of God as a whole, transmitted through the Greek as a whole, used by Jesus Christ and the Apostles as a whole, and enjoyed by the early Church as a whole (both in liturgies and missionizing); and canonized by the Church as a whole. Jesus Christ is the master of the whole scripture.

Breaking with ancient understanding and practice, in the year AD 1534, a Catholic priest claimed that the following inclusions in the Old Testament were not divinely inspired: Tobit, Judith, Wisdom, Sirach, Baruch, I Maccabees, and II Maccabees, including chapters 10-16 of Esther; and chapters 3:24-90, 13, and 14 of Daniel.

It should be emphasized that these subtracted books and chapters were integral parts of the Septuagint preceding Christ. These specified books and chapters were inseparably included and equally valued as Old Testament scripture and asserted as such by Church authorities from the earliest years of Christianity up until Martin Luther's recategorization of them as non-scriptural in the year AD 1534.

Upon publishing his German language Bible, Father Luther, an Augustinian scripture professor, downgraded these books and chapters. He lumped them together and placed them at the end of the Bible with the following title and note: "APOCRYPHA, that is, Books which are not to be esteemed like the Holy Scriptures, and yet which are useful and good to read." Remember: the Jews in the time of Jesus, Jesus himself, the Apostles, including Paul, and the early Church treated these same books without distinction, precisely as inspired scripture.

Over the years, as reprintings and fresh Bible translations rolled off the presses of the world, the stigmatized "Apocrypha" would sink lower and lower in appreciation. With the death label of "Apocrypha," printers eventually relegated the extra books to appendixes. Suffering from "publishing-leprosy," these "untouchable" books and chapters eventually were no longer allowed into Bibles. This is how the seventy-three-book Catholic Bible and the sixty-six-book protestant Bible parted ways. The Catholics had not added books; the protestants had first distanced them from divinely inspired writings and then gradually withdrew them.

Some call these "apocryphal writings" the "deuterocanonical" books of the Old Testament. This means they are like a "second canon." If the term merely indicates a literary division, it has limited validity. But if the term is understood with the connotation of denying the divine inspiration of the seven books in question, it's defective. As such, the term is often just a fancy way to softly distance these books from the rest of scripture. It's a concocted term neither rooted in reality nor ancient. It's fooled many Christians. Jesus and the Apostles saw things differently.

Relevantly, it's enlightening to reflect on Paul's fatherly instructions to Timothy, a close pastoral friend. As a seasoned Apostle, Paul shares intimate advice with the young *episkopos*. The context emphasizes Timothy's role to govern and especially teach in the face of false doctrines. Paul counsels: "*All* scripture is inspired by God and is useful for teaching, for refutation, for correction, and for training in righteousness." (II Timothy 3:16) Here, Paul refers to *all* forty-six books of the Septuagint, not yet including the entire New Testament of course and the very letter that he writes to Timothy! An exceptionally knowledgeable pharisee and Apostle, his *"all"* refers to the forty-six-book whole of the Old Testament scriptures, comprised of the Law, Prophets, and Writings. Paul is basically encouraging Timothy to embrace and use everything. Every book is inspired. Every book has its value and purpose for the Christian, especially in the hands of the *episkopos*, the primary teacher of his assigned area.

(Note: The "Writings" are the third of a threefold Hebrew categorization of the scriptures. Following the Torah and the Prophets, the Writings are also referred to as Wisdom literature. This diverse collection of books contains the Psalms, Book of Job, Proverbs, and the Song of Songs, for example. The Septuagint embraced a scripture collection that included the Wisdom books of Tobit, Judith, Wisdom, Sirach, Baruch, I Maccabees, and II Maccabees, including chapters 10-16 of Esther; and chapters 3:24-90, 13, and 14 of Daniel. Wisdom literature is not necessarily tied to historic periods or personages, although it may be. It essentially represents the accumulation of a long tradition of God's chosen people acquiring wisdom through virtue, trials, sufferings, living experiences, prayer, and repentance. The Wisdom collection of books reflects the practical, daily application of the Torah and the Prophets. Can you imagine the Bible without the Psalms? This hints at the unique divine revelation of the inspired Wisdom books.)

The removal of seven Wisdom books from the Bible is tragic because it deprives the world and Christians of a spiritual treasure bequeathed by God. As such, the removed books belong to you and me. They are God's gift and provision and always have been. But a Catholic priest in Germany 490 years ago initiated their exit from the whole forty-six-book Septuagint.

Imagine attending a celebratory banquet where friendship and savory cuisines abound. The banquet host favors you, sets an honored place for you, and grants all that lay before you. The meal concludes with a scrumptious dessert. A beautiful cake is set before you. Your neighbor then grabs your portion and whispers into your ear that the host prohibits your enjoyment of such a special dessert.

Similarly, God gives his beloved family the forty-six-book Septuagint as a complete spiritual banquet to satiate every spiritual hunger. Whispering in God's name, Father Luther has removed the spiritual dessert placed before you by Jesus himself. He says that Jesus does not wish for you to enjoy the dessert. It's not really part of the meal, he chides. I ask: my dear reader, don't you want your dessert?

Jesus, the Apostles, and the Writings

The New Testament's frequent references to the Septuagint, which include Tobit, Judith, Wisdom, Sirach, Baruch, I Maccabees, II Maccabees, and the complete chapters of Esther and Daniel, suggest the divine inspiration of these books. The New Testament references the Septuagint about three hundred times, including the seven books in question, about seventy times. This establishes a history of apostolicity required for the Church's authoritative seal of divine inspiration.

Upfront, before exploring the nature of these references, here's an abbreviated sample of twenty-four New Testament passages with corresponding references to the Wisdom books in question. This is not an exhaustive list:

Ephesians 6:13-17; see Wisdom 5:17-20

James 3:13; see Sirach 3:17

John 6:35; see Sirach 24:20

Mark 9:48; see Judith 16:17

Luke 13:29; see Baruch 4:37

Romans 1:20; see Wisdom 13:1

Luke 1:52; see Sirach 10:14

Matthew 6:19-20 and James 5:3; see Sirach 29:10-11

I Peter 1:6-7; see Wisdom 3:5-6 and Sirach 2:5

Hebrews 11:35; see II Maccabees 7:1-42

John 6:35-59; see Sirach 24:21

John 1:3; see Wisdom 9:1

Apocalypse 20:12; see Sirach 16:12

Apocalypse 5:17; see Sirach 1:8

Matthew 27:39-43; see Wisdom 2:17-18

Matthew 7:12; see Tobit 4:15

Matthew 9:36; see Judith 11:19

Apocalypse 17:14 and 19:16; see II Maccabees 13:14

Apocalypse 19:11; see II Maccabees 3:25 and 11:8

Luke 24:4 and Acts 1:10; see II Maccabees 3:26

I Corinthians 10:9-10; see Judith 8:24-25

Matthew 27:43; see Wisdom 2:18

Matthew 11:28; see Sirach 24:18

Matthew 6:1-18; see Tobit 12:8

Sometimes, due to a poor appreciation of the "deuterocanonical" books of the Old Testament, difficulties may surface when trying to scrutinize references. Newer Bible translations sometimes minimize the relationships between the New Testament and such "apocryphal" references, which may have lost their place in the Bible. Indeed, some Bibles might not even include the deuterocanonical books any longer. Old concordances may be needed to locate the dwindling cross-references.

A mistranslation of words may indeed weaken related passages. It will be helpful to sometimes compare the actual Greek words in the Septuagint with the words used in the Greek New Testament —noting the meaning of terms during their respective times of usage. Yes, it does take some work and resources.

For example, in the Greek New Testament, there are several appearances of the word *episkopos*. This word means "overseer" or "supervisor" in Greek. It was the position assigned to leaders in new churches. (See chapter two.) The proper English translation of this word is "bishop." Yet, some Bibles swap the translation of the word itself for the meaning of the word. Why? Perhaps some "translating authorities" may prefer not to call attention to the ancient Church's rudimentary governing structure of bishops. The word "bishop" may feel too Catholic, especially if one's church has abandoned such terminology or theology.

Even so, the organic link between the New Testament citations and the Wisdom literature references may not be obvious. An initial comparison then may be superficially dismissed. But the effort invested in "contextual reflection" will produce enlightenment. The following tips may help shed light on the organic links between New Testament quotes and related Wisdom literature references:

When the New Testament reaches back to use something from the Old Testament, it's rarely done in a complete and formally clarified manner. For instance, When Jesus dies on the cross, he says: "My God my God, why have you forsaken me?" (Mark 15:34) This is the opening of Psalm 22:2, a thousand years earlier. Notice that Jesus doesn't clarify the source of his meaningful words. Yet, every attentive listener near the cross knows it, except for some bystanders who misunderstand him. Perhaps Jesus prays the entire psalm; it's not clear. Psalm 22 describes Jesus's suffering on the cross. It ends with the recognition of God's deliverance of people yet unborn. As he dies on the cross, he fulfills the prophecy of the Psalm.

The Old Testament is written for the New Testament. The Old comes in an incomplete and often skeletal form. It comes first and waits for its "Christianization" and full blossom of meaning from the Son of God and his Apostles. Let's consider two examples of how Wisdom literature finds its perfection in the New Testament:

The link between Wisdom 13:1 and Romans 1:20 demonstrates this: "For all men were by nature foolish who were in ignorance of God, and who from the good things seen did not succeed in knowing him who is, (Hebrew sacred name of God, Ex 3:14) and from studying the works did not discern the artisan." (Wisdom 13:1) Then, roughly 160 years later, Paul wrote arguably his masterpiece, beckoning the Romans to Christ: "Ever since the creation of the world, his invisible attributes of eternal power and divinity have been able to be understood and perceived in what he has made. As a result, they have no excuse…." (Romans 1:20)

These two passages of scripture show a similar theme and context. More is gleaned by reading the entire chapters. They each underline God's knowability through the witness of creation. Those who are blind to this reality are foolish, vain, and left to their own doom. Paul does not cite the Book of Wisdom by chapter and verse; he simply, casually reiterates the message in his own words for a Roman audience. No doubt, he was familiar with the Book of Wisdom. Drawing from his lifelong education, he merely tweaked and redirected a gem from the Old Testament to advance the cause of Christ.

(Note: My Catholic Bible includes the following footnote for Romans 1:18-32: "In this passage, Paul uses themes and rhetoric common in the Jewish-Hellenistic mission proclamation, cf. Wisdom 13:1-14, 31, to indict especially the non-Jewish world.")

Another example of the New Testament perfecting a Wisdom literature teaching is when Jesus spells out the meaning of Tobit 12:8 in Matthew chapter six. But to grasp the full significance of Jesus's building upon the old, some background is helpful:

Tobit was a pious and well-off Israelite living in Galilee, where fishermen enjoyed the sun on the sea and where Jesus called Peter, Andrew, James, and John to be Apostles. Yet, Tobit lived there roughly seven hundred years earlier. He was known and respected as a good man, truthful and generous. Tragically, in 721 BC, the North Kingdom of Israel fell to the Assyrians. Jerusalem was sieged, and Tobit suffered displacement. In his early 60's, leaving his whole life behind, the man was taken captive with a crowd and exiled to Nineveh (modern-day Mosul, Iraq.) Although Tobit lost everything and became blind, he held firm to his faith and remained steadfast in his love for all in need. He spent his days finding ways to feed the poor, clothe the naked, and bury the dead.

The Wisdom book of Tobit, likely written around the third or second century BC, relates the amazing story of this virtuous man. The story had been handed down by oral tradition from age to age until God inspired its written form. The Dead Sea Scrolls included four fragments of Tobit in Aramaic (Jesus's own tongue) and one in Hebrew, suggesting the popularity of the work. The quick-read book underlines how God brings good out of everyday trials. No matter what happens; suffering, exile, persecution, death, blindness, poverty, disability, or demonic attacks, God can faithfully turn everything to good and bring about a happily ever after.

The story of Tobit demonstrates the beauty and irreplaceable value of Jewish Wisdom literature for the common believer. Not everyone can be a Moses, or Sampson, or David, or Isaiah. Wisdom literature brings spirituality down to earth and makes the practice of the faith relevant and practical for the everyday man or woman pursuing holiness.

After Tobit encouraged his son to give a great amount of money to a visitor who had blessed the family considerably, God's favor fell upon him. Tobit did not know that his visitor was actually the angel Raphael sent from heaven to test and bless him. Raphael called Tobit and his son together in private, revealed his identity, and offered holy counsel:

Prayer and fasting are good, but better than either is almsgiving accompanied by righteousness. A little with righteousness is better than abundance with wickedness. It is better to give alms than to store up gold; for almsgiving saves one from death and expiates every sin. Those who regularly give alms shall enjoy a full life; but those habitually guilty of sin are their own worst enemies. (Tobit 12:8-10)

Holy advice lasts forever. The faithful would come to treasure prayer, fasting, and almsgiving as the three pillars of Jewish piety. Traced back to Tobit, these three practices grouped together would develop into the cardinal disciplines taught in the synagogues for hundreds of years to encourage piety. During the days of Jesus's ministry, Jewish listeners were keenly aware of the story of Tobit. Along with Adam and Eve, Noah, Job, and Jonah, the story of Tobit likely passed on to every Jewish boy or girl through the lips of a devoted mother. The Jews were intimately familiar with Tobit's contribution to Jewish spirituality.

Jesus preached with full awareness of his listeners and full authority from his Father. He did not need to justify anything he said. This is how he preached with power, not relying on the crutches of specifically cited quotations. What he had to say was more important than anything anyone had ever said. The context of his listeners' education (not necessarily formal) and Jesus's own way of racing into the hearts of his listeners explains much of his preaching style. He knew what each person knew; he knew hearts. Why waste time on establishing his voice on what others have said?

Mindful of this rich context, see how Jesus takes a small piece of Wisdom literature, Tobit 12:8, and brings it to perfection in chapter six of Matthew. The fifth and sixth chapters of Matthew bunch together fundamental moral teachings. Beginning with the sermon on the mount, Jesus recalls long-established moral standards, skipping over specific authors, books, and chapters. (The Pharisees liked to highlight multiple citations from famous teachers to establish their points.) Jesus was not known for this brainy, show-off preaching style.

He merely starts each theme: "You have heard it said...." He then affirms the moral issue at hand, explains its defective understanding and practice, and highlights the perfection of the moral practice God desires. After touching upon the nature of the Law, anger, reconciliation, adultery, lust, divorce, the taking of oaths, retaliation, and the love of enemies, Jesus arrives at firming up the old Jewish pillars of personal spirituality, namely: almsgiving, prayer, and fasting.

Jesus neither cites the Book of Tobit nor the teaching of the angel Raphael. But he does offer commentary, building on the foundation of Tobit and long-established Jewish customs. Jesus recognizes that almsgiving, prayer, and fasting go together. His back-to-back presentation even reflects the order of importance revealed by Raphael. The angel had instructed Tobit: "Prayer and fasting are good, but better than either is almsgiving...." As almsgiving is the best of the three, that's where Jesus starts. Accordingly, he teaches about almsgiving, then prayer, and ends with instructions on fasting. His commentary launches from the parallel structure presented in Tobit.

But there's still more that shows Jesus's fine-tuning of Tobit 12:8-10. Raphael insists that righteousness must accompany almsgiving. It's righteousness, or one's genuine relationship with God, that exalts and perfects the act of almsgiving. It's righteousness that makes almsgiving a beautiful way of loving one's neighbor. Raphael adds: "It is better to give alms than to store up gold."

Jesus underlines these ancient truths and then advances further in the moral order. He points out that the value of almsgiving flows from the inner disposition of the giver's heart. Pure giving, free from ostentatious display, is a manifestation of genuine righteousness. As such, Jesus spells out the righteousness God desires in the act of almsgiving. He shuns giving with the blowing of a trumpet, summoning congratulations and praise for the giver. Almsgiving is supposed to be a modest act of love, not a sinful act of vanity. Here, Jesus brings to perfection the succinct advice offered by the Angel Raphael seven hundred years ago: "Prayer and fasting are good, but better than either is almsgiving accompanied by righteousness."

Jesus also tweaks Raphael's encouragement to give freely rather than store up gold. But Jesus nuances a different kind of "gold storage." He explains that if a person gives out of vanity, there will be no "gold storage" in heaven. Jesus says such sinful almsgiving has "no recompense from your heavenly Father." He emphasizes this teaching twice more. The praise-seeking givers have already received their tinsel rewards on earth. The teaching on almsgiving again repeats the idea: "And your Father who sees in secret will repay you."

Continuing, Jesus adds further commentary on prayer and fasting. Like almsgiving, the customs of prayer and fasting had also suffered corruption. Jesus directs attention to these pious practices as internal, intimate acts before God, not man. He points out the evil of praying and fasting for the sake of appearing holy and gaining the praise of men. Jesus then twice echoes the theme he introduced when speaking of almsgiving. "And your Father who sees in secret will repay you." (Matthew 6:6)

Although more could be said, this targeted comparison between Tobit 12:8 and the sixth chapter of Matthew shows the way the New Testament often references the Wisdom literature of the Old Testament. The references are often subtle and illusive to modern readers two thousand years later. The secret to perceiving the complementary links is to realize that ancient Jewish listeners already knew the Wisdom literature.

Clarifying this point, imagine patriots attending a political rally. From the stage, a speaker bellows: "My friends, don't we have divinely given rights that can't be taken away? Has not God granted us life, liberty, and the pursuit of happiness!?" Notice that the speaker neither references his source of ideas nor quotes verbatim. He didn't need to. Everybody was intimately familiar with the Declaration of Independence. Similarly, the New Testament's references to Wisdom literature often flow likewise. Sometimes, it's less clear than the two examples above; sometimes more obvious.

Translating from the Masoretic Text, Not the Septuagint

Why? Why would a man so audaciously subtract from the whole content of scripture? Concisely summarized, apart from Luther's personal psychological, emotional, and spiritual struggles that certainly imprinted on the way he thought and believed, I believe there were three causes that most significantly prompted Luther to act as he did:

First, bypassing the Septuagint, Luther worked from a shortened version of Hebrew scriptures to translate into German. Second, Luther failed to fully appreciate that the Church alone was authorized by Christ to determine the official canon of the Old and New Testaments. Third, equally theologically erroneous, Luther believed that the content of divine revelation was alterable according to personal beliefs.

Focusing on Luther's first cause of reducing the forty-six-book Old Testament to thirty-nine books, a little historical context explains much. Here, we note the earliest years of Christianity and the initial expansion of the Church throughout the Roman Empire. With a vigorous use of the Septuagint, the early Christians converted great numbers of Jews and pagans.

Oftentimes, hardened Jewish communities recoiled from this perceived threat to both their faith and culture. They drew back from the Septuagint and gravitated to the safety of their own Hebrew scriptures. For the most part, they abandoned the Septuagint, progressively considering it too Greek, too "Christianized," and too persuasive for the Christians' evangelistic purposes.

Jews retreated to old collections of Hebrew scriptures. There was a forty-six-book collection and a thirty-nine-book collection with the widest circulations in pre-Christian times. They picked the thirty-nine-book collection. They did this to preserve their Jewish identity and shield themselves from the corruption of Christianity. Accordingly, they adopted the thirty-nine-book collection that excluded Tobit, Judith, Wisdom, Sirach, Baruch, I Maccabees, and II Maccabees, including chapters 10-16 of Esther, and chapters 3:24-90, 13, and 14 of Daniel.

As such, the Hebrew scriptures "divorced" the "Christianized" Septuagint. The Jews did this to discourage the use of the Old Testament scriptures for Christian proselytizing. Suddenly, it appeared that the Septuagint fell short of representing the original Hebrew texts.

Then, hundreds of years later, during the Middle Ages, the Masoretic Hebrew Text appears in the timeline. This was an authoritative "canonization" of the Hebrew scriptures by Jewish scholars and scribes between the seventh and tenth centuries AD. Continuing with the post-Christian practice of leaving out the seven books, the Masoretic Text continued categorizing such ancient writings as "Apocrypha." Remember: these books were not apocrypha to Jesus, the Apostles, and the early Church.

When Luther translated the Old Testament into German, he went to the official Jewish Masoretic Text as his original source of Hebrew. Setting aside the Greek Old Testament, Luther assumed the Masoretic Text was the best ancient starting point for a genuine translation into common German. In hindsight, this was a questionable academic premise. It overlooked both the critical history of the Christians' Septuagint and the subsequent Jewish reactionary manipulation of the Hebrew texts.

Requisite Apostolic Authority to Canonize Scripture

An innovative presumption of authority was another contributing cause of the thirty-nine-book Old Testament. The Church alone was authorized by Christ to determine the Biblical canon. Neither the Jews nor any unauthorized Christian had such authority. Luther challenged this long-established understanding. He assumed personal authority to remove books that had been formally declared canonical by the official Church repeatedly for 1,152 years. (These years are measured from AD 382 when Pope Damasus I and the Council of Rome confirmed and decreed Athanasius's seventy-three-book canon as the official canon of the Church, up until the publishing of Luther's German Bible in AD 1534.)

Luther valued the experience of private inspiration so highly that he failed to distinguish the drawing line between personal, interior inspiration and exterior, divine revelation. The line between the two was blurred. Personal inspiration certainly has its place in a person's life, but there's a critical distinction that limits the scope and domain of such inspiration. God never inspires someone to oppose what he himself divinely reveals.

For instance, God revealed the Ten Commandments, and they are absolute, no matter if I feel opposite inspirations. God revealed the Church and Church authority to teach, regardless of my personal ideas. Private inspiration can only take me so far in directing my life. I also need the balance of immovable divine revelation. These two things are meant to go together and complement each other. Starting with Luther, private inspiration pushed aside the divine revelation of Church authority, eventually leading to forty thousand Christian denominations.

(Note: Compared to the days of Luther, the Catholic hierarchy today is much more corrupt. It is infected with a homosexual network of greedy, self-serving servants of worldly powers. The present "Pope" is likely an anti-pope and certainly a heretic. There's a large body of cardinals and bishops that have sold their souls to the devil. Where is the safe path during such a storm? Pursue a life of prayer and personal holiness; draw close to the teachings and practices of the ancient apostolic Church, and hold on to the boat where Christ sleeps. Act mightily when the situation calls for it, and courageously resist when authorities usurp more authority than Jesus Christ commissioned.)

In short, Luther did not recognize the exclusive authority of the Church to set the Biblical canon. He established the premise that such authority belongs to any inspired Christian, even you or me. By his premise, even you may exclude the book of Hebrews, the Gospel of John, or Paul's letters to the Corinthians from the Biblical canon. Imagine yourself recategorizing the Gospel of Matthew as apocrypha henceforward. Such is plainly a possible logical deduction of presuming this kind of personal authority.

It's breathtaking to grasp how much authority Jesus gave his Apostles. No other men, ever, have been bestowed with such authority by God. Jesus gave the Apostles the authority to take his place in the world and continue his mission to save man. Of course, all Christians are commissioned by Christ to participate in the mission, yet only the Apostles were deputized and appointed to authoritatively manage it for the universal *Ekklesia*.

Reflect on their wielding of that authority. Boldly assuming charge, they officially cut loose the irreplaceable Mosaic laws like circumcision, ritual ablutions, and restrictive diets. They replaced the Sabbath with the Breaking of the Bread, a radically altered Passover ritual observed on Sunday, the celebratory day of Jesus Christ's resurrection. They moved worship and religious education from the temple and synagogues to the homes of the baptized. They replaced the apostolic reprobate Judas with the disciple Matthias. Understanding the extent of their mission to reach the ends of the earth until Christ would return, they established a Church structure consisting of bishops, priests, and deacons. They forgave sins, just as Christ had empowered them to do. ("When he had said this, he breathed on them; and He said to them: 'Receive ye the Holy Spirit. Whose sins you shall forgive, they are forgiven them; and whose sins you shall retain, they are retained.'") They produced a completely additional set of scriptures.

God himself personally taught and trained the Apostles for three years! Focus on their paramount, official authority to teach the divinely revealed truths passed on to them through the lips of the Son of God made man. This is where the exclusive authority resides in declaring the divine inspiration of the Old and New Testaments. Christ authorized the Apostles to confirm whatever is true about God's revelation to men and even to expel those who oppose God's voice in such matters.

They were the touchstone to determine the valid canonization of scripture. "Amen I say to you, whatsoever you shall bind upon earth, shall be bound also in heaven; and whatsoever you shall loose upon earth, shall be loosed also in heaven." (Matthew 18:18) Notice that Jesus did not hand the Apostles a list of seventy-three divinely inspired books, but he did authorize them and their successors to settle the matter as time advanced. Future bishops would look back to the Apostles to discern divinely inspired writings. And those same bishops would declare with contiguous apostolic teaching authority –the seventy-three-book Bible.

Not believing that the official Church had the authority to set the canon of scripture, Martin Luther assumed that authority for himself. Detaching himself from authentic, historical validity, he believed he could declare a thirty-nine-book Old Testament canon, "amending" the Church's ageless forty-six-book Old Testament canon.

Suffering the corruption of his age, Luther lost the ability to distinguish between the evil abuses of his times (real or imagined) and the validity of divinely instituted Church authority. Luther felt that Church corruption somehow included the historical and successive link back to apostolic times. He threw out the baby with the bathwater.

Surely, the early Church, walking in the footsteps of clear-thinking and heroic Apostles, burst upon the world with orthodoxy and holiness. For hundreds of years, the Church victoriously battled countless heresies and triumphed with unparalleled glory through the bloody waves of martyrs. Who is so blind or prejudiced not to see the beauty of God at work in this early *Ekklesia*?

Canonization According to Personal Beliefs

The third cause of the thirty-nine-book Old Testament was Luther's unarticulated principle that the content of divine revelation was alterable according to personal beliefs. About one thousand and four hundred years before Martin Luther, an earlier heretic named Marcion demonstrated this exact same erroneous methodology in Church history. Marcion had pioneered an odd canon of scripture –according to his personal beliefs. He first believed what he believed and then manipulated the content of scripture to fit his beliefs.

Common sense theology holds that divine revelation has a primacy over personal belief. Objective revelation precedes subjective understanding. God's revelation comes first, and then we accept and conform to it. Otherwise, for example, if the principle is reversed, a sincere man may wake up on any given Tuesday morning and believe that there's no Trinity and accordingly erase every reference in scripture that mentions the "Father." Even further, he may feel compelled by a mal-informed conscience to urge all Christians to believe and erase just as he does.

Recall that Marcion believed the Old Testament God was not the same God taught by Jesus Christ. There were then two Gods opposed to each other: the bloodthirsty Jewish God and the loving Christian God. With this belief in mind, Marcion outlined a canon of sacred writings that removed anything and everything about the evil God. Marcion first constructed a theological conclusion in his head and then manipulated the content of scripture to match his beliefs. Martin Luther did something similar.

In hindsight, Marcion's failed canon underlines an important theological principle. The inclusion, exclusion, or editing of the Bible should not be according to subjective, personal beliefs. God's objective revelation comes first. Our role is to humbly receive his revelation, not shape it to suit our feelings or academic convictions.

Of course, this implies that we might not understand everything that God reveals. We then study, pray, consult, listen to the Church's insights, read what early Church fathers said on the subject, and the like. But we do not simply change the text of God's revelation. Amputating or neutralizing books from the Bible is certainly a form of changing the text of divine revelation. Such editing amounts to encountering God's words and modifying them to fit whatever we want to hear.

Martin Luther created a sweeping re-valuing of scriptural books. For him, the seventy-three books of the Bible were not flatly the divinely inspired writings of God. On the one hand, he believed all scripture was reliable and incapable of error. On the other hand, he compared the books of scripture with each other and tragically concluded levels of inspiration.

He organized and introduced "inspiration-gradations" of scripture accordingly: There were the canonical books of the Old Testament and the seven books he removed and labeled as Apocrypha. Regarding the New Testament, there were three categories. The first were the paramount books of God's work of salvation. These were books inspired to the highest degree. These books were the Gospel of John, Romans, Galatians, I Peter, I John, and Ephesians. The second level of inspiration was the canonical

New Testament books: Matthew, Mark, Luke, Acts, Paul's other letters, II Peter, and II John. The lowest level of "inspired" books, if they had any inspiration at all, fit into a "quasi-canonical" category. These were Hebrews, James, Jude, and the Book of Revelation.

Regarding these "quasi-canonical" books, Luther believed they lacked the same authority as the Gospels. Neither were these books worthy enough for usage to develop Christian doctrines. In short, they were radically defective as far as divine inspiration goes.

But truly, either God inspires a New Testament writer or not. He does not go halfway, leaving us in doubt. Our salvation depends upon the certainty of his revelation. The divine inspiration of New Testament authors is an all-or-nothing authenticity. For instance, a man is either dead or alive, and a woman is pregnant or not pregnant. Certain realities are not subject to a scale of degrees or percentages. God's immovable word is such an absolute reality.

Luther felt Hebrews represented "bits of wood, hay, and straw." Elsewhere, he claimed: "We cannot put it on the same level with the apostolic epistles." James was "an epistle of straw...for it has nothing of the nature of the Gospel about it." He further asserted: "I do not regard it as the writing of an Apostle. It is against St. Paul and all the rest of scripture in ascribing justification to works." It is "straw not worthy to be burned in my oven as tinder." The book of Revelation was "neither apostolic nor prophetic.... I can in no way detect that the Holy Spirit produced it."

Luther's canonization and grading of scripture rested upon his personal version of Christianity. He picked in scripture what seemed central to him and graded the books accordingly. Notice that the Church criteria for canonizing scripture were apostolicity and ancient Church universality in usage, especially in liturgies.

Luther used a different criterion to set his canon. He saw the core of Christianity as saved by faith alone, saved by dismissing Church authority, and saved by personal inspiration. The value of scriptural books was then judged accordingly.

But Christianity is better understood by starting with the premise that every word and book of scripture is equally divinely inspired. From this premise, the inquiring mind seeks to harmoniously unite the seemingly diverse pieces of God's revelation. Luther's approach was to devalue or throw out apparently incongruent pieces that didn't fit his vision of what Christianity was all about.

Luther's view of faith contrasted with works is a good example of this. Faith and works in the New Testament represent two 100% divinely revealed truths. Luther made them enemies of each other, exalting one and neutralizing the other. But if they are equally inspired by God, the proper theological approach would be to discover how they harmoniously complement each other.

Luther's result was an Old Testament with seven books fewer and a New Testament that downgraded four books to a "quasi-canonical" state. Luther believed that the seven books removed from the Old Testament lacked the authority to establish doctrine and that God did not want them in the canon. Regarding the four downgraded New Testament books, Luther attempted to leave them out of his canon, but too many people objected, so he reluctantly included them. Nonetheless, he held that they should be considered not truly inspired.

The primacy of God's revelation, superior to personal interpretation, is a repeated theme in scripture. The certainty of God's revelation in scripture counters the idea of a quasi-inspiration. (II Peter 1:20-21; I Thessalonians 1:13; II Timothy 3:16)

In summary: This section highlights the divine inspiration of all forty-six books of the Septuagint. It introduced Martin Luther because he challenged the established Biblical canon with a pruned thirty-nine-book Old Testament. After explaining why Luther reduced the Old Testament canon, we explained why he altered the New Testament canon, too. While Luther did not change the twenty-seven-book New Testament canon numerically, he did introduce reservations regarding the divine inspiration of four New Testament books.

The Council of Trent

The Catholic priest and scripture professor, Father Martin Luther, was excommunicated in AD 1521. He defiantly refused to recant his writings. The Emperor of the Holy Roman Empire, Charles V, subsequently declared Luther an outlaw and a heretic. Powerful German princes protected Luther from that point forward in his life. He published his Bible thirteen years later, in AD 1534.

The swelling protestant revolt soon motivated the hierarchy of the Church to organize a council to address sorely needed doctrinal, moral, and disciplinary matters. Church anarchy had spun out of control, and a counter-reformation was crucial. The plans and arrangements to initiate a council started, paused, changed, stopped, and failed for a while. Finally, a town in northern Italy (not a unified county at that time), wedged between the Venetian Republic, Austria, and the Swiss mountains, was decided upon. The place was called Tridentinum. We know it as "Trent."

The Council of Trent met for many sessions during a lengthy period of eighteen intermittent years. Although there were only about seven hundred bishops in the entire world at that time, conciliar participation at its best only reached two hundred bishops in attendance. Not unusually, sessions took place with significantly fewer bishops. At the beginning of the council, three papal legates, four archbishops, twenty-one bishops, forty-two theologians, and various representatives from European powers kicked off the counter-offensive. Among a few other themes, the earliest sessions of the Council of Trent focused on repairing the damage done to the Sacred Scriptures.

Although an awful lot could be said about the council, we'll limit our abbreviated coverage to the bare minimum that pertains to the Bible, our primary subject of pursuit. Finally, a messy twelve years after Luther had printed his Bible, the Council of Trent definitively addressed the issue.

The bishops issued a conciliar decree that clarified the canonical scriptures. Essentially, Trent confirmed the identical seventy-three-book canon decreed by the Council of Florence about one hundred years earlier. Yet, Trent added something more. It additionally declared an anathema for those rejecting the seventy-three-book canon. The following is an excerpt from the *Decree Concerning the Canonical Scriptures*, approved and promulgated by the Council of Trent in AD 1546:

The holy, ecumenical, and general Council of Trent, lawfully assembled in the Holy Ghost, the same three legates of the Apostolic See presiding, keeps this constantly in view, namely, that the purity of the Gospel may be preserved in the Church after the errors have been removed.

This [Gospel] of old promised through the Prophets in the Holy Scriptures, our Lord Jesus Christ, the Son of God, promulgated first with His own mouth and then commanded it to be preached by His Apostles to every creature as the source at once of all saving truth and rules of conduct.

It also clearly perceives that these truths and rules are contained in the written books and in the unwritten traditions, which, received by the Apostles from the mouth of Christ himself, or from the Apostles themselves, the Holy Ghost dictating, have come down to us, transmitted as it were from hand to hand.

Following, then the examples of the orthodox Fathers, it receives and venerates with a feeling of piety and reverence all the books of both the Old and New Testaments since one God is the author of both; also the traditions, whether they relate to faith or to morals, as having been dictated either orally by Christ or by the Holy Ghost, and preserved in the Catholic Church in unbroken succession.

It has thought it proper, moreover, to insert in this decree a list of the sacred books, lest a doubt might arise in the mind of someone as to which are the books received by this council.

"They are the following…." The Council of Trent then lists the forty-six books of the Old Testament, including the seven books that had been labeled as apocrypha by Luther and the full books of Esther and Daniel. Next, the twenty-seven books of the New Testament are listed without any indication of categorical or qualitative differences regarding the divinely inspired nature of every book.

If anyone does not accept as sacred and canonical the aforesaid books in their entirety and with all their parts, as they have been accustomed to be read in the Catholic Church, and as they are contained in the old Latin Vulgate Edition, and knowingly and deliberately rejects the aforesaid traditions, let him be anathema.

A second decree immediately follows, entitled: *Decree Concerning the Edition and Use of the Sacred Books*. This covers various observances regarding the printing, propagation, circulation, examination, and approval and requisite respect for the Sacred Scriptures that are subject to Church oversight. As the first two paragraphs of this eight-paragraph decree touch upon errors propagated by Martin Luther, an additional excerpt is pertinent:

Moreover, the same holy council considering that not a little advantage will accrue to the Church of God if it be made known which of all the Latin editions of the sacred books now in circulation is to be regarded as authentic, ordains and declares that the old Latin Vulgate Edition, which, in use for so many hundred years, has been approved by the Church, be in public lectures, disputations, sermons and expositions held as authentic, and that no one dare or presume under any pretext whatsoever to reject it.

Furthermore, to check unbridled spirits, it decrees that no one relying on his own judgment shall, in matters of faith and morals pertaining to the edification of Christian doctrine, distorting the Holy Scriptures in accordance with his own conceptions, presume to interpret them contrary to that sense which holy mother Church, to whom it belongs to judge of their true sense and interpretation, has held and holds, or even contrary to the unanimous teaching of the Fathers, even though such interpretations should never at any time be published.

CHAPTER ELEVEN

The Fixation Period: AD 367 – AD 419

Fixation: Authoritative Repetitions

The term "fixation" is not employed to imply that something is broken or subject to repair. Neither does the present usage of the term refer to psychological, obsessive focus. Rather, "fixation" here describes an action or extended process by which something (the Biblical canon in this case) is made firm and stable. Accordingly, the canon is not only definitively listed but "fixed" immovably in place.

This compact fifty-two-year period marks a grand historical turning point regarding the Biblical canon. Although we placed great emphasis on St. Athanasius's seventy-three-book canon, the fifty-two years that followed his famed festal letter are equally significant. By the end of this period, the seventy-three-book canon would be perennial for all Christians.

We enter a period of history when the identification of the Biblical canon shifts from individual bishops discerning for their own dioceses to councils and synods of bishops discerning for the Church as a whole. Like in a relay race, when the slowing runner hands the baton to the next runner, Bishop Athanasius bequeathed his personal determination of the scriptural canon to the Pope and formal bodies of bishops. They would sprint the rest of the way to the finish line. These authorities then continually confirmed and ratified Athanasius's canon and essentially made it their own. He had finished the leg work; the universal Church would next "institutionalize" the canon, so to speak. Progressively, the fixation of the canon surpassed the standard of a sole, gifted individual and matured into a divinely authoritative declaration of the universal Church.

The imperative step of the Church's definitive canonization of scripture started with the Council (Synod) of Rome in AD 382. This council represents the first time ever that the universal Catholic Church authoritatively decreed the Biblical canon exactly as it is today, distinct from the altered protestant Bible 1,152 years later. This council was convened in Rome by Pope Damasus I, who promulgated the same seventy-three-book canon listed by St. Athanasius fifteen years earlier.

Within a fifty-two-year time frame, one council (actually a synod in Rome), three additional regional synods, and two Popes asserted, reasserted, and ratified Athanasius's list. Following Rome's decree in AD 382, the "Council" of Hippo declared the seventy-three-book Biblical canon in AD 393. Four years later, in AD 397, the "Council" of Carthage declared the same seventy-three-book canon. Pope Innocent I reaffirmed the same seventy-three-book canon in AD 405. Then, in AD 419, another "Council" of Carthage decreed the same seventy-three-book Biblical canon. Once this wave of Church authority swept through Christianity, the Biblical canon rested securely.

(Note: Although the "canonization blitz" pauses here, the Bible story continues: In AD 494, there was another Roman Synod convened by Pope Gelasius I, who listed the same Biblical canon determined by Pope Damasus I. Thereupon followed the Councils of Nicaea II in AD 787, Florence in AD 1442, and Trent in AD 1546. Each of these councils again and again declared the seventy-three-book canon of scripture. The seven hundred bishops of the Council of Vatican I in AD 1870 did the same.)

Consider the stretch of time between Pentecost in AD 33 and the decree of Pope Damasus I in AD 382. That's 349 years of the only existing Catholic Church without a formally and universally promulgated Bible. While variations of scriptures abounded, the successor of St. Peter had not yet formally declared with absolute clarity the seventy-three-book Bible. Once Pope Damasus I did this, many regional Church authorities followed his lead and repeated his declaration. The regional echoes roared from the authoritative voice of Peter.

Drilling down on perspective here, 349 years is the same time frame between AD 2023 and AD 1672. At that time, neither Mexico nor Canada existed as countries, and the Declaration of Independence would not be written and signed for another 104 years. This is worth a great deal of reflection. Similarly, Christians lacked an authoritatively canonized Bible for the first 349 years of their existence. Yet, the Church was in place from the day of Pentecost onward.

This underlines a very important assumption: The Church preceded the New Testament. It preached it, wrote it, disseminated it, interpreted it, collected it into a single book, and finally canonized it. Conclusively, if the Bible is to be understood, the Church must be understood. Similarly, for instance, the father and mother must be understood if the intricacies of the offspring are to be fathomed. The cause explains the effect.

The monumental and truly foundational decree of Pope Damasus I requires a comprehensive critical context to be fully appreciated. Such context should include a rudimentary grasp of papal authority, the uninterrupted line of papal succession, and the attempted Arian coup to usurp the office of the papacy. The following sections address each of these.

Papal Authority: Basic Theology

We said earlier that no unauthorized man, regardless of holiness, intelligence, or inspiration, had the power to determine the official canon of scripture. The best anyone could do was to impart a personal assessment. Many had done so for hundreds of years. No matter his personal beliefs, Luther had stepped beyond the limits of human authority to shoulder such a task. Just as true, St. Athanasius equally lacked the authoritative scope to decree the Biblical canon for the entire world. He was authorized by the Church to teach the ancient Gospel, the best he knew, to his own flock. But a unique authority would be needed to irreversibly canonize the Holy Scriptures. After St. Athanasius had presented his homework, as it were, papal authority alone could determine the official Biblical canon. The Pope wielded the delegated divine authority to settle the matter once and for all, of course harmoniously with Church tradition.

Before anything else, let's demystify the term "Pope." In AD 382, Pope Damasus I, was not called the "Pope" as we exclusively use the term today. During the fourth century, any bishop or priest may have been addressed with the word *"Pappas,"* Greek for "Father." It was a simple ecclesiastical title that expressed affectionate respect. As such, the assigned *presbuteros* of a local church may have been called *Pappas Andreas,* for instance. It referred to a type of spiritual fatherhood. This ancient custom reflects the paternal sentiments of St. Paul for his own converts birthed in Christ. "I became your father in Jesus Christ through the Gospel." (I Cor. 4:15)

A few hundred years after Damasus I, the term "Pope" evolved into a strict usage for the Bishop of Rome in particular. But when he lived, Pope Damasus I was simply referred to as *Episcopus Damasus* (Latin) or the "Bishop of Rome." Perhaps some who enjoyed a more familiar relationship with him called him *Pappas,* too. (Note: We still breathe the vestiges of this ancient custom when we call the pastor of the local parish, Father Smith, for instance. The title "patriarch" also derives from the Greek root word *Pappas*.)

The term "Pope" has picked up some heavy baggage throughout the centuries. In some circles, the term is psychologically inseparable from negative connotations. Granted, popes are human beings, even more, sinners. There have been holy, smart, or dynamic popes. There have also been worldly, or high-handedly political, or obdurately immoral men who have governed as the Bishop of Rome. Some have been more focused on the beauty of paintings and mosaics than the nurturing of holy souls, including their own.

Just so it's important to distinguish between the person and office of the pope. For example, sinful parents do not negate the validity of God's institution of parenthood itself. A wicked president does not prove that the founding father's institution of the office of the President of the United States of America is invalid. Similarly, the distinction between the person and office of the pope should be kept in mind. A bad pope does not prove that Jesus Christ did not institute the office. Consider: Judas's betrayal did not prove he lacked an apostolic office. Sin and even death did not obliterate that office founded by Jesus Christ. Accordingly, the Apostles (by Peter's leadership) replaced Judas with Matthias. (Acts 1:15-26) The apostolic offices entrusted by Christ continue beyond the Apostles.

Pope Damasus's decree of canonization is incomprehensible if seen merely as a person's opinion equal to any others. No, Damasus knew his decree was the authoritative act of an office instituted by Jesus Christ. He knew he was the authorized person who held the office, and he decreed in the name of the office. The very words of Jesus Christ to Peter, the Church's ancient understanding of Peter's office, and the continuation of Peter's office in time all explain Pope Damasus's mindset and his canonization of the Bible.

Cutting to the chase, let's scrutinize Jesus's words to Peter, the scriptural heartbeat that substantiates the doctrine of papal authority:

Blessed are you, Simon, son of Jonah. For flesh and blood has not revealed this to you, but my heavenly Father. And so I say to you, you are Peter, and upon this rock I will build my church, and the gates of hell shall not prevail against it. I will give you the keys to the kingdom of heaven. Whatever you bind on earth shall be bound in heaven; and whatever you loose on earth shall be loosed in heaven." (Matthew 16: 17-19)

In this three-verse passage, Jesus makes three declarations about Peter. Each declaration is immediately followed with a related complementary meaning. Both individually and collectively, the declarations, with their elaborations, revert to the person of Peter and God's power in his life. Viewed as a whole, the verses reveal an astounding act of divine authority deputizing Peter as the head of Christ's *Ekklesia.*

The three declarations are a triple blessing upon Peter. From a plain language perspective, the entire passage speaks of Peter as the primary subject: The first verse identifies, blesses, and compliments him. The second verse renames him and teaches the significance of his new name. The third verse promises Peter authority and explains the promise.

In verse 17, the declaration is that Simon is blessed. The added elaboration explains the nature of Simon's profession. Simon's faith and pronouncement of the Gospel are returned by Christ both as a blessing and an educational opportunity. Jesus clarifies that Simon's profession is not ultimately from Simon; neither by his efforts, nor by his blood lineage, nor by the fleshly fruits of his intelligence. Rather, Simon is blessed precisely because the Father has freely bestowed the gift of faith and its profession upon him. Simon's profession is, above all else, God's work, not man's. Simon can believe and say that Jesus Christ is the Messiah only because God has showered that gift of faith upon him.

This verse foreshadows Simon's new place in life, racing upon him through the next words from the mouth of God. Simon would be sent to teach, not by the strength of his human ingenuity and wits but by the Father's gift of proclaiming the Gospel. Simon's divinely appointed teaching role would fully manifest during his opening sermon after the descent of the Holy Spirit at Pentecost. (Acts 2:14-41) Nonetheless, at present, Jesus encourages him to let the Father proclaim through him. But Simon is clearly not ready for selfless preaching. Notice the stern rebuke of Jesus to Simon when the Apostle operates according to a human way of thinking. (Matthew 16:21-23)

In verse 18, the declaration is that Simon is renamed by God as "Peter" henceforward. Notice that the renaming is preceded by the equivalent of a "therefore." Jesus indicates that precisely because Simon had just received the divine gift of proclamation, he immediately advanced to the next step of God's far-reaching purpose. Jesus wastes no time. Simon's profession of the Gospel is what prompts Jesus to rename him.

Recall that in the Bible, when God renames a person, it's both symbolic and real. He doesn't take names lightly. A new name signifies God's new purpose for a chosen person. In the Old Testament, when he was ninety-nine years old, "Abram," meaning "exalted father," is renamed "Abraham," meaning "father of a multitude." (Genesis 17:1-6)

An angel renames "Jacob" as "Israel." "Jacob" referred to the grasping of the heal of Esau, his twin brother at birth. The name "Israel" refers to a struggle with God and an overcoming. The new name identifies a new role and destiny in life. Jacob henceforth would engage directly with God and come to acknowledge God's lordship over his life. (Genesis 32:27)

As such, the newly given name repurposes the role and mission of the person in God's far-reaching designs. "Simon," meaning "he who hears," is renamed "Peter," meaning "rock." From God's perspective, this is not casual but a momentous repurposing of Simon's life. The new name points to a fresh heavenly destiny on the horizon.

The added elaboration in verse 18 logically follows. Having just re-named Simon, Jesus gives a meaningful glimpse of Peter's new mission and destiny. It makes perfect sense that if a man is given a new name, an appropriate enlightenment of the new name would follow. Jesus will make Peter the "rock" or "building foundation" of his Church. The promise to build upon him stems from Peter's new gift of proclaiming the Gospel. Peter is equipped with the inner gift he'll need to fulfill his new purpose. Jesus then elaborates on the nature of the Church he has in mind, that it will prevail over the demonic powers of evil. This last addition implies the perpetuity of Peter's authoritative office and, therefore, successors.

In Verse 19, the declaration is that Jesus Christ will give Peter authority (keys). When Jesus entrusts the keys to Peter, the bestowal of the keys to Eliakim suggests an Old Testament parallel. The servant, Eliakim, was clothed with a robe, sashed, and entrusted with the keys of authority over the inhabitants of Jerusalem and the house of David. Honorably, this faithful servant (chamberlain) exercised temporary rule in place of David, his master.

"I will place the key of the House of David on his shoulder; when he opens, no one shall shut. When he shuts, no one shall open." (cf. Is 22:15-25) Christ's declaration and elaboration reflect the pattern provided by Isaiah. It would not be difficult for the Apostles to grasp that Jesus sets Peter in place as the new chamberlain over the House of the New David.

Jesus then elaborates, spelling out the kind of authority the keys represent. The binding and loosing metaphor has a rich rabbinic tradition. It refers to the ability to establish, alter, or abolish rules of conduct for the Jewish community. The scribes and Pharisees retained the power of *"Halakah"* as a matter of practical governance. Jesus had excoriated them for abusing the practice, for "tying up heavy loads and laying them upon men's backs," while doing nothing to lighten demands. The pharisaical perversion of *Halakah* had resulted in a religion that was excessively burdensome and impossible to observe without tormenting scrupulosity. The detailed moral conformities required by the Pharisees had mechanized religion and squeezed the joy out of it. It gravitated toward a "check-list-spirituality" rather than an intimate relationship with God.

Nonetheless, in principle, Jesus never condemned the authority and custom of *Halakah* itself. Understandably, there had to be some kind of practical mechanism to regulate religious practice. Wisely then, in verse 19, Jesus uses the commonly known *Halakah* metaphor to entrust Peter with its power for the *Ekklesia*. Whereas Peter's place as the foundation of the Church remained exclusive, Jesus later extended the power of *Halakah* to all the Apostles (Matthew 18:18). Years later, led by Peter, the Apostles as a body demonstrate their undeniable ownership of *Halakah* for the *Ekklesia* when they meet in Jerusalem and liberate both Jewish and gentile believers from the no longer applicable observance of the Mosaic Law (Acts 15:1-29).

(Note: Jesus's preservation of the *Halakah* structure of the Pharisees shouldn't be surprising. Just because a custom or doctrine was practiced or believed by the Pharisees, it was not categorically dismissed. For instance, while the Sadducees claimed orthodoxy by adhering to the Torah alone, some doctrines from the oral traditions of the Pharisees were readily accepted by Christ. Examples of the variance would be the belief in the resurrection of the body, the afterlife in heaven, and the existence of angels, none of which find proof in the Torah, but all of which were accepted by Christ. The Sadducees contemptuously held such things as pure pharisaical innovations that must be rejected. But Jesus recognized the place of oral tradition, too. The Messiah knew how to distinguish between whatever was true or false or harmful for his *Ekklesia*.)

The authority bestowed upon Peter underlines the nature of the Church as authoritative, visible, governable, and institutional, similar to the structure of the Jewish religion, with an appointed head and ruling body that exercised *Halakah*. This shouldn't be rashly doubted, considering that the Jewish religion was both the prefigurement and organic root of the Christian *Ekklesia*. When the Son of God founded His Church, He didn't unconditionally tear down and replace the Jewish *Ekklesia*. Jesus didn't start all over again and build from scratch. Rather, he "Christianized" the theological doctrines, spirituality, liturgy, calendar, feasts, morals, daily customs, and even hierarchical structures that had been established in view of the Messiah's eventual coming and perfecting.

It's appropriate here to at least note a modern, erroneous interpretation of Matthew 16:17-19 to clarify further. Although the above explanation of this passage is rooted in an understanding of the ancient *Ekklesia*, some have advanced a new interpretation of the passage. They hold that the use of the term "rock" in verse 18 does not refer to the person of Peter but to his profession of faith.

However the structure of Jesus's speech and a common sense reading of the passage argue against this stance. Each verse starts with an assertion about the person of Peter and then logically adds something more about that person. If "rock" in verse 18 refers to something outside of the pattern, it would be a forced incongruency of the sentence structure and an odd derivation from the overall pattern of the passage. As such, an inconsistency and ambiguity of language by Jesus regarding such an important matter shared among the Apostles is hardly comprehensible.

Moreover, to support this innovative viewpoint, some people focus on an important (imagined) difference between the Greek words *Petros* and *petra* in verse 18. It's believed that *Petros* means "small stone" in Greek and that *petra* means "large rock." As such, Peter is the "small stone," and his profession of faith is the "large rock" upon which the Church is built. Nevertheless, while this vocabulary nuance existed in some early Greek poetry, it no longer existed during first-century Greek. At that time, the Greek writers of the New Testament used the different but synonymous words as a mere stylistic variation, a routine writing technique to avoid undue repetition.

Besides, as Jesus spoke in Aramaic with Peter, he pronounced the word *"Kepha"* when renaming Simon. In Aramaic, *kepha* meant "massive rock," not "small stone." So, neither does a reference to the Aramaic language support the argument that identifies Peter's profession of faith as a larger "rock" than Peter himself.

Regarding verse 18, putting aside the unusual reading of the sentence and the weighing of old Greek words, there's a theological problem with building a Church upon a man's profession of faith. We're speaking of a Christian *Ekklesia* here, like the former Jewish *Ekklesia*. It's a body with a head that is authoritative, visible, governable, and institutional. A person then must be placed as the head.

Notice that David was a man after God's heart. He performed many good deeds that pleased God. But when God blesses him, David himself is bestowed with authority, and the kingdom of Israel is built upon him. God builds institutions on persons, not performances. Abraham also pleased God with astounding acts of faith. But the nation of Israel is built upon the person of Abraham, not upon his acts of faith. Of course, his faith prompted God to bless him. But the blessing and empowerment of Abraham falls on him as a person, not his profession of faith. The same holds with Peter. Of course, Peter's profession of the Messiah was special and pleasing to God. But it is the person of Peter who is blessed in return —with real authority.

The Rock and the Keys

We had stated that Pope Damasus's canonical decree is incomprehensible without truly grasping the authority bestowed upon him by God. Who did this man think he was to define the Bible till the end of time? This prompted our explanation of the scriptural basis for papal authority. Otherwise, the historic act of the papal signature might be idly skimmed and superficially dismissed. Having covered the foundational theology, let's focus on some cultural context to enrich that theology. Consider it like this: after theological concepts in black and white, a few colored photos illustrate the nuances of papal authority theology.

(Note: The rich cultural and religious nuances of this section are attributed to Jeff Cavins, a protestant minister who had converted to the Catholic Church.)

Gospel flashback: The first time Jesus meets Simon, he says, "You are Simon the son of John (Jonah), you will be called *Cephas* (*Kepha*)." (John 1:42) Upon meeting him for the first time, Jesus reveals to Simon that in the future he will be known by a different name. This both contextualizes and bookends the renaming of Simon.

Andrew had convinced his brother to meet Jesus by saying, "We have found the Messiah." Simon's future new name would linger as a mystery for a long time, as would Jesus's true identity. The two realities were inseparably weaved together in a shared destiny. At last, when Simon finally confesses Jesus as the Messiah, Jesus renames him Peter. The name anoints Simon for the Messiah's future mission to the world.

Deep into his ministry, Jesus and the Apostles hiked north to Caesarea Philippi, fifteen miles from Galilee, about a three-day walk north from Jerusalem. This pagan territory was isolated from everything Jewish. No Jews visited. It was an ideal place for privacy between Jesus and his Apostles, free from the clamor of the crowds and cross-questioning of the Pharisees. The rabbis had forbidden anyone from going near the thoroughly gentile district. Jews commonly referred to the area as the "Land of Darkness." But Jesus was not subject to the Pharisees and had a good reason for venturing there.

A veritable focal point for the worship of demons, Caesarea Philippi's reputation for wickedness was well deserved. On the side of a massive red-rock bluff, resolute pagans had hewn a shrine with life-sized niches for various gods. Far and wide, the location was known as the great rock of pagan worship. Caesar had his own niche. A more prominent niche was dedicated to the Greek god named Pan, the half-goat, half-man god with the flute, the god of sheep and shepherds. The massive rock spread five hundred feet wide and soared 150 feet high. (Note: The average height of a telephone pole is forty-five feet.)

A hollowed cave marked the dead center. And just inside the cave, a water well welcomed human sacrifices offered to Pan. Living victims were sacrificed by ritual drownings. After the submersion, if blood surfaced upon the waters, the offering had not been accepted by Pan. When no sign of blood appeared, Pan accepted the sacrifice, and appeasement prevailed. Above the bottomless well, claimed by those who had attempted to measure it without success, a sign had been etched in stone: "The Gates of Hades." Israel knew this spot of evil as "the gateway to hell."

Jesus was an educational master. (He frequently matched the theme of his discourse with a complementary setting.) Consider his journey to this location like a field trip, yet with mind-numbing gravity. This is the place where he had planned long ago to inaugurate Peter as the head of his *Ekklesia*. He desired a backdrop that would permanently lodge in the memories of the simple fishermen. With their eyes riveted on the demonic rock of evil, Jesus juxtaposed his own rock. No doubt, the Apostles would accrue many years of reflection surrounding the layers of meaning attached to this place and the related declarations of Jesus.

This "field trip" was not an academic exercise. He had asked the Apostles who he was. They started quoting what others were saying. Jesus was not interested in that. So typical of his teaching style, he flipped the theme to something profoundly personal. The long-awaited talk regarding his identity had finally come up, and the Apostles found themselves wrestling with the burning question. Jesus then asked: "But who do you say that I am?" (Matthew 16:15) The question targeted their inner beliefs.

Of course, the impetuous Peter blurts out what he had been gradually discovering. He had seen the wonders and miracles and pondered long and hard. This time, the man who often said what he thought, regardless of the consequences, was correct. This sign of spiritual maturity was enough for Jesus. Simon was ready. As they perched at the frontier of the demonic world, gawking at the massive rock of pagan worship and sacrifice, Jesus turned to Simon and responded: "Blessed are you, Simon, son of Jonah.

For flesh and blood has not revealed this to you, but my heavenly Father. And so I say to you, you are *Kepha* (massive rock), and upon this *kepha*, I will build my Church, and the gates of hell shall not prevail against it." (Matthew 16:17-18) The physical setting colored the meaning of the declaration.

Simon stated who Jesus was. In return, Jesus stated who Simon was. He was the massive rock of God, now pitted against the massive rock of evil. The line had been drawn in the sand; Peter was now declared the defiant, foundational rock of the Messiah's *Ekklesia*. Jesus had brought Peter to the battle line between good and evil and assigned him as the general.

Henceforth, Peter's awareness would grow. Notice the ending words of his first letter: "Be sober and vigilant. Your opponent, the devil, is prowling around like a roaring lion looking for someone to devour." (I Peter 5:8) Equally revealing, notice Jesus's intimate words to Peter at the closing of the last supper: "Simon, Simon, behold Satan has demanded to sift all of you like wheat, but I have prayed that your own faith may not fail; and once you have turned back (from his thrice denial), you must strengthen your brothers." (Luke 22:31-32) Significantly, these words to Peter immediately followed Jesus's instructions regarding the meaning of leadership. True leadership essentially means –wholehearted service. (Luke 22:26) This was a last-minute lesson for the first Pope before Jesus entered his passion.

Of course, there's considerably more symbol and reality here. There's the demon god of sheep and shepherds, now confronted by the Good Shepherd and his soon-to-be replacement shepherd for the salvation of the world. There's also the divine pledge that the gates of hell shall not prevail against the Church, a direct challenge to the pagan's sacrificial gate of hell within the massive rock of evil.

Caesarea Philippi stood as a gateway to a gentile world. It was somewhat of a northern exit point from Israel. After establishing Peter as the head of his Church, Jesus was not finished with the lesson. The Apostles likely hiked further north to Mount Hermon. Starting with Enoch, tradition claims Hermon's 9,200-foot peak as the place of abomination where the fallen angels procreated with human women to produce the "Nephilim." (Genesis 6:4)

Some Biblical researchers believe this is where the transfiguration took place, only days past the Caesarea Philippi visit. (Matthew 17:1-8) The Apostles were destined to travel beyond the Promised Land to bring the Gospel to the gentile world. Just before Jesus ascended to heaven, he commissioned the Apostles to spread the Gospel throughout the world. Surely, they'd remember Peter's appointment at Caesarea Philippi and the transfiguration on Mt. Hermon. They'd remember the northern gateway to an evil world beyond.

Let's return to the significance of Jesus promising to hand Peter the keys. "I will give you the keys to the kingdom of heaven. Whatever you bind on earth shall be bound in heaven; and whatever you loose on earth shall be loosed in heaven." (Matthew 16:19) We previously noted that this verse and elaboration mirror the pattern found in Isaiah 22:22. The handing of the keys to Peter suggest Eliakim's receiving of the keys of the house of David. Yet, we barely scratched the surface of Jesus's reference. Jewish cultural context is indispensable here. Without it, the modern reader barely catches what's really taking place. A flood of meaning rushed into the minds of the Jewish Apostles when Jesus spoke of handing over keys.

The royal steward accompanied the dynastic monarchy of Israel. The king and his royal steward truly governed as a pair. There are examples in modern times. Consider the monarch of Great Britain and the prime minister. Accordingly, the king enjoys full authority, while the appointed minister has delegated power to exercise on the king's behalf. The same kind of governing relationship played out within the Davidic monarchy. As daily affairs go, it was the royal steward who governed.

The appointed royal steward wore a distinguished royal robe and sash. He was a highly respected and honored person in the city of Jerusalem. As he represented the king, people bowed to him whenever he passed. They respectfully addressed him as "Father" as he fulfilled his paternal office. Everyone knew he exercised royal authority, conspicuously worn whenever he walked to and from the gates of the city with gigantic keys slung over his shoulder. The keys fit the locks of the fortified gates of the city. The royal steward unlocked the city gates every morning and locked them tight every evening, exercising his solicitude for the inhabitants.

So, when Peter is promised the keys of the kingdom, a deep-seated cultural awareness is felt by the Apostles. Peter is pledged delegated authority from Christ himself. He is made the royal steward of Christ of the Davidic line. The governorship of daily operations is, therefore, handed over to him. Peter is established in a position of honor. But with honor comes duty. He is put in charge of securing the doors of the kingdom, opening the way for souls to encounter and receive God, and protecting them from the evils (sin, temptation, demonic influence) that try to breach the gates. The Apostles understood the social structure of the royal steward and certainly interpreted Jesus's words to Peter through this cultural lens.

Additionally, the royal steward's authority represented an institutional office. It wasn't a mere personal favor of some kind. The position then had dynastic succession attached to it. If the royal steward died, another was appointed in his place to continue with the king's affairs uninterrupted. So, the Apostles understood that Peter was pledged an institutional governing office, which would continue beyond his own life.

Notice that Jesus does not yet give the keys to Peter but pledges the keys. It's in the future tense. As such, Jesus is establishing a Church governing structure effective upon his absence. Of course, whenever the king was away, the royal steward usually took charge of the city of Jerusalem. Upon Jesus's departure from this world at his ascension, Peter would grab hold of the keys in full and govern the Church. The keys were a provisional arrangement for the Church on earth. At the end of time, when Jesus would return, they would no longer be needed.

(Note: The provisional nature of the Pope's authority is highlighted in "The Last Judgment" fresco in the Vatican's Sistine Chapel, painted by Michelangelo. Jesus Christ himself is judging the world. The souls are separated between the saved and the damned. Peter stands next to Jesus with the keys in his hands. What is he doing with the keys? He is offering them back to Jesus. They were only something to use meanwhile on earth when Jesus was away. Now, all creation was past that. Christ has returned as the judge and separator of souls. So, Peter returns the keys. This is where beautiful art and good theology marry.)

Lastly, before the detail escapes us, in Isaiah 22:15-24, the Apostles knew the circumstances of Eliakim's reception of the keys as the new royal steward. Eliakim received the keys precisely because the previous holder, Shebna, had abused his privileges. So, the authority was stripped away from Shebna and handed to Eliakim. Coupled with Jesus's bestowal of the power of *Halakah* upon Peter, the parallel is clear. The keys of authority will be ripped away from the Pharisees and handed to Peter.

These additional historical and cultural considerations about the rock and the keys complement the basic theological explanation of papal authority given above. Again, we're simply attempting to sketch the nature of the authority received by Peter and "inherited" by Pope Damasus I.

Unbroken Succession from Peter Onward

Not only does scripture and theology explain Saint Damasus, but history equally defines him. He was the 37th Pope in the history of the Catholic Church, succeeding Saint Peter as the first. His unbroken link back to Peter explains the canonization of the Bible. It wasn't a personal act based on whim or smarts. No, it was an institutional act, formal and official, authorized by Jesus Christ through the unbroken line of apostolic succession. Damasus believed he possessed the exact same authority that Peter had received at Caesarea Philippi 350 years earlier.

While building on the academic and pastoral crests of others, Damasus's anointing was not necessarily to shine as the most gifted person in the Church but to lead the way in pronouncing the Gospel to the world. Authoritatively shouting the revelation of the Gospel was inseparably linked with his "inherited anointing."

As such, Damasus's canonization of the Bible was by the authority bestowed upon Peter. This same authority had been passed on to him by papal election. For instance, wouldn't President Lincoln have the same presidential power as President Washington? Similarly, Damasus had the same authority as Peter —and he knew it. This awareness was a deep part of him. Accordingly, a familiarity with the nuts and bolts of apostolic succession is indispensable for understanding Damasus's bold decree regarding scripture.

Apostolic succession is the line of bishops stretching back to the Apostles. This "line" may be described as a continuous, unbroken link of episcopal consecrations and appointments, all rooted in the Apostles as the beginning point. The line of succession preserves the continuous transfer of apostolic authority. In this way, it makes the Apostles present, so to speak, in our modern world. The apostolic successors then possess the same commission and responsibilities that the Apostles originally received, with the same teaching, governing, and sanctifying authority bestowed by Jesus Christ.

This view of the successor bishops as duly installed with the same authority as the Apostles is ancient theology. Peter had made Evodius the Bishop of Antioch. He had also consecrated Ignatius, who would succeed Evodius as the next Bishop of Antioch. Ignatius explained that the bishop had the same authority as the Apostles. At the turn of the first century, Ignatius many times expressed the apostolic teaching that obeying the bishop was the same as obeying the Apostles and Jesus Christ himself.

Tracing the three consecutive bishops that followed Peter should adequately provide a concrete sample of apostolic succession. When Peter died in AD 67, Linus took over as the next Pope. He was the Bishop of Rome from AD 67 to AD 76. After Linus came Pope Cletus, who ruled from AD 76 to AD 88. Next came Pope Clement from AD 88 to AD 97. (Today, we know Clement as Clement I because other newly elected popes would take this same name as their own.)

Easily glossed over when reading, such are the names and dates that historical research presents before our eyes. However, such raw data is insufficient to taste the reality of apostolic succession. We must know something about these men and how they became popes to appreciate their lives. This seems important, simply to demystify the papacy and show that these pious men embraced the very real possibility of dying as martyrs by their papal elections. These were courageous men like the Apostles.

Pause for a moment and reflect not only on the miracles, signs, and wonders of apostolic Christianity but also on our heroes who sacrificed their lives. The Apostles lived in an atmosphere of blood-offering. For professing the Gospel: James (John's brother) was beheaded in AD 42; Andrew was crucified in AD 61; Jude was clubbed to death in AD 62; Philip was crucified in AD 62; James was thrown by the Jews from the pinnacle of the temple in Jerusalem in AD 62; Matthias was hacked to death in AD 65; Matthew was slaughtered at the altar while offering Mass (Breaking Bread) in AD 65; Peter was crucified upside down in AD 67 because he felt too unworthy to die in the exact same way as his Master, Jesus; Paul was beheaded in AD 67, also in Rome, the same year as Peter's execution; Simon was crucified in AD 67; Bartholomew was skinned alive in AD 72; Thomas was stabbed to death in AD 74; and John was dunked alive into a vat of boiling oil before a crowd in the Colosseum in Rome during the reign of Domitian. He survived unscathed and was banished to the island of Patmos, where he wrote his *Apokalypsis*. (The date of the completion of the *Apokalypsis* remains unresolved.)

Linus, Cletus, and Clement were of the same spiritual stock and spittle as the Apostles, ready to testify about Christ unto death. They were brought into Christianity through the ministries of Peter and Paul in Rome, who baptized many in the Tiber River that runs near the Vatican. Learning from these two pillars of the Church of Rome, all three were nurtured in the faith by no less than Saint Peter and Saint Paul.

Originally from Tuscany, Linus lived in Rome. This is the same Linus mentioned by Paul at the end of his second letter to Timothy: "Try to get here before winter. Eubulus, Pudens, Linus, Claudia, and all the brothers send greetings." (II Timothy 4:21) Claudia was Linus's mother, both significant members of the first Christian community in Rome. Linus ended up as Paul's companion in Rome. He died between the persecutions of Nero and Domitian, which suggests that he did not die as a martyr, yet some historians claim otherwise. After his death, Linus was buried near Peter on Vatican Hill, basically a cemetery outside of the Roman city boundaries at that time.

Cletus was a Roman by birth. (Some historic records refer to him as Anacletus, his formal name.) He grew up near Peter's residence in Rome and became a close disciple of his. After Peter baptized him, the Apostle personally educated him in the faith and the ways of Christian virtue. No surprise, Cletus became well known for his profound piety. Standing at the foot of the cross, Cletus personally witnessed the execution of his dear friend, remaining faithful until Peter's last breath. As the roots of Christianity sunk deeper into the city of Rome, Linus had accompanied his mentor, Paul, while Cletus had accompanied his mentor, Peter.

Cletus was the Pope when Emperor Domitian reigned. Domitian was fiercely anti-Jewish and considered the Christians without discrimination as a subset of the Jewish religion. Domitian's approach was to either kill the Jews or subject them to exorbitant taxation. The Christians were targeted as the scapegoats for causing famines, floods, and diseases that sometimes flashed anywhere throughout the Empire.

Soon after coming to power, Domitian declared himself "God the Lord." He passed a law decreeing that "no Christian, once brought before the tribunal, should be exempted from punishment without renouncing his religion." The Christian community met secretly in homes or catacombs. Although the details are lost to history, Cletus's martyrdom is highly probable. His slashed body was found in a Roman dump and soon buried near Peter.

The historical record lists Clement as the fourth Pope. He's also known as Clement I or Clement of Rome. Clement was a close disciple of Peter's, yet amply co-worked with Paul as well. He was the most educationally gifted of the three immediate successors of Peter. The imprint of both Apostles is evident in his monumental letter to the Corinthians. He reflects the style and themes of Paul, compounded with the explicit authority of Peter. This critical letter stands out as Clement's enduring mark in history.

At the end of Paul's letter to the Philippians, a compliment is shared about Clement: "Yes, and I ask you also, my true yokemate, to help them, for they have struggled at my side in promoting the Gospel, along with Clement and my other co-workers, whose names are in the book of life." (Philippians 4:3) During the reign of Trajan, Clement was banished to the Pontus quarries, and later martyred by drowning in the sea, with an anchor knotted around his neck.

That's a quick review of these three contemporary co-laborers with Peter and Paul. But how did the apostolic papal succession take place? Although Peter held the office as the primary Bishop of Rome, he went ahead and consecrated Linus and Cletus as bishops, too. These two friends worked together to help alleviate the many responsibilities that fell upon Peter's shoulders. Today, we call such bishops "auxiliary bishops." (The term "auxiliary" derives from the Latin *"auxilium"* meaning "aid, help, or support.")

As such, Linus and Cletus helped Peter, especially with the priestly ministry and sacramental needs of the Roman Christians. Yet, Peter didn't divide his bequeathed, authoritative office as the singular head of the universal Church. His office was undividable. Yet, this pastoral arrangement did help free him for adequate time to pray, teach, and preach in public. Peter did not want to disengage from his duty to preach the Gospel to first-time listeners in public settings. Meanwhile, the clergy and faithful of Rome came to know and greatly appreciate Linus and Cletus as knowledgeable and holy pastors ever close to their hearts.

Shortly before his death, Peter then consecrated Clement as another bishop. Throughout the years, Peter came to realize that it was Clement, not so much Linus or Cletus, who possessed the qualities best suited as his successor, as the head of the Church. Like Paul, Clement possessed the special gift of profound theological understanding and a wonderful familiarity with the Septuagint. So, Peter made him a bishop and strongly expressed his intentions and hopes that Clement would succeed him in the papal office. Peter even expressed that he handed the power of the papal office to Clement. Then, martyrdom soon raced upon Peter as he continued exercising the papal office.

During an ongoing persecution, the Church was suddenly left with three bishops in Rome, facing the question of succession. The Church, of course, knew the precedent of the Holy Spirit working through an election process, as in the case of Matthias replacing Judas. Of course, Peter had played a key role in introducing that course of action. The Church equally understood that once the papal office became vacant, the replacement had to be a decision made by the living, not the dead. So, the *presbuteroi* of Rome, imploring divine assistance, subjected the succession to the first papal election. Having just lost Peter and Paul, the Church operated underground, now by the hands-on care of Linus and Cletus. It's likely that these two veteran pastors helped organize that first election.

Linus won the election and became the second Pope. He held the office for eleven years. Cletus followed, holding the office for twelve years. History does not record groundbreaking feats of governing of these two Popes. Linus consecrated fifteen bishops. Cletus divided the city of Rome into twenty-five geographic locations and named them "parishes." He then ordained twenty-five priests, one for each parish. In this way, the first two popes that followed Peter focused on the development of the Church in Rome.

When Cletus died, Peter's personal favorite won the third election. Clement was Pope for nine years. It seems a consideration of seniority had played a role throughout the elections of Linus, Cletus, and Clement. The clergy had a long-established affinity for their dear two pastors who had held "auxiliary" authority the longest, assisted Peter the most, and established deep personal relationships with the Christian community. Linus and Cletus had the most administrative know-how for overseeing the Church and had "paid their dues," so to speak. It shouldn't be surprising that they won consecutive votes prior to Clement receiving the required number of votes to become the fourth Pope.

God has his timing that sooner or later unfailingly proves wiser than the calculated choices of men. It was neither by happenstance nor good luck that a grave need of the Corinthians and the occupation of the papal office by Clement coincided. Clement's attempted resolution of their needs occasioned an early demonstration of papal authority that set a significant precedent.

In AD 95, unfortunately, the Church in Corinth still suffered from its distinctive defects. A melting pot of well-meaning Christians from various pagan backgrounds, the local church there still indulged in the vices of factiousness and disharmony. Of course, Paul had worked to resolve these tendencies, apparently now with limited success. Forty-five years after he had founded this cosmopolitan church, the inner strife of the church finally boiled over worse than ever.

Young upstarts had overthrown the legitimately appointed bishops and priests of the church of Corinth. A rebellion had broken out. Schism threatened the Corinthians' survival as a community of Christians. The dispute festered, and the community couldn't find a way to solve their own problem. This prompted some of the more mature leaders to write to the Bishop of Rome for help. Clement must have read their desperate letter with a heavy heart. He had witnessed Paul's persistent struggles to birth the Corinth church. Clement would surely have felt the responsibility to help resolve the tragedy. He responded with an energetic determination, creating the masterpiece epistle of his papacy. He basically picked up where Paul left off. The letter has passed on to history, known as Pope Clement I's Epistle to the Corinthians.

Notice this letter was not an unexpected, unwelcomed assertion of authority. It was not a Pope meddling in another church's affairs. Clement didn't undertake the letter to make his authority felt. Rather, it was a response to a faraway Greek church appealing to Rome for help. The response was plainly the fulfillment of a duty pressed upon Clement. A sign of this is that the Apostle John was still alive, living not that far away from Corinth. The Corinthians' request for an adjudicator bypassed the Apostle John, who lived just down the street, as it were, and shot directly to the distant authority figure of the universal Church, the Successor of the Apostle, Peter.

Clement's vigorous response with a massive letter represents the first instance in the historical written record when a Pope (following Peter) acted with authority over the universal Church. Normally, bishops characteristically taught and governed strictly locally. Clement, however, responded with a gentle heart yet with overtones of authority over the whole Church. He intervened and instructed on a course of action beyond the locality of Rome. Clearly, theologically grounded, Linus, Cletus, and Clement had the same authority. It shouldn't be surprising that Clement was really the first one to display it visibly. Perhaps Peter and Paul saw such a destiny for Clement. His time had come. The following excerpts give a sense of Clement's directives in his letter to the Corinthians:

Christ therefore was sent forth by God, and the Apostles by Christ.... and thus, preaching through the countries and cities, they appointed the first fruits of their labors, having first proved them by the Spirit, to be bishops and deacons of those who should afterward believe. Nor was this anything new, since indeed many ages before it was written concerning bishops and deacons. For thus says the Scripture [in a certain place], 'I will appoint their bishops in righteousness and their deacons in faith.' (Chapter 42)

Our Apostles also knew through our Lord Jesus Christ, there would be strife on account of the office of the episcopate. For this reason, therefore, because they had obtained a perfect foreknowledge of this, they appointed those ministers already mentioned, and afterwards gave instructions, that when these should fall asleep, other approved men should succeed them in their ministry. We are of the opinion, therefore, that those appointed by them, or afterward by other eminent men, with the consent of the whole Church, and who have blamelessly served the flock of Christ in a humble, peaceable, and disinterested spirit, and have for a long time possessed the good opinion of all, cannot be justly dismissed from the ministry. For our sin will not be small, if we eject from the episcopate those who have blamelessly and holily fulfilled its duties.... We see you have removed some men of excellent behavior from the ministry, which they fulfilled blamelessly and with honor. (Chapter 44)

Ye are fond of contention, brethren, and full of zeal about things which do not pertain to salvation. Look carefully into the Scriptures [meaning the books of the Septuagint and the New Testament Gospels and letters read at liturgies], which are the true utterances of the Holy Spirit. Observe that nothing of an unjust or counterfeit character is written in them. There you will not find that the righteous were cast off by men who themselves were holy. The righteous were indeed persecuted, but only by the wicked. They were cast into prison, but only by the unholy; they were stoned, but only by transgressors; they were slain, but only by the accursed, and such as had conceived an unrighteous envy against them.... (Chapter 45)

In short, Clement told the Corinthians they had erred and must reinstate the worthy bishops they had ejected. Of course, he does this somewhat softly but nonetheless with an authoritative spirit. They had asked for help; he decided to stand on the power of his office. Notice that Clement did not respond by directing the Corinthians to their church leaders to resolve their own local problems. He stepped forth to solve the problem.

Clement's letter enjoyed wide circulation and great respect during the post-apostolic years. It was even included in many scripture collections and read in churches, both in the East and West. It showed a continuum of Paul's work caring for the church of Corinth. It equally showed a continuum of Peter's authoritative office. Just like Peter, Clement freely spoke as the holder of the keys. He presumed authority.

The successive line of Linus, Cletus, and Clement underlines how apostolic succession works. This glance at Church history suggests more of the same. Popes would be elected for hundreds of years. Some men would do a little; others would do plenty. But regardless, they'd all keep Peter's authority and continue passing it forward.

Pope Saint Clement I died in AD 97. Three hundred and sixty-three years later, a sixty-one-year-old deacon in Rome was elected the Pope. His name was Damasus, the Pope who officially canonized the Bible in AD 382. The above sections on the theology of papal authority and the introduction to papal succession illuminate Pope Saint Damasus I. They shine a light on his theological beliefs and keen awareness of an unbroken succession back to the Apostle Peter.

Hurricane of Heresies

We've indirectly glimpsed the inner life of Pope Damasus I. His deepest interior awareness was the immovable, profoundly personal belief in his papal status, initiated by Jesus Christ, theologically sustained in scripture, and shown by tradition to have passed on from generation to generation for the salvation of the world. These burning convictions in his heart define his self-perception. This explains some of his reasoning in canonizing scripture. He knew he had the authority to do so. He believed he could determine the Biblical canon precisely because he had the same authority Jesus gave Peter as the head of the Church. Otherwise, his bold decree would certainly seem incomprehensible.

But the story of the canonization of Scripture is still incomplete. Let's step away from Damasus's interior life and into his external environment. Consider his religious and political world. Do you realize that Damasus's declaration of the canon happened in the eye of a religious and political hurricane within the Roman Empire?

Damasus lived from AD 304 to AD 384, dying at eighty years of age. Those years reflect an unrelenting barrage of heresies wrestling to grab hold of Christianity. At the same time, the politics of the times struggled to subjugate Christianity. In chaotic times, God customarily works in hidden silence to bring about his will for the world. He flies beneath the radar until the decisive moment of intervention arrives. As the Church was surrounded by the frightful powers of the age, the seventy-three-book Biblical canon was inconspicuously set in stone.

Damasus's eighty-year lifespan (and subsequent years) manifests a hostile religious environment of menacing heresies. He lived his entire life in the shadow of Arianism. This heresy denied the divinity of Christ, asserting he was a unique creature that once did not exist. According to Arianism, Jesus was not really God's co-eternal and co-equal son; that was just a way of speaking. Of course, making Jesus Christ a mere creature undermined the doctrine and belief in the Trinity. Damasus was twenty-one years old when the Council of Nicaea condemned this heresy. (Not coincidentally, he was a similar age to another secretary and deacon at that time: Athanasius, the destined warrior against the Arians.) Arianism had spread everywhere before the Council and subsequently raged more fiercely afterward. Damasus swam in its aftermath, or perhaps better said, survived. The Arians would even attack Damasus's election and almost seize the papal office.

Besides Arianism, the heresies of Apollinarianism and Macedonianism also flourished during Damasus's adult life. Apollinarianism taught that Jesus Christ had no rational soul. Perhaps he had a purely animal-based soul that enlivened a physical body but no intellectual and deliberative soul like a real man possesses. Jesus's human soul was replaced by the Divine Logos. The result of this was that Jesus Christ was not really a complete man. Jesus certainly looked like a man but essentially was not. Whereas Arianism denied Christ's divinity, Apollinarianism denied Christ's humanity.

Then there was Macedonianism. This heresy attacked the personhood and divinity of the Holy Spirit. According to these heretics, the Son created the Holy Spirit. As such, the Holy Spirit was a creature to God the Father and God the Son. This heresy denied the Trinitarian doctrine of three distinct divine persons, united in one divine essence, where each of the three persons possessed the whole divine nature. (Of course, the fine points of the trinitarian doctrine had not yet been probed.)

Arius died when Damasus was thirty-two years old. Yet, Arius's ideas did not die. They practically resurrected. In AD 340, four years after Arius's death, Pope Julius I invoked a council to tackle the Arian problem all over again. Many bishops showed up, but the Arians had somewhat "boycotted" the event. Without their presence and cooperation, little could be done. Three years later, Pope Julius tried again. One hundred and seventy bishops arrived. There were ninety pro-Nicaean bishops and eighty Arian bishops. Once the Arians realized they were outnumbered, they immediately packed up their bags and journeyed back home. In his mid-30s, securely in the Nicaean camp, Damasus had witnessed both futile efforts.

Fast forward: during his papacy, Damasus repeatedly dealt with the heresies of Apollinarianism and Macedonianism. At sixty-three years old, he held a synod to condemn Apollinarianism. He did the same when he was seventy-two years old and again at seventy-six. When sixty-four years old, he called a synod to condemn Macedonianism. At seventy-six years old, he dealt another blow of condemnation at Macedonianism through the Council of Constantinople in AD 381. Damasus sent papal legates to this council, which also repeated an additional condemnation of Apollinarianism.

(Note: It should be underlined that when a Pope formally condemns a heresy, he does so to protect the ancient Gospel of Christ from innovative errors. Nonetheless, the heresy itself tends to claim its own life. It hatches, gains initial adherents, spreads, and perhaps becomes prevalent before either dying or morphing into another hybrid error. The condemnation presumes concepts and customs dangerously entrenched. Even after the condemnation, a heresy may continue to grow and cause significant spiritual harm. But the clarification is necessary to officially direct the bishops, priests, deacons, and faithful in general to the standard of the ancient Gospel of Jesus Christ. It so happens that the Church's confrontation and condemnation of heresies occasions a continuous refinement of the theological penetration of the Gospel.)

We said that Damasus decreed the seventy-three-book Biblical canon in the eye of a religious hurricane of heresies. Once Arianism, Apollinarianism, and Macedonianism had spread their errors and faced multiple condemnations, a dramatic pause turned to the long overdue authoritative settling of the Biblical canon in AD 382. Suddenly, it struck like lightning, led by Pope Damasus and the Council of Rome. Other synods soon echoed it in various locations throughout the Roman Empire. Then, fresh heresies swept over the Church again. The passing of the hurricane's eye gave way to more thunder and lightning. Soon after AD 382, three innovative heresies rose: Pelagianism, Nestorianism, and Monophysitism.

Pelagianism taught that man can live an upright, moral life without God's help. Man was, therefore, capable of earning salvation by his own efforts alone. In the early 380s, an apparently holy monk named Pelagius arrived in Rome from the British Isles. His teachings on man's ability to live a sinless life without the assistance of grace from Jesus Christ gained wide acceptance among the Roman elite. The spread of these errors mushroomed from there. The heresy took root during the last years of Damasus's life and was finally condemned in AD 416 and again in AD 418. Saint Augustine would fiercely confront these errors that denied the need for the saving grace of Jesus Christ.

Nestorianism derives its name from Nestorius, the Patriarch of Constantinople. He lived from AD 386 to AD 451. Consecrated a bishop in AD 428, Patriarch Nestorius caused one of the most infamous Christological heresies of ancient Church history. Nestorius was adamantly anti-Arian, so he accordingly held firm to Christ's divinity –but in an oddly limited way. He taught that Jesus Christ was essentially not one but two separate persons. There was the human person of Jesus and the divine person of the Son of God. Each had their own nature, human and divine, respectively. Each of these persons acted independently but were united superficially. This heresy grew rapidly but was finally condemned twice, by the Council of Ephesus in AD 431 and again by the Council of Chalcedon in AD 451.

(Note: The Council of Chalcedon clarified the distinctions of person and nature in Christ. Accordingly, Jesus was not two but one divine person. There are, however, two natures, divine and human, united in the one divine person of Jesus Christ. The union of the natures is "without mixture, without change, without division, and without separation," as expressed by the Council. Simply put, Jesus is one divine person who is true God and true man. This partial clarification of the mystery derives from scripture and apostolic tradition.)

The heresy of Monophysitism was also condemned at the same Council of Chalcedon in AD 451. This heresy taught that Jesus Christ only possessed one nature. This nature was either divine or some kind of hybrid of a divine and human nature mixed together. As such, Jesus was not a person with two separate natures, divine and human, implying that he was neither truly God nor truly man. This heresy was a reaction against the Nestorian position that Jesus Christ was two distinct and separate persons. Monophysitism then asserted that Jesus was indeed one person but failed to distinguish two complete and undiluted natures in Christ.

The Political Landscape of Pope Saint Damasus I

Besides the hurricane of heresies before and after the decree of Biblical canonization, there was a political upheaval that almost ripped papal authority away from Damasus I. Unfortunately, it was only through the shedding of blood and the intervention of a Roman Emperor that Pope Saint Damasus ultimately succeeded in the papal office. And, of course, the canonization of the Bible hinged upon that. An Arian faction viciously fought to seize the papacy and rule the Church. But the hand of God was at work. An unbroken line of papal succession remained in place.

Political context is indispensable here. In AD 325, the Council of Nicaea had basically put a small patch on the gushing Church wound of Arianism. It held for a little while. As long as Constantine reigned, the bandage held firm enough. While Constantine and a large majority of the Church in the West adhered to the Nicene creed, the Eastern Roman Empire clung to its Arian tendencies. A shift in the delicate political balance of powers could easily ignite the Arian problem all over again. And that's just what happened.

Soon after his long-delayed baptism, Constantine died in AD 337. This divided the Roman Empire into four blocks, each ruled by a male heir of Constantine. The first son, named Constantine II, inherited France, Spain, and Briton. This son was a solid supporter of the Nicene creed and an anti-Arian. The second son, named Constans, inherited Italy, North West Africa, and Greece. He sided with pro-Nicene Christians.

(Note: although the term "pro-Nicene Christians" is employed here, it's important to underline that these represented the sole, true Church. These Christians, also called the Catholic Church, believed in the divinity of Jesus Christ. The Arians, although sizable, especially in the east, were the offshoot from the true Church founded by Christ.)

The third son, named Constantius II, inherited the eastern provinces, the lion's paw of the Roman Empire at that time. This geographical block included present-day Turkey, Bulgaria, Persia, Palestine, North East Africa, and the coveted gem of the world, the city of "New Rome," in its fifth year as the up-to-the-minute capital of the Roman Empire. This beautifully developing, highly strategic city would soon be called "Constantinople." We know it today as "Istanbul." Constantius II was adamantly Arian and now sat as the "king" in thickly Arian territory. A nephew named Dalmatius inherited Macedonia and a couple nearby provinces. But he was abruptly assassinated by his own soldiers the same year of Constantine's death in AD 337. Dalmatius's territories diverted to Constans.

These inheritances are pertinent because they show how the world suddenly split into two political and religious halves. Politically, the West was ruled by two pro-Nicene brothers. The East was ruled by a third brother, hell-bent on making the whole world Arian. Events would soon transpire that would establish the Roman Empire under a sole Emperor: Constantius II: the Arian!

The firstborn, Constantine II, had felt dissatisfied with his inheritance. He thought he should have received more than Constans. The two brothers bickered. After three years of governing his own share of the inheritance, Constantine II invaded Italy to grab more land. In AD 340, he died during the failed conquest, and his territories passed to Constans. Ten years later, Constans was assassinated by Magnentius in AD 350. The following year, Constantius II defeated Magnentius and claimed sole emperorship over the entire Roman Empire: England to Egypt, Spain to Georgia. The Arians were back, this time with imperial power.

Of course, Constantius II could hardly resist trying to transform Rome and the papacy into an Arian stronghold. His dream was to unite the Christians under the religious banner of a modified form of Arianism. Constantius II would rule the world from AD 351 until his death by illness in AD 361. He knew that the path to an Arian Empire hinged upon the subjugation of papal authority. At that time, Pope Liberius held the papal office. His deacon, Damasus, served as Liberius's competent secretary. Damasus had a front-row seat to the drama about to unfold. Constantius II would pressure Pope Liberius to deny the divinity of Christ.

Constantius's first chess move was to tear down the people's champion against Arianism: Bishop Athanasius of Alexandria. Constantius pressured the bishops of Italy to sign a document to condemn Athanasius. Sadly, many capitulated and signed. But this still fell short of the overall stratagem. Pope Liberius had to join in the betrayal of Athanasius and condemn the Nicene creed. The emperor clearly understood that the Pope was the only ecclesiastical superior above the Bishop of Alexandria. So, Constantius demanded that the Pope issue a public condemnation of Athanasius.

Constantius II sent his prefect with a letter and a fat bribe. The message to the Pope was clear: "Obey and take this!" Refusing to cooperate, Liberius would not budge. Further, the Pope insisted that Athanasius remain untouched, that the emperor's decree against Athanasius be annulled, that a council gather to reconfirm the Nicene creed, specifically without the attendance of the emperor and his entourage, and that the followers of Arius again be anathematized. Constantius's prefect left the bribe, but Liberius threw it across the room, which angered the emperor's delegate all the more. When Constantius II learned of Liberius's response, he soaked in anger.

The stalemate would not last long. The emperor promptly kidnapped and exiled the Pope to Beroea (a city in Northern Greece). Faithfully supporting his friend, Damasus decided to accompany Pope Liberius into exile. Meanwhile, an anti-Pope named Archdeacon Felix II usurped the papal office in Rome. (An anti-Pope is an illegitimately elected Pope.) Constantius II had selected this particular deacon, had him consecrated by an Arian bishop, and set him in place as the stand-in Bishop of Rome. A Roman mess ensued. Some accepted the new Pope; most ignored him and gathered to pray fervently for the return of the real Pope. The clergy of Rome swore they'd never acknowledge Felix II as legitimate.

Emperor Constantius II's next move was to break the will of Pope Liberius and use his "conversion to Arianism" as a tool of propaganda. The Pope had to submit! During his two years of exile, a brand-new creed was devised to replace the Nicene creed. It just needed the real Pope's signature, including a condemnation of Athanasius. Until the signature was secured, Liberius lived under the threat of death. Periodic sums of money were offered to Liberius by the emperor and others, but he always refused the "gifts" and sent them back. Liberius could not be bought.

Looking for a shrewd but sincere way out of his situation, he struggled over the wording of the document desired by the authorities. In the midst of the Pope's personal struggle, Damasus decided to return to Rome and resume his responsibilities beneath the authority of the anti-Pope. His rationale for doing so is blurred. Did Liberius and Damasus have a plan? Did they have a disagreement? History offers no clear-cut answer.

Finally, dejected, coerced, and exiled, Pope Liberius agreed to sign a dubious formula that weakened the Nicene creed that only implicitly disavowed Arianism. The explicit precision of the Nicene creed, designed to combat Arianism with force and clarity, was watered down.

The fresh document conveyed ambiguity rather than outright heresy. It could possibly be interpreted in a heretical fashion or accommodate for an orthodox explanation. He had refused to sign earlier drafts that surely subordinated the Son to the Father. Finally, he settled on a draft that could possibly not deny the truth of Christ's divinity: The Son was similar to the Father "in essence and in all things." This was certainly not the clearest way to assert the co-equality and co-divinity of the Father and Son. But it could lend itself to that explanation. Liberius reluctantly signed it.

Never give in to a tyrant! Liberius would learn the hard way. Because he signed the decree, he was allowed to return to Rome, but Constantius II demanded that Liberius and Felix would rule the Church co-jointly, each with equal, shared power. In AD 357, Liberius entered the city with a great amount of support from the priests and deacons who had sworn not to obey Felix. The faithful felt triumphant and rejoiced. Their prayers had been answered! The true Pope was back home!

Once publicly known, Constantius's condition of joint rule was loudly opposed. The atmosphere filled with a chant: "One God! One Christ! One Bishop!" The chant echoed throughout the streets of Rome! Defiance! The Romans eventually rose against Felix and his supporters and drove them out of the city. Liberius categorically refused a joint rule arrangement. Once Constantius II heard the news and assessed the situation, he backed down.

An amazing moment of grace appeared. The two old friends, Liberius and Damasus, who had known each other as Roman deacons from way back, met and re-enkindled their friendship. Some say they reconciled. A Pope and the next Pope. The Arian ordeal had strained their relationship, not buried it. At this moment, all was forgiven, and they endured as friends until Liberius died in AD 366. Damasus assumed his role as Liberius's secretary.

During the closing years of his papacy, Liberius still suffered his challenges. Emperor Constantius II pressured him again to sign an explicitly pro-Arian formula. The previous disaster of a new creed was not good enough. Pope Liberius held firm this time and refused any cooperation. He had repented of his moment of weakness. He now traveled an uphill journey to repair the damage he caused the Church and mend his own prestige. Giving that signature had humiliated him and caused reserve about his character.

At last, Emperor Constantius II died in AD 361. Liberius immediately and publicly annulled his signature on the document intended to replace the Nicene creed. He reasserted the primary place of the original Nicene creed and reached out to the bishops in Italy who had condemned Bishop Athanasius. He restored the bishops who had surrendered to the Arians as long as they demonstrated signs of sincere repentance and zeal against the encroachment of the Arians.

Within a few years, the Roman Empire would split into two halves again. Valens soon ruled the eastern half of the empire in Constantinople. This Emperor continued to make his Christian subjects into Arians. In a few years, his quest would devolve into a hideous attack on the pro-Nicene adherents in the East. Their churches were confiscated and given to the Arians. Bishops were given the ultimatum to either embrace Arianism or be exiled. Some dioceses valiantly resisted and massacres ensued.

Fortunately, the western side of the empire went in a different direction. Residing in Rome, a forty-five-year-old military general named Valentinian ruled the western half of the Empire. This was a critically beneficial political development for the Church. Emperor Valentinian was a pro-Nicene creed Christian. Pope Liberius died in AD 366, leaving the chair of Saint Peter vacant. This sets the stage for the rise of Pope Saint Damasus I. As Liberius's secretary, Damasus had seen a lot. His life experience would now serve him well.

Arianism's Attempted Papal Coup and Damasus I

Among historians, there's a significant disagreement regarding the immediate aftermath of Pope Damasus's election. Two opinions vie against each other. So, we'll start with the few things agreed upon. Both sides accept that Damasus was validly elected as the new Pope. He won by a large majority. Perhaps this is why the point is not disputed –by historians.

Besides, it is commonly acknowledged that fighting and bloodshed erupted not long after the election. The fight took place between the supporters of Damasus and a "small faction" that almost immediately elected their own Pope, Deacon Ursinus. This deacon was promptly made a bishop in an irregular fashion, ignoring the strict Roman custom of receiving the consecration through the Bishop of Ostia. The clergy and faithful who had supported Liberius's deacon secretary, Ursinus, had their own man consecrated by the Arian-leaning Bishop of Tivoli.

The pivotal, unresolved question is: who started the fight? Some say the supporters of Ursinus initiated the violence. These were over-zealous adherents of the deceased Liberius, who couldn't stomach Damasus. Others say everything started either with Damasus or his crazed supporters. Some of these accusers maintain that Damasus gathered a group of thugs and hunted down the objectors. Historians on both sides gravitate to the number of 137 killed, although not all agree with this estimate. A few historians note that this inflated number comes from a highly prejudiced historian against Damasus. As such, the often-repeated number escaped the scrutiny of later historians. One decent historian thinks only a few people died.

The skimpy details raise more questions than answers. "A small faction of Ursinus supporters" and "137 killed" don't seem compatible. If the number is accurate, how many more were injured? If the number is accurate, it seems like an awful lot of bloodshed. If so, it's questionable if a somewhat non-confrontational, poet-like, modest secretary had the grit to instigate a course of rampage so violently out of Damasus's character. Although possible, it doesn't seem probable.

Nonetheless, it's not surprising that the election had volatility behind it. Liberius had made enemies among both the Arians and the pro-Nicene Christians, too, by flipping and signing the compromised Arian creed. Additionally, Damasus had his enemies. He had waffled back and forth, supporting either Liberius or Felix II. Finally, he ended up with Liberius again. Damasus's shifting allegiances didn't help him. Where did he truly stand? Both Liberius and Damasus offered reasons for Christians to doubt or oppose them. It was in this atmosphere that the election took place. The whole election ordeal was certainly related to the personal trials that both Liberius and Damasus suffered under Arianism. Neither one of them survived the scourge of Arianism without battle scars.

Prompted by the combatant encounters, two priests against Damasus appealed to Emperor Valentinian to help settle the conflict. Perhaps they expected the emperor to side with them. But he resolutely decided in Damasus's favor, asserting that the man was validly elected. Emperor Valentinian then went further. He banished Ursinus from Rome and drove his chief followers out of the city. Later, Ursinus would "convert" entirely to

Arianism and encourage smear campaigns against Damasus, accusing him of adultery and murder, among other things. Damasus would suffer from such personal attacks on his character for years.

(Note: It so happens that when God marks a person for a critical salvific mission, the devil tries to disrupt it. Damasus was chosen to establish the seventy-three-book Biblical canon; the devil deduced this and tried to prevent his papacy. It's not that the devil knows the future as God does —seeing it as the present laid bare before him. But the devil can have a decent idea of the future by penetrating the causes of things and logically knowing how nature plays out. Grasping the histories, tendencies, beliefs, essences, virtues, vices, and convictions of a person offers the keen intellects of demons surprisingly good shots at predicting the future. I believe this happened with Damasus. Much demonic attention focused on him. God destined him to set the canon of sacred scripture until the end of time. The demons saw the organic development of the Bible for hundreds of years. They saw Damasus's love of the scriptures and gift of the written word. They saw the friendship and common interests of Athanasius and Damasus. They had a sense of the probable. Why not nip the possibility in the bud by robbing him of his papal office? And why not use the momentum and backlash of Arianism for this purpose? The demonic denial of Christ's divinity had already proven to be a usefully destructive force in Liberius's and Damasus's lives.)

The year following Damasus's papal election, in AD 367, in Egypt, Saint Athanasius of Alexandria promulgated his groundbreaking festal letter that canonized the seventy-three-book Bible. Attributed to the great respect Christianity granted the hero, the circulation of Athanasius's letter rocketed far and wide. It no doubt reached the hands of Damasus in Rome. Six years later, Bishop Athanasius, the champion against the Arians, died. Damasus promptly gathered a synod in Rome the following year, AD 374, and proclaimed the New Testament canon. Did Athanasius's death urge the Pope forward? It seems so. It was the same twenty-seven-book New Testament canon determined by Saint Athanasius. (This is an example of how a Pope builds upon and anoints the work of a good theologian.)

An Emperor and a Patriarch Prompt a Papal Response

Fast forward six years: In AD 380, both Gratian and Theodosius jointly declared Christianity the empire's official religion. Gratian was the Roman Emperor of the West; Theodosius was the Roman Emperor of the

East. The Imperial decree asserted that the followers of the recognized official religion are called "Christian Catholics." It noted, too, that all other Christian sects are considered heretical and that the adherents of such sects should fear both God's chastisement and imperial punishment. This position of the State telegraphed the imminent death blow to Arianism.

Theodosius's edict, called "De fide Catholica," included clarifications: It indicated that the Church of Rome was the custodian and guarantor of the one orthodox faith —spelled out at the Council of Nicaea in AD 325. It further noted that the official religion was that which "the divinely inspired Apostle Peter passed on to the Romans and which the Pontiff Damasus and Peter, the Bishop of Alexandria, follow." (In the east, Arian readers would certainly note that Theodosius equated orthodox Christianity with the two widely-known advocates of pro-Nicene praxis.)

Some mistakenly view this political move of the Roman Empire as the official establishment of the Catholic Church. But Christians had been called Catholics since the end of the first century. Additionally, the recognition of Peter and his successors as the heads of the Catholic Church is firmly rooted in ancient Christianity. Accordingly, the Roman Empire didn't start the Catholic Church; it adopted it as its official religion, mandating adherence to its beliefs and practices. This was an Empire's new secular law for its citizens.

This historical development begs for distinctions. It's good when secular authorities agree with the divine revelation and Gospel of Jesus Christ. To confirm the divinity of Jesus Christ is good. To confirm Jesus's establishment of the Catholic Church, led by Peter and his successors, is good too. To curb the proliferation of heresies that inflict great damage upon souls is also good.

Yet, there are a few red flag distinctions here. This political development introduced new problems for Christianity. In less than a hundred years, Christians went from running and hiding from persecutions to standing with equal rights alongside pagans to now enjoying the status of the official religion of the empire. Two enduring problems would emerge from this sudden political twist.

The adoption of Christianity as the official state religion begged the question regarding who was really in charge: the state or the Church? Who held the highest authority? Who had the final word over the other? Was Christianity a Church-inspired assembly or a state-driven apparatus? Accordingly, a perpetual struggle was initiated, whereby each side would continually step on the other's toes, asserting jurisdiction over human souls. This conflict would recurringly erupt, in one way or another, for the next 1,644 years until today.

(Note: Perhaps a modern comparison regarding the Church in America may help. The founding of a church happens in a self-contained and independent manner. It need not forge any link with a secular government. Nevertheless, a church may establish itself also as a 501 (c)(3) tax-exempt entity. As such, when the civil status is established, it does not mean that the church was founded at that time. No, the church preexisted the civil status that was added later, for better or for worse. Similarly, when the Roman Empire imposed Catholicism as its official religion, the Church had preexisted before the secular governmental status was added.)

Yet, another problem appeared that Christianity thus far did not know. If Christianity was mandated by a secular power, where were the limits of such a governmental law? Christianity presumes the revelation of Christ as the touchstone of belief, truth, and moral conformity. The genuine practice of Christianity equally presumes interior beliefs, conformities to conscience, and free choices of inner acts of love in a faith-based relationship. Can a secular authority possibly exercise jurisdiction to mandate such things inside the human heart? Not at all. So, when the Roman Empire mandated the practice of Christianity, it overstepped its realm of authority. The living of Christianity (or any religion) can't be forced by a secular government. It does not have the authority to do that. A secular government's scope of authority lies elsewhere. It can't civilly legislate how the heart is to believe and love. Ideally, the state would stay engaged within the proper parameters of its authority to encourage its citizens to freely choose Jesus Christ, but without a punitive mandate.

These inherent, unavoidable contradictions of the State's mandating of Christianity were not yet significant. The inevitable consequences of the new law were not yet tested. Certainly, good would flourish from the new law, but new difficulties would eventually emerge too. The checking of heresies (especially Arianism) was the key concern at that historic moment in AD 380. A couple of years later, Damasus would add his two cents regarding this political development.

Meanwhile, in AD 381, another issue surfaced that would draw Damasus's attention. Emperor Theodosius made the political decision to appoint his own new Patriarch of Constantinople. He acted independently and without the participation and blessing of the Church. Many bishops strongly disagreed with the appointment and how it took place in a non-traditional manner separate from the Church's own internal government. They requested a council with bishops from both the West and the East to deal with the matter properly. Amazingly, Emperor Theodosius agreed to the request.

Gratian and Theodosius then convoked a Church council of 150 eastern pro-Nicene bishops in Constantinople. Arian-leaning bishops also attended, but smaller in number. This council had a two-fold purpose. The first was to provide an ecclesial forum by which the Church might confirm the appointment of the next orthodox Patriarch of Constantinople. Equally, the council was convoked to condemn Arianism, Macedonianism, Apollinarianism, and other heresies. The intent to squash heresies was commendable; the state's intervention to influence a patriarchal appointment was questionable.

Following the doctrinal work of the council, which wonderfully affirmed the personhood and divinity of the Holy Spirit, a Church organizational issue came up. A declaration burst forth that assigned the Bishop of Constantinople preeminence of honor after the Bishop of Rome. Because Constantinople was the "New Rome," its Patriarch should have the second place of honor in the Church, following the Bishop of Rome.

There were two subtle problems with this stance. The first was the unspoken premise that the order of preeminence of the episcopates corresponded with secular seats of power. But the Bishop of Rome's preeminence was based not upon the supremacy of the city of Rome but on the succession of Saint Peter. The second problem was that the declaration unjustifiably reordered the ranks of the ancient patriarchates of the East. (Unfortunately, later in history, some would construe this Eastern canon to mean that the Pope and Patriarch of Constantinople were equal in all things.) Meanwhile, the defects of the declaration (referred to as the third canon of Constantinople) caught Pope Damasus's attention. He would soon contribute his correction.

Damasus Clarifies Papal Authority and Decrees the Canon

In AD 382, Pope Damasus I tailored a succinct response to both the fresh secular status of the Church and Constantinople's claim of the second place of honor and importance in Christianity. Damasus declared the bare minimum to sketch the parameters of his authority. The primacy of the Apostolic See was now buttressed by the imperial acts and edicts of the state. But Damasus indicated that the supremacy of the Roman Church was distinct from such worldly decrees. This supremacy rather was based on the very words of Jesus Christ to Saint Peter, upon whom He entrusted the building of his Church. So, Damasus distinguished a theological justification for his supremacy, not a political or conventional basis for authority.

Further, answering the rationale for the third canon of Constantinople, Damasus pointed out that the primacy of the Apostolic See had nothing to do with any rank or honor attached to the conventions of secular prestige. "Yet, the Roman Church is not set ahead of the other churches by any synodal decrees, but rather by the Gospel's words of our Lord and Savior did it take hold of the primacy: 'Thou art,' he says, 'Peter.'" Pope Damasus strongly rejected the idea that the primacy of Rome revolved around a secular measurement of the greatness of this or that political capital.

That same historic year, within the context of a small council (more accurately, synod) held in Rome, the Pope decreed the Church's definitive Biblical canon for both the Old and New Testaments. This canonization of scripture then spread to the Catholic churches throughout the Roman Empire and beyond. Behold, Pope Damasus's official list:

Genesis	Song of Songs	Acts of the Apostles
Exodus	Wisdom	Romans
Leviticus	Sirach	I Corinthians
Numbers	Isaiah	II Corinthians
Deuteronomy	Jeremiah	Galatians
Joshua	Lamentations	Ephesians
Judges	Baruch	Philippians
Ruth	Ezekiel	Colossians
I Samuel	Daniel	I Thessalonians
II Samuel	Hosea	II Thessalonians
I Kings	Joel	I Timothy
II Kings	Amos	II Timothy
I Chronicles	Obadiah	Titus
II Chronicles	Jonah	Philemon
Ezra	Micah	Hebrews
Nehemiah	Nahum	James
Tobit	Habakkuk	I Peter
Judith	Zephaniah	II Peter
Esther	Haggai	I John
I Maccabees	Zechariah	II John
II Maccabees	Malachi	III John
Job	Matthew	Jude
Psalms	Mark	Apocalypse
Proverbs	Luke	
Ecclesiastes	John	

(Note: To avoid confusion, the seventy-three books listed above do not represent Damasus's list exactly as promulgated. Some of the names of the books are now a little different, accounting for modern English. The manner of counting the books varies, too. For example, Damasus listed "Kings (four books)." But the above list spells out those four books: "I Samuel, II Samuel, I Kings, II Kings." Damasus also listed "Solomon (three books.)" But the above list again details those three books: "Proverbs, Ecclesiastes, Song of Songs." Again, Damasus lists "Ezra (two books)." But those two books are listed above as "Ezra, Nehemiah." Damasus listed "Jeremias (one book), with Ginoth that is, with his lamentations." But the above list differs. It breaks down this old list into three separate books: "Jeremiah, Lamentations, and Baruch." This is so because the Septuagint presents the books of Lamentations and Baruch as integral ending parts of the book of Jeremiah. As such, Damasus had intended the complete writings of Jeremias. Likewise, Damasus listed fourteen Pauline epistles, considering the book of Hebrews included accordingly. The content is the essence of the declaration, not so much the numerical listing.)

The canonical list given above is the second part of the Acts of the Council of Rome, decreed in AD 382. This document of the scriptural canon is entitled *De libris recipiendis vel non recipiendis*. For untold years, it has been familiarly known as the opening part of the Gelasian Decree. The Gelasian Decree was not the papal original but part of a private compilation by Gelasius (not Pope Gelasius), composed in Italy in AD 495.

Saint Jerome

Saint Jerome was baptized by Pope Liberius in AD 360. Twenty-two years later, the historic year of the papal canonization of scripture, Jerome served as Damasus's secretary in Rome. The climactic assertion of the content of the Bible didn't mean that Damasus's vision was complete. Now that the list of books was officially declared by Rome, the Pope's focus shifted to another aspect of biblical development: a decent Latin version.

Especially throughout the fourth century, the Western Roman Empire experienced a significant evolution of spoken language. It shifted from Greek to predominantly Latin. As the Greek Bible remained firmly in place in the East, the swiftly developing culture hoped for a better Latin version of the Bible in the West.

There was considerable disarray regarding the Latin translations of the scriptures. Many such were amateurish. Equally substantial, Damasus and Jerome recognized the many variances of disjointed translations as problematic. Which translation was superior and dependable? A single, uniform, official whole was sorely needed. Sure, Latin translations of this or that book already existed, made by various localities over a long period of time. Still, Church unity in the face of unending heresies and the preservation of divine revelation begged for a standard and authoritative Latin version.

The new Latin version of the Bible would end up with the name "The Vulgate." "Vulgate" simply meant "common." So, the Latin revision referred to the official Bible in the common language of the time. It didn't withdraw or replace the Greek scriptures; it merely added a Latin version. It basically cleaned up the *Vetus Latina* piecemeal translations (not yet compiled in a single volume) made by devout Christians over many years. The *Vetus Latina* did not derive from careful studies by competent linguists of ancient manuscripts. Rather, this set of scriptures consisted of unofficial and unauthorized colloquial translations from the available circulating Greek scriptures. Damasus would kick off a process (deliberate or not) that would gradually change all such "unprofessional" translating efforts.

It so happened, furnished by God's providence, that Jerome was at hand. Damasus's immediate need was immediately covered. Jerome was uniquely suited for the job and available. He was a scripture scholar with a profound grasp of Latin, Greek, and Hebrew, sitting at Damasus's right hand. Of course, Pope Damasus commissioned Jerome to roll up his sleeves and revise the existent Latin language Gospels. Without hesitation, Jerome embraced the momentous work, fine-tuning the Latin while double-checking with the original Greek Gospels.

Jerome had spent his youth devoted to the routines of grammarians, linguists, and rhetoricians. God had now placed him in a position to encourage his natural gifts for the salvation of souls. The touch of an outstanding linguist and scholar was indispensable for the important work at hand. By AD 383, Jerome had finished revising and improving the translation of the Gospels from Greek into Latin. After beholding this advancement and likely holding the Latin treasure in his hands, Damasus soon died in AD 384.

With the tenacity of a bulldog, the hard-headed Jerome relentlessly translated the rest of the Bible over the next twenty years. Yet, the original papal commission was only for the Gospels. The translation of the rest of the Bible would be predominantly Jerome's initiative. Lacking a specific papal mandate for the rest of the Bible, Jerome's work henceforward would have to stand on its own merits.

Often, any given secretary of a Pope succeeds as the next elected Pope. Electors tend to favor the element of continuity. However, this did not happen with Jerome. A different man was elected, named Siricius –who disliked Jerome. This shouldn't be too surprising because Jerome was, frankly, often a hard man to get along with. Additionally, after the new Latin Gospels made their way throughout the city of Rome, there was a great amount of criticism against Jerome. Some did not want to let go of the Greek, others resisted the unexpected, different words of the new translation. You can't please everybody!

These developments influenced Jerome to make a major change in life. As hard as he labored, it seemed that few appreciated his efforts. As soon as the new Pope took office, he packed his bags, shook the dust from his feet, and journeyed east. Jerome finally settled in the town of Bethlehem in AD 386. There, he lived the rest of his life like a hermit in a humble abode, scribbling away. Jerome finished the translation of the Latin Bible in AD 405. He had abandoned Rome but clung to the unique vision of his life.

During those austere but focused years, as his Old Testament advanced in Bethlehem, Jerome started to visit with rabbi scholars for consultative purposes. Some difficult Hebrew texts (Job in particular) called for the input of Hebrew experts. While relying upon the Septuagint as his primary source, Jerome slowly gravitated to a raw translation from the Hebrew. He went from translating from the Septuagint alone to letting the Hebrew texts exert their influence to favoring a direct translation from the Hebrew into Latin, bypassing the Septuagint altogether.

Jerome arrived at the conviction that a decent Latin translation of the Old Testament demanded more than merely revising already existing translations. His gradual abandonment of the Septuagint and reliance upon the Hebrew as a starting point was an unpopular course of action. Christians had held the Septuagint as especially inspired for untold years. Many thought it questionable to work from the Hebrew alone. None other than Saint Augustine had expressed the same reservation at that time. But Jerome ignored the chatter and stuck to his opinions and methodology. Many Christians denigrated Jerome for not holding the Septuagint in high enough esteem.

It so happened that the learned rabbis had persuaded Jerome beyond the nuances of words and structures of sentences. They had equally impressed upon Jerome their canonical ideas too. Jerome and the rabbis found an agreement in this: The Hebrew canon, without the books of Wisdom, Sirach, Tobit, Judith, Baruch, and first and second Maccabees (the seven deuterocanonical books), represented the true Hebrew text from which to base a translation. According to the traditions of the rabbis, these books were devoid of God's inspiration precisely because they lacked Hebrew original texts.

(Note: In principle, this stance is based on faulty theology, as shown by God's inspired word of the New Testament, originally written in Greek. The Holy Spirit can divinely inspire the written word, either in Hebrew or Greek.)

Siding with the rabbis' perspectives, Jerome operated under the persuasion that the Septuagint was nothing more than a loose translation of the Hebrew text. The Greek translation ultimately rested upon the original, inspired Hebrew text. Even further, Jerome became convinced that the specific Hebrew text possessed by the rabbis was indeed the authentic collection of the Hebrew books of the Bible. Of course, these lacked the deuterocanonical books.

Jerome was apparently unaware that the Hebrew scriptures of his time represented a truncated version of the Old Testament produced in the second century. Back then, because the Septuagint was such a powerful tool of evangelization, the Jews mutilated their own scriptures as a reaction to Christian missionizing. For more than two hundred years, the Jews had become accustomed to their "non-Christianized version of scriptures." The fact had been lost to history. And Jerome accepted the rabbis' canon.

Accordingly, for scholastic considerations, Jerome strayed away from the recent decrees of Saint Athanasius and Pope Saint Damasus I, which specifically included these seven books in the official canon of the Catholic Church. The Church had based its conclusions on traditions back to Apostolic times, including the universal usage of the "deuterocanonical books" in liturgies. Corresponding to the rabbis' views, Jerome came to agree that the "extra books" may be referenced and read for the edification of Christian readers. But the Church should neither consider them canonical nor use them as sources of fundamental Christian doctrine.

So, how did Jerome handle this conflict? Basically, he translated the books but devalued them in the eyes of the readers. Jerome was accustomed to adding brief introductory prologues to each book he translated. The purpose of this was to provide an orientation for the reader. Now, when it came to the deuterocanonical books, Jerome allowed his private opinions to show. While these extra books made it past his translating, his prologues downgraded them to "Apocrypha." They may be read for edification but not to establish doctrine.

The tragedy here is that Jerome held the Jewish canon in higher esteem than the Christian canon. He relied upon his education, less so the recent decrees of the Church regarding the canon. This set up a canonical anomaly that would echo throughout history. Eventually, Martin Luther would use Jerome's viewpoint as a historic justification for advancing the protestant reduced canon.

Meanwhile, Jerome did receive pushback from the bishops of his age for his radically unorthodox approach to the canon. In particular, the great Saint Augustine ignored Jerome's ideas and promoted the official canon of the Catholic Church as promulgated by Saint Athanasius and, by the Council of Rome in AD 382, by Pope Saint Damasus. In this light, the regional Councils of Hippo and Carthage speak volumes. All three councils ignored Jerome's canon and confirmed the canon decreed by papal authority. Although the Church eventually accepted Jerome's Latin translation of the Old Testament, it never accepted his canon.

Despite the hesitancies of Jerome, the Church officially and consistently stated and restated the same canon declared by Pope Damasus in AD 382. As such, the Councils of Rome in AD 382, Hippo in AD 393, Carthage in AD 397, and Carthage in AD 419 affirmed and reaffirmed the divine inspiration of the canon, the deuterocanonical books included. Interestingly, the same year Jerome finished translating the Old Testament in AD 405, Bishop Exuperius of Toulouse wrote to the Pope requesting a clear list of the canonical books of the Bible. Pope Innocent I wrote back to the bishop, reaffirming the same canon of Pope Damasus I.

CHAPTER TWELVE

The Muratorian Fragment:
Roughly AD 390

A Minuscule Fragment, Lacking Substantial Context

The Muratorian Fragment is an eighty-five-line piece of writing that describes a sketchy "New Testament canon." Both the beginning and ending parts are missing. Unfortunately, without a contextual introduction and conclusion, the ultimate purpose of the work wants for clarity of intent. It doesn't start with the declaration: "The Christian's Official Canon of the Divinely Inspired Books of the New Testament." Fittingly labeled a "fragment," the pithy five hundred and twenty-one words take five minutes to read.

Ponder the first two lines of the fragment: *(...quibus tamen interfuit et ita posuit tertio euangelii lebrum secundo lucan.)* Translation: *(...at which nevertheless he was present and so he placed [them in his narrative.] The third book of the Gospel is that according to Luke.)* By context, the opening lines suggest that the author just finished talking about the Gospels of Matthew and Mark, and now moves on to the Gospel of Luke.

Accordingly, the next six lines of the fragment share snippets about the Gospel of Luke. The author says that Luke was a physician and companion of Paul. He adds that Luke wrote his Gospel in his own name. He further includes that Luke did not see the Lord in the flesh, but came to know the events he recorded through others who had known the Lord. After these six lines, the author continues by launching into the Gospel of John. The lines of Latin carry on, a book and corresponding comment at a time.

For a long time, many scholars surmised the fragment was written around AD 150 – AD 200. Yet, a fresh breakaway batch of scholars deduced a considerably later production period around the later AD 300s or early AD 400s. Because the support finally appears stronger for a later period, an approximate AD 390 writing date seems generally accurate.

Named after the Scholar who Discovered it (in a Library)

The scrappy excerpt has neither an author nor a title attached to it. It, therefore, derives its name from Lodovico A. Muratori, a much-respected Italian historian. A Catholic priest and scholar, Father Muratori, discovered the fragment in the thick pages of a late seventh or early eighth-century codex in the Ambrosian Library of Milan. The fragment had quietly slept for over a thousand years, snuggled between various tracts and creeds collected from the second to fifth centuries.

Consider the historical period when the "Muratorian Fragment" was tucked away. It was a frightening world of Islamic armies conquering Christian strongholds: Northern Africa, Palestine, the Holy Land, and even parts of Spain and France. Perhaps a Catholic monk prudently made a Latin codex of ancient writings to help preserve a piece of Christian heritage.

Realizing its significance and antiquity, not long after discovering it, Father Muratori published the piece in AD 1740. He believed it possibly represented a second-century attempt at a New Testament canon. If so, it would be the earliest canon that closely reflects our present-day New Testament.

The original source of the fragment is unknown. As only the defective and amateurish Latin translation exists, Father Muratori believed the original must be in Greek, authored by a hardly-known priest in Rome. Both speculations are uncertain.

Today, the Muratorian Fragment is particularly important because teachers and preachers often extol it as a golden proof of Christians' claim for an early New Testament canon. Such enthusiasts feel confident that the fragment tangibly argues against the slow, tedious, organic settling of the twenty-seven-book canon in AD 367.

They say it supports a universal, well-articulated canon that appears abruptly in the timeline roughly two hundred years earlier, possibly around AD 170. Thus, the Muratorian Fragment is seen as decisive evidence that St. Athanasius's canon is less groundbreaking than otherwise thought.

New Testament Books: Valued by Church Usage

So, let's consider the nature and apparent function of the fragment, identify the fragment's acceptable twenty-two books, and scrutinize a probable time period of production. Precisely because the fragment persuades many to believe in a "lightning-speed" canon appearance historically, a pursuit of the details is pertinent. After a thorough discernment, this fragment will actually further confirm the gradual development of the twenty-seven-book New Testament.

The Muratorian Fragment is often referred to as a canon of the books of the New Testament. Of course, books are listed, noted, and identified, but not in the framework of presenting "divinely inspired writings" by name. It would be a sloppy summary to assert that the fragment is a list of divinely inspired writings, as little such contextual claim is included in the eighty-five lines.

Instead, the fragment better reflects a survey of Christian written materials with basic historical or theological comments attached to each entry. It's like an introduction to Christian written materials to provide a reference for the uninitiated. Perhaps it was intended to guide catechumens regarding existent Christian writings.

For instance, a professor might provide a reading list for the new students of a course. The listing of each book might include the professor's concise orientation remarks that clarify the value, author, or perspective of this or that book. This is the feeling that comes across when reading the Muratorian Fragment. Its aim is less to declare than to educate.

As the author lists the books, the value of a book might be earmarked as special with a variety of expressions. In this regard, no less than four times the worthiness of a book is linked to its place in the Church. As such, it encourages the premise that there's no canon of inspired books without the authority of the Church to include or exclude. As such, books are considered "divinely inspired" that are accepted for formal use by the Church.

Examples: Paul's letters to Philemon, Titus, and Timothy "are held sacred in the esteem of the Catholic Church." Paul's letters to the Laodiceans and Alexandrians are "forged in Paul's name to[further] the heresy of Marcion, and several others which cannot be received into the Catholic Church." Jude, John I, and John II "are counted (or used) in the Catholic [Church], as is [the book of] Wisdom, written by the friends of Solomon in his honor." "We receive only the apocalypses of John and Peter, though some of us are not willing that the latter be read in Church."

The Church is identified as: "the One Church spread throughout the whole extent of the earth." The value of the books then is measured by their acceptance or disapproval by this one Catholic Church. The context of a book's value is Church acceptance while not explicitly spelling out that a book is divinely inspired. Again, this kind of presentation smacks of educating a catechumen as he or she prepares for baptism and formal entry into Church membership. Or did the fragment serve the function of noting which books may or may not be used in the Church?

The Identification of Accepted Books

The following Church-accepted twenty-two books are included in the Muratorian Fragment: The Gospels of Matthew (implied), Mark (implied), Luke, John; Acts, Romans, I Corinthians, II Corinthians, Galatians, Ephesians, Philippians, Colossians, I Thessalonians, II Thessalonians, I Timothy, II Timothy, Titus, Philemon, I John, II John, Jude, and the Apocalypse of John. The Book of Wisdom is included, making a total of twenty-three books for Church use. Except for the Book of Wisdom, no reference is made to any other books of the Old Testament.

The following five books are not included in the fragment: James, I Peter, II Peter, III John, and Hebrews. No indication is forthcoming even about the existence of such books. Neither is there accompanying commentary to share any rationale for their absence. Perhaps these books were actually included in the wider work, but it was abruptly cut short. Interestingly, in the middle of the third century, Origen had signaled elements of reservation surrounding these same books. Is there a link between Origen and the Muratorian Fragment?

The Apocalypse of Peter and the Shepherd of Hermas are listed as lacking unanimous consent. This "unanimous consent" seems to mean the consent of the Church in a universal manner.

Having considered the nature and likely purpose of the fragment and identified its list of twenty-two books, we can now scrutinize a possible production period. I had proposed above: something around AD 390. Let's explore this possibility.

Arguments for a Late Production Date

Scripture scholars are pretty much evenly divided regarding the production period of the Muratorian Fragment. Half say the second century; the other half say the latter half of the fourth century. Finally, it's emerging that the fragment likely represents a fourth-century author "back-dating" to substantiate an early precedent for a later position on the New Testament canon.

In this instance, "back-dating" specifically means that a fourth-century writer inserted misdirection that suggests a New Testament canon from the second century. In this regard, a growing number of reputable scholars view the Muratorian Fragment as a "fraud," "hoax," or, more politely, an "anomaly" as they wrestle with an inexplicable text.

Welcome to the Wild West of "belated apocrypha!" Ages ago, our contemporary parameters that delineate and discourage plagiarism did not yet exist. Copying, exaggerating, anonymous borrowing, tweaking, elaborating, lifting, and assigning a false name all unfortunately existed.

It seems that the unknown author (or translator) of the Muratorian Fragment, with horrendous Latin, incorporated passing commentary that today confusedly hints at a second-century production and simultaneously points to a fourth-century production. Nonetheless, the arguments for a fourth-century production seem stronger. The fine points of the arguments are slowly swaying a consensus toward this latter production date.

Three distinguished scripture scholars initiated the reassessment of the production date for the Muratorian Fragment:

In 1973, Professor Albert Sundberg Jr. bravely challenged the 233-year grand assumption of a second-century production date of the Muratorian Fragment and called for a reexamination of the production date and origin. Sundberg affirmed a fourth-century production from an Eastern (Syrian/Palestinian) provenance.

In 1992, Dr. Geoffrey Mark Hahneman grabbed the baton from Sundberg and ran ahead. His research culminated with the publishing of *The Muratorian Fragment and the Development of the Canon*, published by Clarendon Press Oxford. The following excerpt from the introduction offers an orientation of this research:

Sundberg's hypothesis deserves serious study and consideration because the date of the Muratorian Fragment is so crucial to the common understanding of the history of the New Testament. The present work will confirm Sundberg's argument that the traditional dating for the Fragment cannot be sustained. Based upon a careful analysis of its traditional dating and its place in the history of the Canon, it will suggest an Eastern provenance and a fourth-century date for a revised history of the New Testament canon and will sketch a development of the Christian Bible that is more gradual in its formation, and that culminates, not at the end of the second century, but in the midst of the fourth.

In 2018, another scripture scholar, Clare K. Rothschild, dedicated ten years of focused research on the Muratorian Fragment. Her thoroughness included a personal examination of the original document in Italy. In the *Novum Testamentum*, volume sixty, she released her conclusion with an academic paper entitled: *The Muratorian Fragment as a Roman Fake*. After a ton of research, she wasted no words!

Other scholars jumped on board, and the number is still growing. These researchers include Robert Grant, J.K. Elliott, and G.A. Robbins. Side-stepping a mountain of scholarly technicalities, let's note a few of the internal arguments found in the Fragment itself –that corroborate a fourth-century production date.

In the Fragment, lines seventy-three to seventy-six relate: "But Hermas wrote the *Shepherd* very recently, in our times, in the city of Rome, while bishop Pius, his brother, was occupying the [episcopal] chair of the Church of the city of Rome." Pius was the bishop of Rome from AD138 to AD 155. In antiquity, it was held that the *Shepherd of Hermas* was written in the first or early part of the second century by an unknown author. Not until the late AD 300s are there any references in literature of the identity of the author of *The Shepherd of Hermas*, precisely as the brother of bishop Pius of Rome.

It seems unusual for the Fragment to have identified the author of *The Shepherd of Hermas* so early and accurately in history, only to have the information lost again and not mentioned in other writings for the next two hundred years.

In the Fragment, lines eighty-four to eighty-five relate: "....together with Basilides, the Asian founder of the Cataphrygians..." Who were the Cataphrygians? These were the Montanists of the second century. The name change did not occur until the fourth century. At the presumed time of the writing of the Muratorian Fragment, the term Cataphrygians was not in use.

In the Fragment, lines eighty-one to eighty-five relate: "But we accept nothing of Arsinous, Valentinus, or Miltiades, who also composed a new book of psalms for Marcion, together with Basilides, the Asian founder of the Cataphrygians..." Here, Miltiades is associated as a heretic with

Marcion. But this same Miltiades is praised by Tertullian and Eusebius as a hero, opposed to the heretics of his generation. It is not until the latter half of the fourth century when Miltitudes began to be called a heretic.

In the Fragment, lines sixty-eight to seventy relate: "Moreover, the epistle of Jude and two of the above-mentioned [or, bearing the name of] John are counted [or, used] in the catholic [Church]; and [the book of] Wisdom, written by the friends of Solomon in his honor." The inclusion or categorizing of the Book of Wisdom with the books of the New Testament only starts appearing in the fourth century by Eusebius and Epiphanius.

In the Fragment, lines sixty-three to sixty-five relate: "There is current also [an epistle] to the Laodiceans, [and] another to the Alexandrians, [both] forged in Paul's name…." This letter to the Laodiceans is dated as a fourth-century document, not a second-century document.

It certainly makes sense to speculate why the subject matter of the Fragment was out of sync with other writings of the time. Whereas the fourth century abounds with written materials that touch upon a universal canon, the second century has no parallels.

It seems anomalous for an isolated writer in the middle of the second century to put together a universal canon that other writers henceforward knew nothing about. Such an innovative, off-topic writing feat at that time surely should have shown a few historic repercussions among other writers.

In the middle of the third century, Origen had traveled and searched far and wide for every piece of information he could get his hands on to move toward shaping a universal canon. How is it that he did not come across the "Muratorian Fragment" (of course, not by name). Perhaps, plainly, it had not yet been written.

In conclusion, it's not difficult to understand that the initial face value assessment of the Muratorian Fragment found in a Latin codex in the seventeen hundreds suggests a second-century production period. Nonetheless, today's deeper analysis places the production period highly likely in the fourth century.

CHAPTER THIRTEEN

Ancient Liturgical Context

The Passover: Scripture, Sacrifice, and Communion

There were two fundamental differences regarding the Jewish ancient use of scripture (the Old Testament). The synagogues used the scrolls of the scriptures primarily as teaching references. Here, the scriptures rested in the hands of the "professionals." The Pharisees publicly read passages and propounded further. Yet, the scriptures also had a ritual or liturgical setting that burst forth in the private homes of the Chosen People, most demonstrably during Passover. The written word served as a basis for a great amount of memorization. During the Passover, each family told the story of Exodus and sang Psalms. If someone had enough education and access to scrolls, home readings would reach the ears of fervent listeners and enrich their cherished celebration of liberty from slavery.

The practical distinction between these usages was very real in Jewish culture. The synagogues did not replace the one and only temple in Jerusalem where sacrifices took place. Rather, each village synagogue represented a subsidiary place of education and prayer. For instance, on any given Sabbath, a Pharisee might read scriptural passages related to the Sabbath rest and then follow with a long list of derived distinctions, applications, and clarifications.

Accordingly, a Pharisee might clarify if it was permissible to eat an egg laid on the Sabbath, as it was the product of forbidden labor. Or perhaps he'd discuss if it was permissible to gargle with vinegar because of a sore tooth on the Sabbath, as medicinal healing was a labor procedure. The same question applied to soaking an injured foot in water. This was a medicinal labor, especially if you moved your foot around. Anything from a sea of rabbinic precepts was fair game to lay upon the listeners. Could you tie a knot on the Sabbath? Could you walk a thousand steps? Could you light a fire, prepare food, draw water, write literally two letters, sew two stitches, put out a lamp? Such hair-splitting casuistry tended toward dry, technical, and stifling legislation that defined religious observance as void of interior peace.

In a best-case scenario, the synagogue experience would nurture a familiarity with scriptural sources and encourage a satisfying spirituality. For the most part, the synagogues offered the basics regarding the Jewish faith, with an emphasis on knowledge and laws, not so much heart-driven spirituality. People had to find this kind of inner fire elsewhere. It did exist, but it was rare. The core group of Apostles had discovered it in Saint John the Baptist, who thundered far beyond the status quo of the synagogues.

Home-based reliance on scripture was a different experience from synagogue learning. Primarily from memorized scriptural passages of historical narratives, the words of the prophets, the Psalms, and wisdom literature, genuine spirituality had a chance of blossoming, untethered from the speculative meanderings of Pharisees. The home ritual setting of the Passover celebration offers a fair example of such use of scripture and the nurturing of a profound relationship with God. A brief description of the Passover unfurls a rich context of scripture usage in the average ancient Jewish home.

By the time of Jesus, the Passover had enjoyed an institutional history that shaped Jewish identity and spirituality. For more than a thousand years, families had gathered around their home tables on the 14th of Nissan (around the end of March or the beginning of April) to celebrate their independence. God himself had told Moses exactly how to conduct the celebration.

On that day, Jews had crowded into Jerusalem from the far-reaching tentacles of the Roman Empire. By early afternoon, a member of the household would select a one-year-old male, unblemished lamb. The lamb would then be ritually sacrificed at the temple and carried home with some of the blood in hand. Upon arriving home, the blood would be brushed on the front door lintel and side doorposts. This was done in memory of the first Passover when the angel of death *passed over* the Israelite houses marked with lamb's blood.

The lamb was placed upon the fire as a sacrificial offering to Yahweh. While smiling faces rushed to the shops to pick up any missing prescribed items for the celebration, homes were scrutinized and swept free of lingering leaven. By twilight, the streets of the city filled with the appeasing aroma of roasted lamb floating everywhere. Passover was comparable to our Christmas Eve and Independence Day, married on the most anticipated night of the year.

The night began when family members and guests would enter the home. The lowest person in the household would wash everyone's feet. (This custom was not exclusive to Passover.) The feast participants would relax barefooted either on pillows or upon a low divan that surrounded a table that stood around eighteen inches high.

The Passover celebrated the historic liberation of the Jews by Yahweh from slavery in Egypt. The festal celebration was paced with four distinctive cups of ritual wine, dividing the feast into a fourfold structure. The feast obliged every participant to drink the four ritual cups without exceptions. The youngest kids enjoyed a substitute grape juice with perhaps a drop or two of wine. Each male could only participate in the Passover if circumcised. Of course, this was the permanent mark of belonging to God's own people. Each cup of wine distinguished a particular promise that God had made to his chosen people.

The first cup of wine (the *kiddush*) marked the opening prayer. Spoken over the first cup, this prayer recognized Yahweh's promise to remove and set apart his own people from the entrapment and burden of Egypt. It voiced the opening blessing of the celebratory feast. With this cup, the group shared bitter herbs to recall the bitterness of slavery. Unleavened bread was also served with a dipping sauce. Unleavened bread reminded the Jews of not having time to add yeast and wait for the rising of the dough. God had given this instruction because they had to quickly flee Egypt to seize their liberation.

(Note: The Israelites had suffered the bondage of slavery for four hundred years. By comparison, counting back four hundred years from 2024, the Pilgrims on the Mayflower had just landed on the shores of the New World. So, the Israelites had been slaves for roughly twelve generations. Year after year, most of those families had been born into slavery and died as slaves. They had known no other life. They had grown beyond a million strong by the time Moses led them out of Egypt.)

The second cup of ritual wine (the *haggadah*) was poured, and a prayer with extended hands was pronounced over it. This initiated the proclamation of the Passover narrative, according to Exodus, chapter twelve. This cup recognized Yahweh's promise to deliver His people. He is praised for the long-awaited deliverance, finally pledged to take place immediately. The opening food items were now removed from the table. It was time to focus on the meaning of the celebration.

At this point of the meal, typically, the youngest member of the family or group would ask questions of the oldest, who would answer by reading or referencing the age-old scriptural narrative. It could be that the son of a family would ask the father to relate the meaning of the feast and recount the story of Exodus. Then the "Little Hallel" was sung. (Psalm 113) This was the educational part of the meal.

A grand recounting of the history of Israel from Abraham to Moses and the giving of the law proceeded. The scriptural references flowed, either explicitly or subtly, by inference. It could be nothing but the dramatic story of the Egyptian plagues, the angel of death, the outstretched arms of Moses, the parting of the Red Sea, and the passing of an entire nation to freedom, not sparing the details of God's intervening power and mercies. Here is a wonderful use of scripture by a family, distinct from the readings and "sermons" at the synagogues.

In the case of the Last Supper, it likely would have been the Apostle John (the youngest) asking Jesus such questions, who would have expounded the account. (Imagine in American culture, after the family clinks glasses, the child might ask Dad about the meaning of the feast of Thanksgiving. The father would launch into the account of the Pilgrims and Indians and their historic feast together while adding his own side commentary. By comparison, something similar happens at this second cup of ritual wine at the Passover.)

Following this educational part of the meal, the main feast arrives. The ritually roasted lamb is respectfully rested in the middle of the spread, now surrounded by many specially prepared and symbolic holiday foods. After the meal winds down, the third cup of ritual wine (the *berakah*) is poured. This is called the "blessing cup." It recalls Yahweh's promise to redeem and take back his Chosen People who are rightfully his. Gratitude and thanksgiving are offered for his mighty act of rescue. After the blessing, the cup is drunk, and the Great Hallel is sung. (Psalms 114-118)

These Psalms praise Yahweh for rescuing his people. Thanksgiving is given for the gift of salvation. No more cups of wine are allowed from this point forward until the ritual fourth cup officially ends the meal. The sacrificial lamb and its consumption represent a union established between Yahweh and his own. The use of scripture at this meal is inseparable from the context of God uniting his people with himself. Scripture is used for that intent. Accordingly, the use of scripture is less focused on study and more oriented toward devotion.

The fourth and last cup (the *zebah todah*) of the Passover praises Yahweh for promising to establish a perpetual covenant between his people and himself. Equally, it celebrates the completion of this covenant. The Passover then concludes with the declaration: "It is consummated!" This means not only that the Passover is officially finished but more so that the covenant of mutual acceptance of Yahweh and his people is confirmed on the spot. It is done! It is finished! Now, a familial relationship between God and his rescued people endures.

Jews from all of Palestine and the diaspora crowded into Jerusalem every Passover to celebrate this feast. The inner courtyard of the temple resembled a slaughterhouse, streaming with the blood of lambs and goats. More than a couple hundred thousand ritual, sacrificial victims were carried home to roast for the evening celebration. (In AD 65, Emperor Nero had counted 255,600. In AD 70, two hundred and seventy thousand were counted before the razing of the temple that same year by the Romans.) It was an ageless, institutional event that stemmed from the very voice of God. As Yahweh had spoken to Moses and Aaron: "This day shall be a memorial feast for you, which all your generations shall celebrate with pilgrimage to the Lord, as a perpetual institution." (Exodus 12:14)

The Four Last Supper Deviations

The Last Supper and Passover are not synonymous, though the terms are sometimes used that way. The Last Supper was Jesus's last meal. This same meal also happened to be the Jewish Passover feast Jesus had with his apostles before his passion and death. This meal took place on Thursday evening. The next day, Jesus was crucified. The Gospels of Matthew, Mark, and Luke (the Synoptics) reflect this calendar of events.

Even so, the Gospel of John narrates something different. It relates that the Passover began the Friday evening of Jesus's death, the day following the synoptics' claim. Why? Skipping the details, this discrepancy boiled down to a disagreement between the Pharisees and the Sadducees, who had affirmed different dates for the Passover that year. John's Gospel reflects the Sadducees' date; the synoptic Gospels reflect the Pharisees' date, the traditional 14th of Nissan. This was the calendar date when most of the Jewish population observed the Passover. The general population was more inclined to follow the official traditional date and the Pharisees' calendar rather than the Sadducees' date.

Having sketched the theology and customs of the Passover celebration, it's critical to see how the Passover of Christ's Last Supper differed. While the basic Passover structure remained in place, Jesus nonetheless introduced a few radical changes. We'll note the changes without explanations. Once the changes are indicated, we'll backtrack to probe the meaning of the innovations. Apart from the washing of the Apostles' feet by Jesus and the betrayal of Judas, there were four momentous changes during the Last Supper. These were deliberate deviations introduced by Christ, breaking away from ageless traditions of the Passover celebration.

The first deviation was Jesus's discourse after the pouring of the second cup of ritual wine. If locked into the traditional theme, he should have dedicated his words to the proclamation of the Passover narrative. He would have outlined Yahweh's historic and miraculous intervention to rescue the Israelites. But nothing was said of Egyptian slavery, Moses, the angel of death, the parting of the Red Sea, the chasing of the chariots, nor the arrival of God's chosen people on the shores of the other side. Total silence on the fixed and highly anticipated theme!

The second deviation surrounded the pouring of the third cup of ritual wine. This "blessing cup" (*berakah*) was unfailingly dedicated to thanking Yahweh for his wondrous rescue. But Jesus went in an entirely different direction. Suddenly, breaking with the customs and precepts of the Paschal dinner, he introduced a radical change:

> While they were eating, Jesus took bread, broke it, and giving it to his disciples said, 'Take and eat; this is my body.' Then he took a cup, gave thanks, and gave it to them, saying, 'Drink from it, all of you, for this is my blood of the covenant, which will be shed on behalf of many for the forgiveness of sins. I tell you, from now on, I shall not drink this fruit of the vine until the day when I drink it with you new in the kingdom of my Father.' Then, after singing a hymn, they went out to the Mount of Olives. (Matthew 26:26-30)

Differentiating a bit from Matthew's narrative, Mark and Luke each add their own details. Mark adds that "they all drank from it." (Mark 14:23) Luke adds that once Jesus had distributed the bread, He said: "Do this in memory of me." Additionally, he shares the detail that the "cup is the new covenant in my blood, which will be shed for you." (Luke 22:19-20)

Jesus's third deviation from the strictly structured Passover meal was an instruction to the Apostles to maintain the change just introduced. "Do this in memory of me." (Luke 22:19) Accordingly, the Apostles are commanded to permanently alter the Passover celebration. Henceforth, the "blessing cup" would be superseded with the offering of the new covenant of his body and blood.

Jesus's fourth deviation was the skipping of the fourth cup of the meal. After the third cup of the Passover, Jesus declares that He will not drink of the fruit of the vine again until entering his Father's kingdom. The Great Hallel is sung, and Jesus and his Apostles walk out of an unfinished ceremony. As such, the presider (Jesus) of the celebration does not properly close the Passover feast. He does not declare: "It is finished!" The confirmation then of the Old Covenant between Yahweh and His Chosen People is left hanging and unaffirmed.

Consider the context of Jesus's deliberate omissions and radical alteration of the third cup, replacing an immovable custom initiated by God himself with a freshly commanded new custom. Reflect upon the moment and setting. Around 11:00 p.m., Jesus knew He had about sixteen hours to live. He had visited Earth to redeem humanity. The sacrifice of His life was immediately upon him. This was the decisive moment (His last will and testament, so to speak) when He needed to complete the arrangements with his immediate "family" for His divine life –through His humanity-- to reach all mankind till the end of time. He wasn't about to just leave His words behind.

A pivotal moment in world history had arrived. The Old Covenant of the Jews was now replaced with the New Covenant. Jesus's alterations of the Passover celebration fulfilled the prophecy of Jeremiah made 620 years earlier, foretelling the replacement of the Old Covenant with the New. Christians would eventually consider Jeremiah's prophetic words as "the Gospel before the Gospel:"

> …I will make a new covenant…. It will not be like the covenant I made with their fathers the day I took them by the hand to lead them forth from the land of Egypt, for they broke my covenant, and I had to show myself their master, says the Lord. But this is the covenant which I will make with the house of Israel after those days, says the Lord. I will place my law within them and write it upon their hearts; I will be their God, and they shall be my people. No longer will they need to teach their friends and kinsmen how to know the Lord. All, from least to greatest, shall know me, says the Lord, for I will forgive their evildoing and remember their sin no more." (Jeremiah 31:31-34)

Besides this old prophecy, Jesus had recently uttered his own complementary prophecy to a Samaritan woman at a water well. He indicated that the time is at hand when the true worship of God will break free from Jewish exclusivity and no longer need the temple of Jerusalem: "Believe me, woman, the hour is coming when you will worship the Father neither on this mountain nor in Jerusalem…. But the hour is coming, and is now here when true worshippers will worship the Father in Spirit and truth…." (John 4:21-23)

These prophecies suggest a path forward to understanding the Last Supper. Through the lens of these prophecies, let's now backtrack and consider the meaning of the four deviations.

The First Deviation: The New Covenant Discourse

The first deviation was Jesus's omission of the traditional proclamation of the Passover narrative. But this does not mean that He had little to say. Realizing the importance of relating Jesus's last discourse at such a monumental moment, John devotes no less than five chapters to the words of Jesus from the beginning of the Passover to the eleven Apostles' exit from the upper room to the Garden of Gethsemane. The Gospel of John shares a substantial 3,510 words in this singular setting, mostly words pronounced by Jesus.

Nowhere in the Gospels is there such a captured, detailed account of a single discourse by Jesus. Different from the accounts of the synoptics, who had presented Jesus's transformation of the bread and wine into his body and blood, John adds the complementary discourse of Christ at the table that evening. If the transformation of the bread and wine represents the precious diamond of the evening, the discourse represents the handcrafted cathedral setting for the crown jewel.

This discourse is neither a farewell address nor a spontaneous love letter that flutters about like a butterfly nor a last will and testament. Though these elements are laced within it, they do not comprise the expansive, underlying theme. Without denigrating the limits of the Old Covenant, Jesus uses the discourse to lay bare the heartbeat of the New Covenant. He completely overshadows the pillars of the Old Covenant.

At this moment, Jesus looks less to the past and more to the future. Nothing is said of the old Passover, the rescue, Moses, the opening of the Red Sea, the Decalogue, circumcision, or a hundred other distinguishing events of the Chosen People's liberation. Leaving behind the limits of the old, Christ's discourse shifts to the New Covenant! The all-encompassing theme is that of love. Jesus speaks of intimacy, friendship, and sharing in the inner family of the Father and Spirit. He defines love, commands it, demonstrates it, and associates future persecutions and suffering with it. He pledges the Holy Spirit's help. By the end of the discourse, Jesus speaks directly with His Father and asks Him to consecrate the men surrounding Him.

The Second Deviation: Consecration of the Bread and Wine

The second Passover deviation dealt with the "blessing cup" of the feast. It so happened that Jesus had remotely prepared his Apostles for the mystery of the Eucharist. The unexpected pronouncements over the bread and wine that evening must have evoked an unsolved riddle that had been filed away in the minds of the Apostles during their "ministerial education." Their memories would have dug up the feeding of the five thousand, and then the four thousand, and the bread of life discourse. Indeed, how could they forget the abandonment of all those disciples who had refused to believe that Jesus could give his body to eat and his blood to drink? With that unforgettable head start, the Apostles could now begin to unravel the mystery of the moment.

But before the memories kicked in, the historic, cultural, and theological context of the Passover suggested much regarding Jesus's "bread and wine innovation." From the time these grown men were little boys skipping to Jerusalem for the Paschal feast, they knew the kind of sacrifice the Passover represented. The Jews detailed several categories of animal sacrifices for various purposes. Each type of sacrifice had its specific nature and strict ritual. Knowing where the sacrifice of the Paschal lamb fit into the overall sacrificial categories oriented the Apostles to grasp the "bread and wine innovation."

Consider sacrificial holocausts. This is when the animal was completely destroyed by fire. It represented the offeror's complete submission to God. Lifting the whole victim up to God underlined the Most High's supreme sovereignty. Nobody was allowed to eat anything of this kind of sacrifice.

Then, there were expiation sacrifices. The purpose of these was either to absolve sin or make up for the injuries done by sin, or fulfill restitution. Sin offerings were regulated by the status of the person who offered them. For instance, a person of wealthy status would offer a bull; a "middle-class" sinner might offer a lamb; a poor person could be allowed to offer two turtle doves to be purified from sin. (For instance, after giving birth, a woman was considered unclean and in need of a purification sacrifice to be offered. If poor, two turtle doves would be a sufficient sacrifice in this case. See: Luke 2:22-24.)

Further, a more serious injustice, like stealing the neighbor's goat, required the victim of injustice to be paid back fourfold. After paying this restitution, a sacrificed animal would be offered to God as a reparation offering. By definition, the expiation sacrifices were partially burned for God and partially eaten by the priests who expedited the sacrifice at the temple.

There were also sacrifices called either peace offerings or fellowship of-ferings. These were not required by any transgression of the law. They were purely voluntary, motivated by personal devotion. These sacrifices intended to recognize, confirm, or promote a friendly, peaceful relationship with God. Underlying expressions of praise and thanksgiving motivated them. Such sacrifices were commonly offered simply to fulfill a vow, give thanks to God, or for any reason to promote unity with God. The distinctive feature of the peace offering was the communal sacrificial meal. This was the distinguished sacrifice where the family ate the sacrifice offered. The purpose of the consummation of the sacrifice was to bring about commu-nion with God.

Belonging to this *shelamim* category, the Paschal sacrifice manifested the communal meal as the principal part of the offering. At the Passover, consuming the lamb and drinking the wine was, therefore, integral to the sacrifice of the night. The eating of the sacrifice was accordingly insepara-ble from the very nature of the offering. The sacrificed food was sacred. No leftovers were allowed. Whatever could not be consumed had to revert to the fires of sacrifice offered to God. Furthermore, this Paschal offering was an extraordinary, divine prescription. Hence, if you were a Jew, you had no choice in the matter. If a male, of course, attendance required circumcision, ritual cleanliness, and the consumption of the lamb and wine. The Passover then was a special, required peace offering for the chosen people as a whole.

These seemingly scattered pieces of context explain the heartbeat of the Last Supper. The Old Covenant is replaced with the New. This is the key to fitting together the puzzle. A peace offering meal, rather than a holocaust or expiation sacrifice, was chosen as the didactic framework to help grasp the New Covenant. The Paschal meal was chosen precisely because it was the ancient ritual most meaningfully adapted into the new ritual. Remember, a prefigurement is designed to help recognize its pro-phetic and perfect fulfillment. So, the Old Covenant's Passover ritual was divinely designed to receive its fulfillment from the Messiah. The old ritual celebrated freedom from physical slavery; the New Covenant celebrates freedom from the slavery of sin.

The Old Covenant had its old sacrificial lamb. The New Covenant has its new sacrificial lamb: Jesus. The roasted lamb on the table was replaced with the consecrated bread distributed from the hands of Jesus, the new "Lamb of God." Among his followers, no more sacrificial lambs would need to be slain forever. Just as the Old Covenant lamb must be eaten, so now, the New Covenant lamb must be eaten. The Old Covenant's purpose in eating the sacrifice was to confirm a union with God. The New Covenant's purpose in eating the New Lamb is the same, yet much more efficaciously.

The history, regulations, and setting of the Last Supper were chosen and orchestrated from eternity to establish the institution of Christ's Eucharistic presence on earth until the end of time. At the Last Supper, Jesus bequeathed to humanity His continued presence on earth in such a way that it would be forever hidden from the proud and faithless while embraced by the humble and faith-filled.

The above paragraphs sketch the meaning of Christ's deviation regarding the "blessing cup" of the Last Supper. New Testament passages wonderfully harmonize with this explanation of the ancient Jewish "liturgy" and Christ's innovation. While shelving an exhaustive theological argument, it's nonetheless pertinent to note a few complementary scriptural references:

Consider Jesus's birth. (Luke 2:6-20) As God himself chose the details surrounding his own human birth, the details must be taken as meaningful and not coincidental. God does everything with a purpose. As a youth, King David had lived as a shepherd in Bethlehem, watching over his father's flock. Bethlehem sat about six miles south of Jerusalem. During ancient times, its rolling hills and many flocks contributed to a "feeder system" to supply the temple with sacrificial lambs. There were hundreds of households in the rural area, perhaps up to a thousand by the time of Jesus's birth. The area was known for its spread-out grazing terrains and bounteous shepherds, who were generally looked on with disparagement. The shepherds were held in such low esteem their testimonies were not allowed in the courts.

Some hills managed a few partially carved-out caves, somewhat fortified. These served as places to escape the rain for the "shepherd network." The "dug-outs" were undeveloped, dirty, dung-filled places, even if they were cleaned up a bit and supplied with hay when needed. No doubt, baby lambs, meant for eventual temple sacrifices six miles north, were born in these convenient partial shelters. The Lamb of God chose to be born precisely where sacrificial lambs were born. Further, Bethlehem means "House of Bread." The baby Lamb of God was then placed in a manger, a spot designed for offering food for consumption. As such, Jesus's birth and death preached the same consistent and elegant sermon: he is both lamb and bread.

The multiplication of the loaves and fishes is a miracle of provision, turning a modest lunch into a hardly manageable river of abundance. From five loaves and two fish, Jesus fed five thousand men. Including women and children, the total probably neared fifteen thousand people. After everyone's hunger was satisfied, the leftovers amounted to twelve full wicker baskets of bread. The miracle demonstrated Jesus's power to provide for the needs of the moment, regardless of impossibly insufficient means at his disposal. Perhaps much of the crowd, stuck in a desert meadow outside of Bethsaida, perceived only the material dimension of the miracle that dusk.

Yet, there was much more to the physical wonder. Like the Manna from heaven, the miracle was equally a veiled prophecy that prefigured the multiplication of Jesus's own body to feed the entire population of the world, everywhere, for all time. Although all four Evangelists relate this event, as usual, it required the spiritual ruminations of John to draw out the profound meaning. He links this miracle with the second Pasch that Jesus would celebrate with his Apostles. There were large crowds of travelers en route to Jerusalem to purchase their lambs and prepare for the Passover feast. This transpires one year before the Last Supper. (Matthew 14:13-21; Mark 6:32-46; Luke 9:10-17; John 6:1-15)

As John recounts, the miracle of the multiplication inevitably prompted the famous "bread" of life discourse. (John 6:22-71) The day after the miracle, as the crowd reassembled and hunger returned, Jesus again engaged with his listeners. Their full bellies had wanted to make him a king. But Jesus would have nothing to do with that. The deeper purpose of the miracle was to forthrightly declare the doctrine of the Eucharist for the first time. The bottom line: Jesus proclaimed that His body is food and His blood is drink, and His body must be eaten and His blood drunk if a person is to have eternal life. The Apostles, except for Judas, believed without the assistance of understanding. Such was their matured, childlike faith in Christ. A year later, the Last Supper would answer the "how" question. Meanwhile, the Apostles would have a year to reflect upon the Lord's radical and mysterious words.

The "bread of life" discourse must have sounded unbelievable, like the ridiculous rantings of a madman. It hit people's ears harshly. Murmuring and quarreling festered. For instance, of the eighteen terms available in

Greek for the word "eat," John chose *"trogo."* Nothing could have been more literal and less metaphorical. The nuances of the word captured the idea of "ripping," "tearing," "chewing," or "gnawing," like a dog does with a bone pinned in the grip of his paws. Further, as the Jewish law strictly prohibited the drinking of blood, the instruction must have sounded scandalous to pious ears. A large contingent of the crowd, and many disciples, could not accept this teaching and decided to abandon Jesus. Scripture relates that Jesus foresaw the division, yet this did not deter him from proclaiming the truth exactly as he wanted it to be heard.

(Note: Some assert that the entire discourse on the bread of life is purely figurative. They construe a metaphorical sense of the discourse when Jesus adds: "It is the spirit that gives life, while the flesh is of no avail. The words I have spoken to you are spirit and life." (John 6:63) Yet, these are expressions that explain the mystery, not contradict, nor deny it. Dealing with his listeners' resistance, Jesus hints at a way forward to grasp the mystery. But a big chunk of the crowd remained unbending. Moreover, the proper method of scriptural interpretation identifies complementary scriptural references and confirms a consistent pattern of belief and practice by the ancient Church. In this case, both approaches confirm the literal sense of the bread of life discourse. Note also that the disciples who couldn't believe in the literal meaning of Jesus's words separated themselves from following him.)

(Additional note: It's difficult to express the unique essence of Holy Communion. While respecting the role of faith and man's free choice to humbly surrender to this doctrine, Jesus offers an insight. Two back-to-back statements slightly lift the veil of the mystery. Jesus states: "Whoever eats my flesh and drinks my blood remains in me and I in him." (John 6:56) He almost immediately adds: "It is the spirit that gives life, while the flesh is of no avail. The words I have spoken to you are spirit and life." (John 6:63) Both statements are true. They do not cancel each other out. They are not contradictory. Jesus is saying that the flesh itself, independent from His inner spirit, is not what gives life. It's His inner spirit that gives life. For example, recall the story of the woman with the hemorrhage. A crowd presses upon Jesus, yet a woman of faith wanting to be cured only touches his clothes and is healed. Jesus reacts by asking who touched Him? The Apostles answered: "You see how the crowd is pressing upon you, and yet you ask, 'Who touched me?'" But when the woman of faith touched his clothing, Jesus was immediately aware that power had gone out from Him and cured the woman. (Mark 5:25-34) Reflect, it was not the clothing that healed. Similarly, upon receiving Communion, it's not the flesh that gives life; it's the spirit of Jesus that enters the communicant and gives life. The flesh acts as a conduit of the spirit, just as the clothing of Jesus acted as a conduit for his curing power to enter the woman. As such, Communion is not about a body giving bodily life but the spirit of Jesus touching the spirit of the communicant through the body. The body of Jesus acts as a "go-between" or "instrument" for Jesus's spirit to rush into the communicant who believes in him and desires Him to enter. During Communion, Jesus's spirit invades and merges with the communicant's spirit. "I in him." While each retains their proper independence, Jesus's spirit and the communicant's "touch each other." His body is the doorway for the union of His spirit with the soul of the communicant.)

The Gospel of Luke and Acts reveal the earliest references that touch upon the "Breaking of the Bread." Luke relates the story of two disciples on their way to Emmaus on the day of the Resurrection. Jesus ends up walking with them and explains the scriptures to them, yet they don't recognize him. By the end of the day, together for a meal with this man who understood scripture so profoundly, Luke relates: "…he took bread, said the blessing, broke it, and gave it to them. With that their eyes were opened, and they recognized him, but he vanished from their sight." (Luke 24:30-31) Luke relates this as the first instance following the Last Supper when Christ's new ritual is repeated, even with the same ritualistic pattern. As such, Jesus demonstrates that He becomes present and known through the new ritual.

Acts expands upon the early and eager embrace of the new ritual: "They devoted themselves to the teaching of the Apostles and to the communal life, to the breaking of the bread and to the prayers…. Every day they devoted themselves to meeting together in the temple area and to breaking bread in their homes." (Acts 2:42-46.) The new ritual is described as an early and integral part of embracing Christianity.

From the Last Supper onward, after twenty years of Christians Breaking Bread in their homes, the Apostle Paul authoritatively expounds:

The cup of blessing [once the third cup of ritual wine at the Passover] that we bless, is it not a participation in the blood of Christ? The bread that we break, is it not a participation in the body of Christ? Because the loaf of bread is one, we, though many, are one body, for we all partake of the one loaf. Look at Israel according to the flesh; are not those who eat the sacrifices participants in the altar? So, what am I saying? That meat sacrificed to idols is anything? Or that an idol is anything? No, I mean that what they sacrifice, [they sacrifice] to demons, not to God, and I do not want you to become participants with demons. You cannot drink the cup of the Lord and also the cup of demons. You cannot partake of the table of the Lord and the table of demons…. (I Corinthians 10:16-21)

Above all else, Paul does not say that the consecrated body and blood are strictly symbolic. He does the opposite. He identifies the bread and wine as a literal, real sacrifice. He underlines that the Christian can't go to the temple and eat a sacrifice offered to a god and then attend the Breaking of the Bread in a Christian's home down the street and eat the sacrifice (bread and wine) offered to the Christian God. By "participation" in the body and blood of Christ, he means "consumption of the sacrifice."

Paul then teaches another aspect of the Breaking of the Bread ritual:

Therefore, whoever eats the bread or drinks the cup of the Lord unworthily will have to answer for the body and blood of the Lord. A person should examine himself, and so eat the bread and drink the cup. For anyone who eats and drinks without discerning the body, eats and drinks judgment on himself." (I Corinthians 11:27-29)

In short, he instructs how to make a worthy communion. Whoever eats the bread must believe that it is the body of Christ. Whoever drinks the wine must believe it is the blood of Christ. Otherwise, when eating and drinking are just like any other eating or drinking without recognition of the sacrifice consumed, God's judgment falls upon that soul. Holy realities must be recognized as such and treated accordingly.

In summary, we explained the second deviation of the Last Supper: the consecration of the bread and wine into the body and blood of Christ. We then demonstrated cross-scriptural insights related to Christ's actions and words at the Last Supper. Although the second deviation and third happen practically simultaneously, we categorize them separately to emphasize their distinct natures. The second deviation is a personal act of Christ worked at the Last Supper. In contrast, the third deviation is a deputizing and commanding of the Apostles to repeat this act in the future.

The Third Deviation: "Do this in Memory of Me"

It was daring enough that Jesus radically altered the scrupulously venerated Passover ritual. Yet He continued beyond the replacing of the Passover narrative and the changing of the bread into His body and the wine into His blood. He next commanded and institutionalized the innovation surrounding the third cup of ritual wine. Henceforward, not only Jesus but his Apostles would carry on this New Covenant ritual and pass it on: "Do this in memory of me."

After almost twenty years of presiding over the Breaking of Bread ritual, Paul reflects on his own deputization to maintain and nurture this Apostolic praxis:

> For I received from the Lord what I also handed on to you, that the Lord Jesus, on the night he was handed over, took bread, and, after he had given thanks, broke it and said, 'This is my body that is for you. Do this in remembrance of me.' In the same way also the cup, after supper, saying, 'This cup is the new covenant in my blood. Do this, as often as you drink it, in remembrance of me.' For as often as you eat this bread and drink the cup, you proclaim the death of the Lord until he comes." (I Corinthians 11:23-26)

Paul speaks of a command here to do as Jesus did. Consider this in slow motion. Try not to run ahead. The first thing Jesus did was to declare the bread to be otherwise, and the same with the wine. God causes what he declares. "Let there be light." And there was light. Observe Jesus's miracles. His words are efficacious; they bring into being divine commands. "May no fruit ever come from you again." And the fig tree immediately withered. "Stretch out your hand." The man stretched out his hand and was cured. Jesus rebuked the winds and the sea, and there was great calm. Whatever he commands happens. At the Last Supper, notice that Jesus declares that the bread is His body; the wine is His blood. At that instant, reality changes by the command of God. A miracle happens. The difference between this wonder and the others mentioned is that when the bread and wine turn into the body and blood of Jesus, there is no tangible or perceptible indication that a miracle occurred. But it did.

Specifically, Paul refers to receiving the command: "Do this in memory of me." As such, Jesus commands the Apostles to do what He just did, not merely to say what he said. And what did he just do –but a miracle? He then commands the continuation of the miracle. It was not the first time the Apostles were ordered to venture forth and do miracles. He commanded not a symbol but a reality. There are untold instances in the scriptures when God commanded men to do the miraculous. Moses could part the Red Sea precisely because God commanded it. The Apostles could cast out demons and heal because God commanded it. When God commands someone to do a miracle, He at the same time empowers the act. Otherwise, no man can do a miracle apart from the power of God working through him.

Yet, there's still more mystery veiled in this command to the men sitting in the immediate presence of God. The clock was ticking. Jesus had roughly sixteen hours left to live. The empowering of the Apostles to turn the bread and wine into the body and blood of Christ establishes a new kind of priesthood. The Old Covenant and Old Sacrifice had their established priesthood. The three go together: covenant, sacrifice, and priest. With the command, "Do this in memory of me," the Passover covenant, Passover sacrifice, and Levitical priesthood are replaced by the New Covenant, new sacrifice, and new priesthood.

The Book of Hebrews infers this when it shines a light on Jeremiah's prophecy of a New Covenant, saying, "When he speaks of a 'new' covenant he declares the first one obsolete. And what has become obsolete and has grown old is close to disappearing." (Hebrews 8:13) And when the Old Covenant falls, so does the old sacrifice and old priesthood. Either the three stand together or fall together. For instance, from the Last Supper onward, Jesus, the Apostles, or the early Church never again participated in Jewish animal sacrifices with the assistance of the old priesthood at the temple. All of that is finished. Because of the New Covenant and new unbloody sacrifice, the old priesthood, along with its detailed precepts about sacrificing animals, no longer endures. Of course, the Romans' razing of the temple in Jerusalem in AD 70 would dramatically echo God's intent for a new priesthood.

From the days of Moses onward, technically speaking, only a male from the tribe of Levi could be a priest. Further, the Old Covenant priests had no choice in the matter. Their entire tribe was dedicated to the priesthood. The Levitical priesthood then was hereditary. A man was born into it. But Jesus was born of the house of Judah, so was barred from the Jewish priesthood. Yet, Jesus was a priest by His very essence, far beyond any Levitical priest ever could be. As God and man, Jesus stands in the gap between heaven and earth, drawing Adam's race to his Father and bringing his Father to all men. His sole and perfect mediatorship defines His priesthood. He, therefore, does not need to be born of the tribe of Levi to be a priest. He is the eternal priest from the moment of his incarnation.

Psalm 110 alludes to the different type of priesthood of the Messiah: "Like Melchizedek, you are a priest forever." (Psalm 110:4) This succinct prophetic line suggests an abundance of information about Christ's priesthood. The book of Hebrews applies this prophecy to Jesus and further expounds:

> If, then, perfection came through the Levitical priesthood, on the basis of which the people received the law [of the Old Covenant], what need would there still have been for another priest to arise according to the order of Melchizedek and not reckoned according to the order of Aaron? When there is a change of priesthood, there is necessarily a change of law [of the Old Covenant] as well. Now he of whom these things are said belonged to a different tribe, of which no member ever officiated at the altar. It is clear that our Lord arose from Judah, and in regard to that tribe, Moses said nothing about priests. It is even more obvious if another priest is raised up after the likeness of Melchizedek, who has become so, not by a law expressed in a commandment concerning physical descent but by the power of a life that cannot be destroyed. For it is testified: 'You are a priest forever according to the order of Melchizedek.' (Hebrews 7:11-17; also cf. Hebrew 7-10 for a thorough context.)

Melchizedek goes way back to a world before the Israelites. He was a contemporary of Abram, even before "Abram" received the new name of "Abraham." Just a little knowledge of Melchizedek goes a long way to grasp the unique priesthood of Jesus Christ. Of course, the priesthood of Melchizedek prefigures the priesthood of Christ. (Genesis 14:17-20)

Without a genealogy, both Melchizedek's origins and ultimate end are shrouded in mystery. His priesthood, then, is not disrupted by death. Not bound to a role exclusively for Israel, he serves as an intercessory priest for all. He was not born into a priesthood but was personally chosen. He is greater than Abraham, who pays tithes to him. His sacrificial offering is that of bread and wine, though perhaps not exclusively. These traits offer a little glimpse of the special, non-Levitical priesthood of the Messiah to come.

So, as Jesus presides at the Last Supper, He does so as a new kind of priest prophesied ages past. He is the true high priest who offers a new kind of sacrifice. He is equally the slain victim offered to the Father. And He is the irreplaceable and unrepeatable sacrificial lamb consumed as a confirmation of communion with God.

His command, "Do this in memory of me," signifies an empowering of the Apostles to participate in his own priesthood. Equally, this command commissions the Apostles to bring this new ritual to the world. By the ministry of the Apostles, this New Covenant sacrifice and meal would defy place and time. By divine design and power, it would become present to Christ's entire body everywhere. Paul reflects this view when he says that he received the ministry of the Breaking of the Bread and passes it onward, too. (I Corinthians 11:23-26)

The Fourth Deviation:
Linking the Passover with the Cross

Jesus's fourth deviation of the Last Supper was the omission of pouring and drinking the fourth cup of ritual wine and the omission of the presider's accompanying declaration. The fourth cup (*zebah todah*) praises Yahweh for establishing a covenant with his chosen people. Its drinking signifies the confirmation and celebration of the Old Covenant.

The pouring and drinking, along with the presider's announcement, conclude the Passover feast. The presider says, "It is finished." There's a lot packed into this three-word declaration. It means that the meal is over, the covenant endures, and the covenant of mutual acceptance between Yahweh and his people is officially confirmed. Like a celebratory toast, it's somewhat like a grateful, happy, victorious recognition of the agreement between God and his people.

This is what the fourth cup should have been and what was expected by the Apostles that evening. But the Last Supper took another wild turn. After the Apostles consumed the sacrificial lamb, participated in the new "Breaking of the Bread" ritual, and drank the blessing cup (of blood), Jesus made an abrupt announcement: "'I tell you, from now on I shall not drink this fruit of the vine until I drink it with you new in the kingdom of my Father.' Then, after singing a hymn (the Great Hallel), they went out to the mount of Olives." (Matthew 26:29-30)

What happened? At this moment, Jesus and the Apostles skipped the last cup of ritual wine; they picked up their belongings and exited. The presider (Jesus) did not yet officially conclude the Passover, leaving the celebration open-ended. It would continue until Jesus would drink the fourth cup and announce the completion of the celebration. Within the hour, the spilling of blood would begin: the oozing of blood through Jesus's skin. His blood offering began in the Garden of Gethsemane. "According to the law almost everything is purified by blood, and without the shedding of blood there is no forgiveness." (Hebrews 9:22)

If there's a key to grasping the above four paragraphs, it's this: Jesus's sacrifice doesn't begin at Calvary. It begins at the Last Supper in the upper room with his Apostles. Additionally, this Passover sacrifice doesn't end when everyone stands up and leaves the room. The sacrifice that started in the room ends at the moment of Jesus's death on the cross. It's one continuous sacrificial offering, tied together by four cups of ritual wine.

At the beginning of His crucifixion, Jesus is offered wine mixed with gall. This was the Roman executors' concoction of wine with myrrh, a narcotic. Jesus happens to taste it. He then deliberately refuses to drink. No, he had already surrendered to the chalice of suffering three times in the Garden of Gethsemane. Avoiding even the smallest dose of personal comfort, he chose to suffer for our sake.

After three hours of agony upon the cross, knowing that the moment of death was racing upon him, Jesus finally welcomes the fourth cup of ritual wine. At the foot of the cross, witnessing Jesus's crucifixion and hearing every word, the Apostle John recalls our Lord's last words:

After this, aware that everything was now finished, in order that the scriptures might be fulfilled, Jesus said, 'I thirst.' There was a vessel filled with common wine. So, they put a sponge soaked in wine on a sprig of hyssop and put it up to his mouth. When Jesus had taken the wine, he said, 'It is finished.' And bowing his head, he handed over the spirit. (John 19:28-30)

Jesus then finished the Passover upon the cross. He took the fourth cup of wine and made the pronouncement of sealing the Covenant. But in this case, he sealed not the Old but the New Covenant. This is reflected too by the veil in the temple ripping in half at the instant of his death. "And behold, the veil of the sanctuary was torn in two from top to bottom." (Matthew 27:51) This veil separated the common people from the Holy of Holies, where dwelt the presence of God. The tearing from the top meant that the removal of the veil was God's own work to make the holy presence of God accessible to all.

It may seem that when Jesus says, "It is finished," this refers to his work of saving the human race. Yet, this work will not be finished until the Resurrection. Through his death, Christ freed us from the slavery of sin; through his resurrection, he restored to us the privileges lost by sin. (Romans 4:25)

(Note: The development of the theology of the fourth cup must be attributed to Dr. Scott Hahn, a former Presbyterian minister turned Catholic theologian.)

The Place of Scripture: Immediately following Pentecost

Mindful of the preceding mountain of liturgical context, we can now better appreciate the place of scripture among the earliest Christians. We are speaking of that historic window of time from Pentecost to the completion of the Gospels and Paul's letters. Pentecost took place in AD 33. The Gospels and Paul's letters were complete by AD 60, and the entire New Testament by AD 70. Possibly, John's Apocalypse stretched further in time. (Chapter fourteen spells out the details regarding the re-dating of the New Testament.)

Immediately after Pentecost, Christ's followers were labeled the "New Way." They were disdained as a Jewish sect who insisted that Jesus Christ was the Messiah and that he was somehow still alive. Simultaneously, the "Christians" attracted crowds because of their boldness for good, their shining lives of virtue, and their miracle working. The believers met in homes for educational and worship purposes. The synagogues progressively rejected these "Jewish heretics."

They could hardly afford the extravagant expense of making a personal copy of an Old Testament scroll. A few amateur, common-sense researchers have estimated that the cost of copying an average-sized scroll at that time would have been similar to $1,750.00 USD today. (AD 2020 prices.) As such, a Christian community would have required donations from many believers for such an undertaking. Or a wealthy patron would have adopted the project and covered the cost. (In today's terms, for instance, this would be like paying the cost of your monthly mortgage and then some to obtain a copy of the book of Genesis. Imagine that! Today, you can buy a Bible for a couple of bucks at the local Goodwill.)

As Christians often sold their possessions and houses for the needs of the poor and for the needs of the believers at large, it's likely that some resulting income would have been applied to obtaining the essential items required for the exercise of the faith. Surely, this would have included the most basic of scrolls. Perhaps a nice table, a dignified chalice, and a scroll of the Psalms would have been on any list of liturgical needs. Initially, synagogues became places where conversions to Christ could be nurtured. But this didn't last long, as the Jewish authorities soon closed their doors to "New Way spokespersons." So, the Christians hit the public squares, just as Christ had taught his Apostles to do. Closed doors could not stop these fervent believers!

Given the 3%-15% literacy rate throughout the Roman Empire at the time, most fresh converts to Christianity couldn't proficiently read. So, the believers came to the weekly (or more often) "Breaking of the Bread" ritual to listen to scripture, learn the faith of Jesus Christ and his Apostles, and participate in the reception of the New Covenant's sacrificial communion.

The Christian use of scripture at that time grew organically out of the Jewish use of scripture. Its usage was devoted to nurturing the spiritual life. The primary manifestation of this use was rooted in the "altered Passover." Christians inherited the ancient Jewish habit of exposure to scripture. As such, the Christian believer often listened to the revelation of the Old Testament writings. The "Breaking of the Bread" ritual still maintained the basic division of the Passover. The first half of the ritual was educational, whereas the second half was sacrificial.

From the Last Supper onward, the use of scripture shifted from the embrace of the Old Covenant to the New. The pursuit was no longer to cement the faithful's identity and purpose in Jewish history, culture, and belief. Jesus himself shifts the use of scripture to himself. Henceforward, the educational part of the "Breaking of the Bread" became to pursue the full revelation of the Messiah and to understand the New Covenant to the fullest. The purpose and end of scripture quickly developed into Christ-centeredness.

During the earliest years of the Breaking of the Bread, the Septuagint exclusively was used in the liturgies. This made perfect sense because many potential or fresh Greek-speaking converts lacked familiarity with the Hebrew language. Greek flourished everywhere. The readings were focused on understanding Jesus and nurturing a salvific relationship with him. When this or that scroll was read at the first part of the liturgy, the intellectual pursuit was to discover the meaning, richness, and nuances of the New Covenant, as continually prefigured and prophesied in the Old Testament texts. It was soon appreciated that the Old Testament truly belonged to Christianity. Its full meaning was only possible from a Christian perspective.

This went on for the first seven to twenty birth years of Christianity without even a fragmentary New Testament yet. Painting with broad brush strokes here, the heart of the New Testament, the Gospels, and the Pauline letters appeared as follows: From Pentecost onward, there was a period of the oral Gospel, supported only with Septuagint usage. Then, between

AD 40 and AD 60, both the Didache and the Gospel of Matthew appear. At that time, the Didache was known as "The Teaching of the Twelve Apostles." Between AD 40 and AD 65, the Gospels of John and Mark next appear and begin their universal circulation at liturgies. Following a period of intense travels, Paul then wrote two letters to the Thessalonians in AD 50 – AD 51. They proved so useful that copies were made and circulated. Everybody could learn from them, not just the Thessalonians.

After a writing pause, Paul explodes with other letters between AD 55 to AD 58. Luke follows with his Gospel between AD 57 and AD 60 and his Acts between AD 57 to 62. Accordingly, throughout this lengthy period until AD 70, the New Testament was in the process of coming together from a loose circulation of Gospels and letters copied and recopied and shared between Christian communities. Some of these communities had a few copies of writings, others had gathered most of the writings available. Perhaps influential cities like Alexandria, Antioch, and Rome were the first places where copies existed as a bound set.

From AD 40 onward, the Septuagint and the periodically produced Gospels and letters were publicly read during the educational first half of every Christian liturgy. This is how the readings of the New Testament found their humble beginnings, primarily at the weekly gatherings of the Breaking of the Bread. Consider that the liturgy preceded the reading of the written Gospels by a couple of decades. The context of the readings, old and new, was always the Breaking of the Bread, the cherished praxis of the Christian communities. The place of ancient scriptural usage was consistently ancillary to the central act of consuming the Body and Blood of the New Covenant.

Chronologically, the development of scriptural usage and liturgical practice proceeded in the following order: First, the age-old Passover celebration includes the reading (or narration) of events in the book of Exodus. Second, the Septuagint is translated primarily from Hebrew in Alexandria, Egypt. Third, Jesus founds his Church upon Peter at Caesarea Philippi. Fourth, at the Last Supper, Jesus initiates the foundational Christian liturgy and commissions his Apostles to preserve and spread it. Fifth, the initial Christian communities observe the Breaking of the Bread liturgies, principally using the Septuagint during the educational part of the ritual. Sixth, the Apostles and initial disciples spread the oral Gospel while establishing local Bishops as a primitive Church structure far and wide. Seventh, the Gospels and Pauline epistles are written, passed around, and incorporated into the readings done at local liturgies. Eighth, local Bishops independently discern inspired writings from apocrypha for the good of their local communities.

Ninth, in AD 367, Bishop Athanasius lists the seventy-three books of the Bible. Tenth, in AD 382, Pope Damasus I declares these same seventy-three books as the official Bible set by Papal authority. Carefully note the progression of history here: Church authority, liturgical development, and an episcopal governing network precede the first drop of ink applied by Matthew on *papyrus* in AD 40. Paul's first letter to the Thessalonians was still ten years down the road.

As the Breaking of the Bread develops, its own stable character emerges as thoroughly Christian and progressively less and less Jewish. Yet, the basic Passover twofold division of an opening educational part and the chief sacrificial part remains firmly in place. The Christians meet in homes to worship. (Church structures built exclusively for that purpose were still more than a hundred years away.) Reflecting on today's common practices, Christian worship only by the use of scripture, song, prayer, and preaching would have been conspicuously incomplete by ancient Christian worship standards. Scripture was welcomed at that ancient time to help worshippers experience something greater than education and inspiration –the fervent consumption of the sacrificial lamb.

It didn't take long for some diversification of liturgies to appear, first in Jerusalem, Greece, Antioch, Egypt, and Rome. Ancient diversified rites soon developed, such as the Coptic rite, the Byzantine rite, the Armenian rite, and more. These reflected the cultures where the liturgies adapted. Nonetheless, even as diversifications appeared, common features were universally observed. Regardless of the location, every Eucharistic liturgy manifested the following progression: an opening purification rite, an opening prayer, various readings that included Old and New Testament sources, the offertory of the bread and wine, the consecration of the bread and wine into the Body and Blood of Christ, the prayer of the "Our Father" as a preparation for receiving communion, the reception of communion by the baptized, and lastly, a formal dismissal by the presider.

Relationship Between the Church and the Bible

This chapter traced the emergence of the Christian liturgy from the Last Supper onward. It then clarified the accompanying path that scripture took on that same journey. Between the Last Supper and the canonization of the seventy-three-book Bible, the New Testament was piece-by-piece born and immediately incorporated into the context of Christian worship. As such, from its practical beginnings, the New Testament accompanied the liturgy. The sacred scriptures and Eucharistic liturgy quickly, inseparably, and harmoniously thrived together.

During the earliest years of Christianity, due to the non-existent state of manufacturing a "book," the excessive expense to produce a scroll, and a widespread low literacy rate, private ownership of an Old Testament scroll by a person of modest means was out of the question. Christians would have to wait until the year AD 70 before the last book of the New Testament would be written, and AD 382 for absolute clarity on the content of the Bible. Moreover, the common usage of codices (ancient, stitched books) was still a long way into the future. During the days of the Apostolic fathers, a privately owned Bible wasn't even imagined. The only path for exposure to scripture was by attendance at the weekly Eucharistic liturgy. No Bibles sat at the bedside stands of devout Christians.

Consider the closing lines of Saint Paul's First Letter to the Thessalonians: "Greet all the brothers with a holy kiss. I adjure you by the Lord that this letter be read to the brothers. The grace of our Lord Jesus Christ be with you." (I Thessalonians 5:26-28) Although Paul does not explicitly ask that the letter be read at the weekly liturgy, he indeed knows that the Sunday liturgy is when everyone gathers, if not more often. It seems his closing is not an afterthought but an instruction. As such, this suggests that New Testament books may have been written precisely for readings at liturgies.

During the ancient days of Christianity, for the common believer, scripture was only found in a liturgical context. The Septuagint, Paul's letters, the Gospels, and the other books of the New Testament were used during the educational part of the eucharistic liturgy. This use of scripture was oriented to help the Christian fully participate in the consummation of the sacrifice. Accordingly, the place of scripture was secondary to the consuming of the Body and Blood of Jesus. Of course, the written and spoken word are ancillary to the divine person of Jesus Christ, present in the Eucharist.

A few rudimentary conclusions can be drawn. The Church preceded the Bible. The Church produced the Bible, notwithstanding the role of the Holy Spirit, who inspired the human authors. The Church wrote, disseminated, copied, organized, and canonized the Bible. The Church used the Bible as a liturgical instrument in the context of participating in the New Covenant sacrifice and subsequent Holy Communion.

CHAPTER FOURTEEN

The New Testament:
Dating and Historical Context

Re-dating the New Testament

The question about "when" is extremely important. When was the New Testament written? The closer the author to Jesus Christ, the greater the credibility of the written testimony. Such closeness should reflect if there was a proximate, intimate friendship in time and place with Jesus. For instance, let's say someone writes the story of your life. Your best friend's memories will be more credible than a distant author who writes two hundred years in the future. Jesus's best friend, the Apostle John, captures this truth at the end of his Gospel:

> It is this disciple who testifies to these things and has written them, and we know that his testimony is true. There are also many other things that Jesus did, but if these were to be described individually, I do not think the whole world would contain the books that would be written. (John 21:24-25)

John expresses that his words are credible precisely because he had personally known and lived with Jesus Christ. He adds that everybody who knows him knows he is truthful.

The same holds true with all the Apostle authors: Matthew, John, Peter, James, and Jude. The Apostle Paul is a special case. He dramatically encountered Jesus at the turning point of his life and learned from most of the Apostles, adding all they shared to his vast education. Mark worked side by side with Peter, writing down Peter's account. Luke worked side by side with Paul, writing down in an organized manner the memories and testimonies of many of the Apostles, including the testimony of the mother of Jesus summarized in the first two chapters of his Gospel.

Such insights are historically traceable to Church traditions. Yet, it's important to note that Biblical scholars, over the past hundreds of years, strayed far away. Without venturing into too many details here, such "scholars," believing too enthusiastically in the power of their own reasoning and abandoning the premise of faith in Church traditions, had made a mess of dating the New Testament. According to these "intellectuals," only a handful of New Testament authors can be completely trusted as original and early testimonies. Some of these terribly misled "scholars" even began figuring things out based on the premise of negating the existence of supernatural realities.

Based upon fixed historical dates, much can be puzzled together regarding when the twenty-seven books of the New Testament were written. The dates of the authors' deaths are excellent starting places. Long-standing local traditions offer either undisputed dates or dependable approximations. Once these death dates are established, it is easy, of course, to conclude that the author could not have written anything after death. This simple consideration narrows things substantially.

Based upon the death dates and various traditions when the authors of the New Testament lived their post-Pentecost endeavors, we can confidently approximate when the New Testament was written. It so happened that within a thirty-year period, AD 40-AD 70, the content of the New Testament was written to completion. This short time span may even have been more contracted. This historical window of time represents the thoughts and cooperation of holy men looking ahead. More so, it represents the God of forethought bestowing a barrage of inspiration upon his young Church to provide a sure source of revelation for all time. Suddenly, in an explosion of God's grace etched upon papyrus, the oral Gospel gave way to the written Gospel.

After his work in Arabia, Parthia, Armenia, and Ethiopia, Matthew died a martyr in AD 65 while celebrating the liturgy. He finished his Gospel between AD 40 - AD 60. Mark died as a martyr in AD 68 in Alexandria, Egypt. While serving as Peter's secretary, Mark recorded Peter's oral account of Christ's life. This Gospel was finished between AD 45 - AD 60, with the latter half of this time frame more probable. Luke either died as a martyr shortly after Peter and Paul's deaths in AD 67 or died in AD 84 in Boeotia. Luke had traveled with Paul and learned greatly from him. He knew Greek very well and possessed a profound knowledge of the Alexandrian Septuagint. He finished his Gospel between AD 57 - AD 60 and the Acts of the Apostles between AD 57 - AD 62. Paul even referenced him a few times in his letters. John died in AD 98, in Ephesus. He finished his Gospel between AD 40 - AD 65. He finished his three letters between AD 60 - AD 65. He finished the book of the Apocalypse between AD 68 - AD 70, or perhaps later.

Peter was martyred in Rome by an upside-down crucifixion in AD 67. He didn't think himself worthy to die the same way his Master had died. After serving as the first Bishop of Antioch, he served as the first bishop of Rome from AD 54 - AD 67 while preaching in the public areas of the city for thirteen years. He finished his two letters while living in Rome sometime between AD 62 - AD 65. Paul died as a martyr by beheading in Rome in AD 67. He finished his thirteen pastoral letters within an eight-year period, from AD 50 - AD 58. James, the cousin of Jesus, became the first bishop of Jerusalem. He died a martyr in AD 62, thrown from the peak of the Temple. He finished his letter between AD 47 - AD 48. Jude also died a martyr that same year, in AD 62. After working in Syria, Phoenicia, and Armenia, Jude was clubbed to death. He finished his letter between AD 61 - AD 62. The book of Hebrews was likely finished in AD 67.

Besides the fixed markers of death dates, various early Church Fathers substantiate the true authorship of the Gospels of Matthew, Mark, Luke, and John. Of course, such ancient assertions indirectly establish a dependable, if not precise, time frame when the authors wrote. The same holds true for the other authors of the New Testament, but the ancients' references to the writers of the Gospels are expectedly emphasized.

Around AD 120: At the turn of the century, a Greek Father, the Bishop of Hierapolis, noted something curious about the Gospel of Saint Mark. The bishop's name was Papius. He had worked alongside Saint Polycarp. Both Polycarp and Papius had learned matters of the faith directly from the Apostle John. Papius served as a bishop near Laodicea and Colossae (in modern-day Turkey), where Saint Paul had founded Christian communities in recent memory.

Papius explained that Mark was indeed Peter's secretary and wrote down what Peter preached, but not in a strict chronological order reflective of Christ's life. He further stressed the accuracy of Mark's Gospel, based on the testimony of apostolic sources. He commented on other Gospels, too, acknowledging their existence, truthfulness, and authorship. Luke, he claimed, was the preferred Gospel in the Pauline Church of Ephesus. He added that the Gospel of Matthew was personally written by Matthew, originally in Hebrew, but translated according to the local needs of various churches. Papius referred to our Lord as "The Truth" following the expression of the Gospel of John and frequently cited other favored expressions of John.

In AD 155, in his *First Apology* addressed to the Roman Emperor Antoninus Pius, Saint Justin Martyr concisely refers to the Gospels as the "memoirs of the Apostles." Along with a detailed description of the early Christian liturgies, he notes that these Gospels were read in common within the context of those same rituals. Justin's student, Tacian, more precisely identifies these Gospels as a set of four numerically in his work entitled *Diatessaron*. This title means "Through Four." It refers to the Gospels of Matthew, Mark, Luke, and John.

Around AD 180, the Church Father, Saint Irenaeus, added further details surrounding the organically transmitted, traditional heritage of the Gospels. He traces his understanding back through Polycarp to the Apostle John. Note how traditions work. Irenaeus states what he was taught by Polycarp; Polycarp preserves and teaches what was explained to him by the Apostle John.

So, Irenaeus confidently spells out further details that had been passed on to him. He underlines that Matthew's Gospel was written first. He wrote (finished) it while Peter and Paul were still alive and doing ministry in Rome. Mark wrote his Gospel right then and there in Rome as he listened to Peter's oral preaching of the Gospel. Mark indeed served as Peter's faithful secretary who worked alongside him. Irenaeus adds that Luke was Paul's traveling companion along with Barnabas. It's also noted that John wrote his Gospel while living in Ephesus. Another complementary tradition situates John in Ephesus, yet for a different reason. He lived in a home there, tending to the needs of Jesus's aged mother.

In AD 190, Saint Clement of Alexandria noted that Mark's Gospel was based upon Peter's preaching. He explained, too, that the Gospels of Matthew and John were based upon their own personal recollections of living with Jesus Christ. He added that Matthew originally wrote in Hebrew.

Around AD 215, Tertullian divided the Gospels into two sets: those written by Apostles and those written by Apostolic men. The Apostles Matthew and John wrote as Apostolic witnesses. The Apostolic men, Mark and Luke, wrote as men closely associated with the Apostles, especially with the Apostles Peter and Paul.

For hundreds of years, the true authorship of the Gospels was unquestionably attributed by the early Church to Matthew, Mark, Luke, and John. Then, in AD 400, the heretic Faustus the Manichean doubted it. The Great Saint Augustine countered Faustus's objection with the following argument:

> Why does no one doubt the genuineness of the books attributed to Hippocrates? Because there is a succession of testimonies to the books from the time of Hippocrates to the present day, which makes it unreasonable either now or hereafter to have any doubt of the subject. How do we know the authorship and works of Plato, Aristotle, Cicero, Varro, or other similar writers but by the unbroken chain of evidence?

The chain of ancient sources proves authenticity. If this is true regarding the great works of antiquity, it is similarly valid regarding the authors of the Gospels.

Note the principle of antiquity at work here. The Church has always looked back toward the real, historical Christ and his Apostles to verify things. The Church has a long track record of consistently applying this principle in multifaceted ways. How do we know that the Pope is truly linked to Christ's delegation of authority? We trace the continuous link of succession all the way back to Peter. As we've seen in previous chapters, this same principle of antiquity was also depended upon to determine the canon of scripture in AD 382. The Church glanced back to sift the Apocrypha away from the truly inspired writings of ancient times. The writings closest to Christ made the list of inspired New Testament writings. The inspired list stemmed from authors who knew Christ and by their writings prayerfully employed during the ancient Church liturgies.

Hence, the principle of antiquity is applied to the dating of the New Testament. There is a long-established Church tradition that attributes the New Testament books to their original authors, whose names have always been part of the book titles. For instance: "The Gospel of Luke," "The Letter of Paul to the Romans," and more. These were not marketing titles! They were identifying indicators of the works. The earliest Christians knew the authors and believed that those same men wrote what they claimed.

This section on the re-dating of the New Testament is plainly a reminder of what the Catholic Church, founded by Jesus, has always believed. Rationalist biblical scholars are no match for the ancient common understanding of the average Christian during the days when Matthew,

Mark, Luke, John, Paul, Peter, James, and Jude wrote. On the one hand, the Church stands firm with the evidence of recorded ancient traditions. On the other hand, the rationalists have no evidence of late dates and substituted authors. Their theories fade on suppositions.

Regardless of the modern pitfalls of dating the New Testament, there is a singular, fresh argument by a modern scholar worthy of attention. His name is Dr. John A. T. Robinson. His key insight about the re-dating of the New Testament harmonizes wonderfully with this present section on the same theme. Of course, claiming a very early production period with nothing written beyond the year AD 70, Robinson's stance contradicts the consensus of generations of Bible scholars. His research is highly recommended: *Redating the New Testament,* by John A. T. Robinson, 1976, by Wipf and Stock Publishers.

Robinson's position, backed by 369 pages of fine research, is that the fall of Jerusalem and the razing of the Jewish Temple in AD 70 would certainly have been indicated somewhere in the twenty-seven books of the New Testament if they had been written after the event. Yet, every book is entirely silent on the matter, even when it is prophesied by Jesus in the Gospel of Matthew and when the book of Hebrews underlines God's "retirement" of the Jewish temple and its accompanying blood sacrifices.

These astounding facts, and Robinson offers many more, provide a context that naturally shouts for acknowledgment and expression by the authors of that time. Consider some comparisons: Imagine a knowledgeable witness of the beginnings of the South Pacific War in 1941. Such a military man writes a book on the subject in 1945. Wouldn't it seem unusual if nothing was mentioned about the attack on Pearl Harbor by the Japanese? Or, for instance, a researcher in 2003 produces a book on Islamic terrorism. But nothing is said about the attacks on the Twin Towers in New York in 2001 by Islamic terrorists that happened only two years before publication. The fall of Jerusalem offers such powerful context for the writers of the New Testament if they indeed wrote after the event. The Evangelists typically went out of their way to highlight whenever Christ fulfilled a prophecy. Why did they not point out that Jesus not only prophesied the fall of Jerusalem but that the prophecy was actually fulfilled?

If written late, it's odd that the most datable and climactic event of the period, eminently pertinent to the Apostles, is silent regarding such a timely and meaningful substantiation of Christianity's message to the Jews especially. If written late, the fall of Jerusalem in AD 70 and the collapse of institutional Judaism based on the temple would have offered the authors a historic fact to sustain their point that Christ replaced the old covenant with the new or that Christ had prophesied the destruction.

Although such arguments do not prove the writing of the New Testament before the year AD 70, they nonetheless offer a view complementary and supportive of Church tradition. Besides, if the New Testament was written before AD 70, the silence is easily explained.

A Bible Context Timeline

There are many Bible timelines. Appropriately for their purposes, they tend to focus on the hard facts: Who wrote which book, and when? Who translated this or that book? When was the book placed in the codex, and where? What words did the translator choose from all possible words? Most summary timelines plainly relate to the consecutive dates of people and events. Each date dispassionately follows another, lacking additional information to foster comprehension. Context would do that. But that would make any list excessively long. Of course, a dry timeline is adequate when a skeletal listing is skimmed, but context is needed for profundity.

The following list then gathers the contextual elements of Biblical development presented in this book, abridges them, and lays everything out in a strict chronological order. The aim is to take a step back and behold the whole picture of the ancient Bible. Appreciating the interconnectedness of dates and seeing the causes and effects of people and events brings clarity.

The development of the New Testament took hundreds of years. It was a slow and organic process. It's one thing to simply accept this on faith. It's another to see it by understanding the causes and effects of contextual, historical developments. For instance, Pope Damasus I promulgated the biblical canon in AD 382. This fact is somewhat empty until the context of papal authority and papal succession is understood —as it was in ancient times.

A heads up: Some dates may be slightly off or approximations. This is due to the varying opinions of historians. The methodology of selecting dates tried to identify the most ancient substantiations unless exceptional research proved otherwise. (The dating of the Muratorian Fragment is an example.) Sometimes, less certain dates found a stable place by comparison to more certain dates agreed upon by multiple authorities.

Because the following list is essentially a review of previous material, reformatted chronologically, it would benefit to first read the book for an immediate comprehension of the timeline. Otherwise, here is the summary:

1400 - 100 BC: Beginning with Moses's contributions to establishing the first five books of the Bible, Genesis, Exodus, Leviticus, Numbers, and Deuteronomy, the Hebrew Old Testament is written, piece by piece, by different authors.

1,000 BC: King David writes and sings his Psalms.

280 BC - 100 BC: The Greek Old Testament (Septuagint) of forty-six books is produced in Alexandria, Egypt, including the so-called "deuterocanonical books."

250 BC – AD 100: The Dead Sea Scrolls also include several of the "deuterocanonical books" mixed among the other Hebrew-inspired writings.

100 BC onward: The Septuagint is widely circulated and commonly used as the primary set of scriptures for Jews and Jewish converts within the Greek-speaking Roman Empire. The Septuagint will become the most frequently referenced set of scriptures used by Jesus, the Apostles, the authors of the Gospels, the Apostolic Fathers, and the early Church. This set of scriptures includes Tobit, Judith, Wisdom, Sirach, Baruch, I Maccabees, II Maccabees, and the complete books of Esther and Daniel.

AD 30: Jesus begins his public ministry and calls the twelve Apostles.

AD 32: At Caesarea Philippi, Jesus appoints Peter as the head of His *Ekklesia*, effective from the moment of His ascension into heaven.

AD 33: Jesus initiates the New Covenant with its communion ritual as the official rite of worship for His *Ekklesia*. At the Last Supper, Jesus perfects the Passover celebration, molding it into a Christian liturgy to be used by His Church.

AD 33: Jesus commissions his Apostles to preach the Gospel and baptize –to the ends of the earth. He ascends into heaven. Note:

Jesus never says anything about writing the New Testament. This will be a gradual Church development that will climax in AD 382.

AD 33: Under Peter's leadership, Matthias replaces the fallen Apostle, Judas.

AD 33: On the day of Pentecost, Peter converts three thousand souls to Christianity.

AD 33 onward: The new Christian liturgy, "Breaking of the Bread," is established as the principal form of regularly observed Christian worship every Sunday.

AD 33 onward: Apostles and Disciples spread the oral Gospel. Obeying the commission of Christ, the Apostles and Disciples burst upon the world with great, expansive power. Keenly aware of their mission, they preach the oral Gospel in modern-day Syria, Armenia, Lebanon, Iran, Turkey, Iraq, Egypt, Ethiopia, Tunisia, Afghanistan, India, Greece, Italy, India, Spain, Romania, Ukraine, Britain, and Ireland.

AD 33 onward: As the Church expands geographically, a provisional Church organizational structure develops, primarily consisting of *episkopi* (bishops) and *presbuteroi* (priests).

AD 33 onward: Following Jesus's example, the Apostles mostly reference the Septuagint when evangelizing. Additionally, the Apostles, Disciples, and early bishops habitually use the Septuagint during Church liturgies.

AD 33 – 50: During this period, as pieces of the New Testament began to emerge, the Church suspends the obligation to follow the Mosaic laws, withdraws from synagogue attendance, establishes worship services in the private homes of baptized Christians, replaces the Sabbath observance with Christian Eucharistic Liturgies principally on Sundays, if not more often; establishes its presence in at least nineteen countries (as identified today); establishes the Church in Rome and Antioch, both by Peter's leadership; establishes an authoritative network or provisional governing structure of bishops, priests, and deacons; and presumes the liturgical and evangelistic usage of the Septuagint as a Christian inheritance. Note that before the New Testament began, the Church functions with bold authority and refined self-awareness. The Pauline letters and written Gospels are a purposeful work of the Church –as it looks to the future.

AD 34: The first deacon and Christian Martyr, Saint Stephen, is stoned to death for preaching the Gospel of Christ. Saul approvingly witnesses the event. "Saul" would later be renamed "Paul." This event led to much Jewish opposition against the "New Way" and a gradual resettlement of Christians fleeing north to Antioch.

AD 35: Saul, a respected, well-educated, industrious Pharisee, labored against the newly developing Christians. On a journey to Damascus to help persecute the "New Way," "Saul" encounters the risen Christ. "Paul" immediately converts and becomes the 13th Apostle. His initial education in Christianity comes from the other Apostles. Consider that Paul benefited from fifteen years of conversations with Apostles, meditating, praying, thinking, and preaching before he decided to put the faith into writing.

AD 40: Somewhere around this date, at Antioch, the "Disciples" are first called "Christians."

AD 40 – 60: Matthew completes his Gospel.

AD 40 onward: The separate New Testament books, one by one, are incorporated into Church liturgies as they circulate. They are read publicly along with the Septuagint during the first half of liturgies. It seems that Matthew's Gospel was the first written Gospel publicly read at Christian liturgies.

AD 40 - 60: The Didache is written and circulated. This is the first known catechetical guide, especially for new converts to Christianity. It presents some basic teachings regarding Christian practices, morals, and the sacraments. It explains the choice between life and death, the way of virtue or the way of vice.

AD 40 – 65: The Apostle John finishes writing his Gospel, likely during the latter half of this time span.

AD 42: After preaching the Gospel in Spain, the Apostle James is martyred by beheading. This is the brother of the Apostle John, not the writer of the letter of James in the New Testament.

AD 43 – 49: Peter establishes the Church in Rome. Yet, due to an unreconcilable Jewish disturbance in the city, the Jews, the "New Way," and Peter are expelled from Rome by AD 49. There was some kind of ongoing disorder caused by "a man named *Chrestus?*" Peter leaves and attends the Apostolic Council described in Acts, chapter 15, which deals with circumcision and baptism.

AD 45 – 60: Mark completes his Gospel, likely during the latter half of this time span.

AD 47 – 48: The Apostle James, the cousin of Jesus and first Bishop of Jerusalem, writes his pastoral letter.

AD 49: After the Apostolic Council in Jerusalem, Peter heads north and assumes the leadership of the Church in Antioch as their first bishop. He offers pastoral care, especially to the Jewish Christians who had fled Jerusalem. Peter stays in Antioch until AD 54. Surely busy enough, he nevertheless waits for the opportunity to slip back into Rome!

AD 50: Paul's first letter to the Thessalonians is completed. This was his first written contribution to the New Testament.

AD 50 – 51: Paul's second letter to the Thessalonians is completed.

AD 51 onward: Apocrypha is written and circulated throughout the known Christian world within the Roman Empire.

AD 51 onward: Local bishops discern for their communities which circulated writings represent the true faith taught from the beginning and are therefore acceptable to be publicly read at liturgies and which writings are doubtful and therefore restricted from liturgical use. These later questionable writings would later be categorized as "apocrypha," a term that usually connotes something either fraudulent or unorthodox, or not sufficiently ancient to establish credibility, or simply not recommended to be read at liturgical settings.

AD 54: Emperor Nero assumes power and revokes the expulsion of the Jews from Rome. Peter, therefore, returns to Rome to complete its foundation and nurture its development. He becomes well known for preaching at the Tiber and baptizing there. Peter would have thirteen years to root Christianity in Rome before his martyrdom, not far from the Egyptian obelisk towering in the middle of Saint Peter's Square today. That obelisk witnessed his crucifixion.

AD 55: Paul completes his first letter to the Corinthians.

AD 55: Paul writes and sends his first letter to Timothy.

AD 56: Paul completes his second letter to the Corinthians.

AD 56: Paul completes his letter to the Galatians.

AD 57: Paul completes his letter to the Romans.

AD: 57: Paul writes to Titus. Paul appoints the Greek Titus, the *episkopos* (bishop) of the island of Crete. Titus then appoints *presbuteroi* (priests) subject to his own supervision.

AD 57 – 60: Luke completes his Gospel.

AD 57 – 62: Luke finishes writing the Acts of the Apostles.

AD 58: Paul completes his letter to the Philippians.

AD 58: Paul writes to Philemon.

AD 58: Paul completes his letter to the Colossians.

AD 58: Paul completes his letter to the Ephesians.

AD 58: Paul writes and sends his second letter to Timothy.

AD 60 – 65: The Apostle John writes his three pastoral letters.

AD 61: The Apostle Andrew is martyred by crucifixion.

AD 61 – 62: Jude completes his pastoral letter.

AD 62: The same Apostle Jude is martyred by being clubbed to death.

AD 62: The Apostle Philip is martyred by crucifixion.

AD 62: The Apostle James [the lesser] is martyred by being thrown from the pinnacle of the temple in Jerusalem and then beaten to death with a club. (This was the James, who was the first Bishop of Jerusalem.)

AD 62 – 65: Peter completes and circulates his two letters.

AD 65: The Apostle Matthew is slaughtered at the altar while "Breaking Bread."

AD 65: Matthias was hacked to death.

AD 64 - 68: Nero launches his persecution of the Christians in Rome. They had been blamed for a six-day fire that ravaged the city. But the fire had been started by Nero himself. Christians were crucified, beheaded, tortured, hunted like game, and used as living torches. This persecution represented a blanketed, full-blown slaughter of Christians.

AD 67: The Apostle Simon is crucified.

AD 67: The book of Hebrews is likely completed.

AD 67: Saints Peter and Paul are martyred in Rome: Peter by crucifixion upside down and Paul by beheading.

AD 67 – 76: Following Peter, Linus becomes the second Pope of the Catholic Church. He had been made a bishop by Peter, studied under him, and worked with him in Rome. Linus had been brought into the faith through the ministries of Peter and Paul, who had baptized many in the Tiber River near Vatican Hill. Linus had also co-labored as a ministerial companion with Saint Paul.

AD 68 – 70: John likely completes the book of the Apocalypse.

AD 69 – 79: Emperor Vespasian executes his persecution of the Jews and Christians.

AD 70: The Roman General Titus besieges and destroys Jerusalem, razing and burning the Jewish temple to the ground. A half million Jews and Christians perish.

AD 72: The Apostle Bartholomew is skinned alive.

AD 74: The Apostle Thomas is stabbed to death.

AD 76 – 88: Succeeding Pope Linus, Pope Cletus takes over. Cletus is Roman by birth and had at one time lived near Saint Peter's residence in Rome. Peter had baptized him and personally educated him in the faith. Peter also appointed Cletus as a "helper" bishop in Rome (along with Linus) to care for the sacramental needs of the faithful while allowing him to have more time to pray and preach the Gospel publicly. Cletus had faithfully stood at the foot of the cross until the end when Peter, his dear friend, was crucified upside down in Nero's Circus.

AD 81 – 96: The Roman Emperor Domitian reigns. He launches a vicious persecution of the Christians. By AD 95, during this same persecution, the Apostle John is dunked in a vat of boiling oil but survives. Domitian then exiles John.

AD 88 – 97: As the fourth Pope, Clement succeeds Cletus. Like Linus and Cletus, Clement, too, is a close disciple of Peter and a co-worker of Saint Paul. Pope Clement is banished to the Pontus quarries and later martyred by drowning in the sea, with an anchor knotted around his neck.

AD 95: Prompted by the inner rebellion of the Corinthian community, some members of the Church appeal to Pope Clement to help resolve their problem. He responds with a massive letter, which is the first instance in the historical record when a Pope (following Peter) acts with authority over the universal Church.

AD 98: This year marks the end of the Apostolic age, when the last Apostle, John, dies in Ephesus.

AD 98 – 117: Under the reign of Trajan, another persecution of the Christians takes place.

AD 107: For the first time in the written historical record, Christ's Church is called Catholic: "Wherever Jesus Christ is, there is the Catholic Church." (*Saint Ignatius of Antioch's Letter to the Smyrnaeans, chapter 8:2*) As the third bishop of Antioch, Ignatius uses this term in several of his letters as if it's in common usage for a long while. He equally emphasizes the importance of obeying the local bishop as if a Christian were obeying the Apostles. He includes the teaching that Jesus Christ is truly present in the Holy Eucharist when the bread and wine are consecrated at the liturgy.

AD 110 – 140: During this period, including before and after, the Jews "mutilated their own scriptures" as described by an Apostolic Father. The Jews replaced the Septuagint, made in Alexandria hundreds of years earlier and used by Jesus and his Apostles, with a newly adapted Palestinian Septuagint. Just as much, they reverted to the frequent usage of a particular Hebrew set of scriptures. Significantly, both of these scriptures did not accept the so-called "deuterocanonical books." These developments were related to a conscious effort made by the Jews to undermine the successful use of the Jewish scriptures to make Christian converts. After the destruction of the Temple in Jerusalem, Jewish leadership progressively gravitated toward re-claiming Jewish exclusivity over their own scriptural heritage. They wanted to "de-Christianize" the scriptural support of the new sect (Christians) that proclaimed a "false Messiah." After a fresh set of Jewish scriptures came about, Jews would later accuse the Christians of embracing a defective and inauthentic Old Testament scriptural basis for their beliefs.

AD 117 – 138: Additional persecutions of Christians continue after Trajan during the reign of Emperor Hadrian.

AD 144: The heretic Marcion attempts to make his Biblical canon. He couldn't reconcile the revelation of the Old Testament with the New Testament and concluded that because these Gods were so different, there must be two Gods. Of course, Marcion's failure did encourage bishops to envision a shared, accurate list of inspired writings.

AD 153 – 155: Saint Justin Martyr writes his "First Apology." As part of his legal defense, Justin explains his beliefs and describes the Christian liturgical service. As such, he explains that the bread and wine turn into the flesh and blood of Jesus and that this becomes communion for the Christians, who are changed by its reception. It makes sense that such an explanation is used as a legal argument precisely because a common accusation against Christians during the many persecutions was their practice of "cannibalism."

AD 161 – 180: Persecutions of Christians continues throughout the reign of Marcus Aurelius. Although this emperor enjoyed a reputation as a thoughtful and cultured ruler, the Christian persecutions nonetheless continued.

AD 170 – 190 (approximately): Saint Irenaeus asserts that the four Gospels of Matthew, Mark, Luke, and John are inspired and canonical, excluding all other Gospels circulating. He explains why. These four Gospels go back to an apostolic tradition of usage, especially at liturgies. He also lists twenty-one books in an early canon that would all end up in the official New Testament, yet leaving out Philemon, Hebrews, James, II Peter, III John, and Jude.

AD 200 – 367: Local bishops discuss possible canons. During this period, Christian writings were gathered, and the Apocrypha sifted. A common aim emerges to determine a definitive, universal list of inspired writings.

AD 235 – 238: The emperor Maximinus the Thracian launches his own persecution of the Christians.

AD 240: Origen, a speculative scholar who taught at the great Catechetical school in Alexandria, attempts to determine a universal canon. He divides the possible New Testament sources into either inspired books or questionably inspired books. At the same time, he advances his own opinion of some specific books he believes inspired: Barnabas, the Didache, and the Shepherd of Hermas. Yet, his academic list is never promulgated by the authority of a local bishop charged with teaching the orthodox faith to his own flock of believers.

AD 249 – 251: Emperor Decius persecutes the Christians. This exceptionally bloody persecution swept throughout the entire empire. Christian worship is outlawed. Unless captured Christians paid homage to the Roman gods, they were forthrightly killed on the spot. Remember that regarding all the persecutions, Christians were viewed as "heretics" by Roman society. Hence, the Christians' primary crime against the state was opposition against Roman polytheistic beliefs and practices. Such opposition convicted Christians of the crime of "atheism."

AD 253 – 260: Emperor Valerian persecutes the Christians.

AD 293: Apart from private homes, the first building is constructed for the specific purpose of Christian worship. Recently discovered in Aqaba, Jordan, it originally accommodated sixty worshippers.

AD 303 – 306: Although he became the emperor for the western half of the Roman Empire in AD 284, Diocletian did not initiate his persecution until the oracle at Didyma urged him to do so in AD 303. Diocletian then targeted the clergy and any faint beginnings of worship structures. At least in the West, Constantine came to power in AD 306 and immediately stopped the persecutions and restored confiscated properties to the Christians. Yet, the persecution continued to flourish until AD 312 in the eastern half of the Roman Empire.

AD 313: The two Roman Emperors, Constantine for the west and Licinius for the east, meet in Milan and jointly proclaim the "Edit of Milan." This proclamation established religious toleration for Christianity and other religions within the Roman Empire, making all religions and practices of worship legal. It ends the persecution of Christians and declares a general state of religious freedom. No doubt, this decisive moment in history is influenced by Constantine's favorable disposition to Christianity, nurtured by his devout Christian mother, Saint Helen.

AD 318 – 322: Constantine initiates the construction of basilicas in Rome to honor the Christian religion. Over the burial sites of Saint Peter and Saint Paul, he starts constructions to honor these two great saints of Rome and the universal Church. Soon, other basilicas would follow, one to Saint John the Apostle and another to the Blessed Virgin and Mother of Jesus. During this time period and earlier, there is a trend to adapt the humble homes of Christians into the first Church buildings of Christianity. Of course, the intermittent Roman persecutions for hundreds of years had delayed this cultural development.

AD 324: Constantine becomes the sole Roman Emperor. He immediately devotes his energies to organizing the Council of Nicaea to resolve the issue of Christian disunity between Orthodox believers and Arians.

AD 324: The year before the Council of Nicaea, Eusebius, the Bishop of Caesarea in Palestine, brushes up his Church History with corrections and updates. In that masterpiece of his life, he organizes New Testament writings into four categories: books that are accepted, disputed, rejected but not discarded, and books that are heretical. He remains on the academic level without the use of his episcopal authority as an act of governing his flock.

AD 325: At the Council of Nicaea, three hundred and eighteen bishops condemn the heresy of Arianism. The Council creates the Creed of Nicene to clearly state the divinity of Christ: "…God of God, light of light, true God of true God, begotten not made, of the same substance with the Father through whom all things were made…."

AD 337: The Roman Emperor, Constantine, is baptized on his deathbed. His death causes the division of the Roman Empire into four parts, each ruled by its own Emperor.

AD 351 – 361: The Roman Empire again is ruled by a sole emperor, Constantius II. Unfortunately, he is a zealous Arian. His interests are to confirm Arianism and influence the papacy to function in a pro-Arian manner.

AD 352: Pope Liberius is kidnapped by Constantius II for not cooperating in making the Church pro-Arian. The Pope was then exiled to Beroea, Greece, and an anti-Pope was set in his place by the Roman Emperor, Constantius II.

AD 366: There's an attempted papal coup, but the validly elected Pope, Damasus I, successfully retains his office and power.

AD 367: Saint Athanasius promulgates an official seventy-three-book canon for his diocese in Alexandria, Egypt.

AD 367 – 419: This is the period of "fixation" when the Biblical canon is stabilized by several Church councils, all reiterating the same seventy-three-book canon.

AD 374: Pope Damasus proclaims the New Testament canon consisting of the exact twenty-seven books listed by Saint Athanasius.

AD 380: Two Roman Emperors, Gratian for the west and Theodosius for the east, jointly declare Christianity as the official religion of the Roman Empire.

AD 381: The Council of Constantinople confirms the divinity of the Holy Spirit. It also condemns Apollinarianism, the heresy that asserts Jesus has no rational soul. Ultimately, this heresy means that Jesus lacks a true human nature. The council also condemns Macedonianism, the heresy that insists the Holy Spirit is not a person and is created.

AD 382: At the Council of Rome, Pope Saint Damasus I promulgates the official Biblical canon of seventy-three books for the universal Church.

AD 383: Saint Jerome finishes his translation of the four Gospels from Greek into Latin.

AD 390: This year approximates the production date of the Muratorian Fragment. The fragment is an incomplete listing of the books accepted by the Catholic Church, found by Father Lodovico Muratori. He discovered it in a codex in the Ambrosian Library of Milan, Italy, in AD 1740. A second-century production date had been long presumed. Yet recently, upon closer examination, the AD 170 date simply did not hold up to the rigor of a critical analysis.

AD 393: The Council of Hippo, in Africa, reaffirms the official canon of the Catholic Church as the same canon decreed by Pope Saint Damasus I in AD 382.

AD 397: The Council of Carthage, Africa, reasserts the same canon propagated by Pope Damasus only fifteen years earlier.

AD 405: In Bethlehem, Saint Jerome finishes his translation of the Bible into Latin, later called "The Vulgate." He had started by translating from the Septuagint and later switched to a direct translation from the Hebrew. He introduced each of the "deuterocanonical" books with prologues that questioned their inspired status. 1,119 years later, Martin Luther would follow Jerome's precedent and do the same. Unfortunately, both men drank from the same poisoned well. They had translated from a post-apostolic Jewish "original" source that had truncated scripture by leaving out seven truly inspired books, as officially promulgated by the Church.

AD 405: Pope Innocent I reaffirms the same seventy-three-book Biblical canon declared by Pope Damasus I, the Council of Hippo, and the Council of Carthage.

AD 416: Pelagianism is condemned. This is the heresy that taught man can live an upright, moral life without God's help.

AD 419: Another Council of Carthage again asserts the same Biblical canon decreed by Pope Damasus I.

AD 431: The Council of Ephesus condemns the heresy of Nestorianism. This heresy taught that Jesus is essentially two distinct persons, one human and one divine. While these two persons remain separate and distinct from one another, they are superficially united.

AD 451: The Council of Chalcedon again condemns the heresy of Nestorianism and defines how the human and divine natures in Christ are united in one divine person. This council also condemns Monophysitism. This heresy taught that Jesus Christ only had one nature, a hybrid of a divine and human nature mixed together.

AD 797: The II Council of Nicaea confirms the seventy-three-book Bible.

AD 1442: The Council of Florence confirms the seventy-three-book Bible.

AD 1534: A Catholic priest in Germany, Father Martin Luther, a scripture scholar, prints his German-translated Bible with prologues that deny the divine inspiration of certain books. This applied to seven books and parts of two other books that he labeled Apocrypha. These books included Tobit, Judith, Wisdom, Sirach, Baruch, I Maccabees, II Maccabees, chapters 10-16 of Esther, and chapters 3:24-90, 13, and 14 of Daniel.

AD 1546: The Council of Trent confirmed the same seventy-three-book canon of scripture that had been decreed and promulgated by Pope Saint Damasus I in AD 382. Numerous councils of ages past had confirmed the same.

AD 1870: The Council of Vatican I confirmed the seventy-three-book Bible.

CHAPTER FIFTEEN

Making the Ancient Bible My Ow

Moving from Theory to Practice

We swam at length in the huge swells of ancient Bible context. We opened the Bible in a multiverse of contextual worlds: ecclesial, historical, political, canonical, doctrinal, and liturgical. A special emphasis was given to the appointment of Peter as the head of Christ's Church; the exalted place of the Septuagint (Alexandrian) for early Christians; the rapid expansion and proliferation of bishops and their role of discerning the authentic books of the Bible for their local communities; the long process of arriving at the Biblical canon; the integral link between emerging New Testament writings and their insertion into the new Christian liturgy founded by Christ at the Last Supper; and the climactic promulgation of the seventy-three-book Bible by Pope Damasus I. The origin of the Bible is hardly comprehensible without an appreciation of this rudimentary context.

Each of these age-old veins of culture clarified how the Bible was born and ended up in our hands today. However, even though we covered much ground, much more ancient context has been left almost entirely untouched. But we nonetheless introduced a productive avenue to understand the place of scripture –precisely by penetrating the context surrounding its birth, circulation, and canonization.

Still, in the world of possible contexts, we have barely touched the tip of the iceberg. Any curious soul could easily discover more about the development of the Bible by studying within the parameters of wider fields of context. Some unexplored contexts (largely absent in this present book) might include the Dead Sea Scrolls, the early art depictions in the catacombs, the writings of the Apostolic Fathers, the earliest Christian architecture, the earliest creeds confessed by Christians, and the doctrinal content embedded in the details of the Roman persecutions. We lightly brushed up alongside a few of these contexts in this book but left such rich deposits of understanding in large part unmined.

Each additional ancient contextual setting would yield further fruit, underlining the causative link between the Catholic Church and the production and usage of the Bible. The great philosopher Aristotle held that something cannot be profoundly understood unless its origins are grasped. So, we've probed the truth of this premise by studying Biblical context.

Seeing Biblical context is one thing; living it is another. The ancient Bible is still not fully understood until it is lived. You can know how to ride a bike in theory. You can know how to bake a cake in theory. But unless a practical habit takes over, do you really know how to ride a bike or bake a cake? That's called practical knowledge, added to theoretical knowledge. This distinction can be applied to familiarity with the ancient Bible.

So, we are now ready to take a giant leap of belief. It's a jump from theory to practice, or better, knowledge to faith. How can I live the ancient Bible of Christianity? The Bible is designed by God as an instrument of conformity to revealed faith and morals. It's a "how to do" type of book, partially. Granted, there's more to the Bible than that. We're merely accentuating the Bible's practical end of personal holiness.

It's not enough to only know the truth while conveniently leaving conformity behind. The demons that roam the world must be considered among the brightest of "scripture scholars." See how Satan quoted scripture to Jesus after His forty-day fast in the wilderness. But what good was Lucifer's Biblical knowledge and ability to quote at will? By not conforming his will to the divine will, he missed the whole point of Biblical knowledge —not by stupidity but by deliberate mutiny. So, we can fall similarly, knowing the chapters and verses of a thousand doctrines while resisting to walk the humble surrender of personal repentance and conversion.

Which Bible to Read

In his Psalm, David links an upright life with walking the ancient revelation of God. He alludes to the virtuous walks of Moses, Abraham, and Noah. "Probe me, God, know my heart; try me, know my concerns. See if my way is crooked, then lead me in the ancient paths." (Psalm 139:23-24) We can learn much from this prayer. This section aims at putting the ancient into practice.

If I'm to live the ancient Bible, I must define it, put it into my hands, and do what it says. Not all Bibles are the same. Not all represent the ancient revelation of God, as they should –perfectly. Some Bibles are missing books, others question the inspiration of books, and still others mislead by poor translations. Even worse, some Bibles add "scholarly comments" that plant the seeds of doubt regarding supernatural content. Such Biblical commentary, for instance, might deny that Moses truly parted the Red Sea or that Jesus worked true miracles.

What current English translation and version of the Bible then would be closest to the ancient Bible and free from poisonous commentary? We would define the ancient Bible as follows: the Greek Old Testament used mostly by Jesus, the Apostles, the early Church, the authors of the New Testament, and the Apostolic Fathers, notwithstanding the Hebrew scriptures in use at that time and referenced by these same sources.

The Old and New Testament seventy-three-book canon declared by the Catholic Church and formally promulgated by Pope Damasus I in the year AD 382 represents the ancient Bible. Clarifying further, the ancient Christian Bible is principally in the Greek language, used in Christian liturgies, and includes as divinely inspired the following books and parts: Tobit, Judith, Wisdom, Sirach, Baruch, I Maccabees, II Maccabees and the complete chapters of Esther and Daniel.

Having defined the ancient Bible, where can I find the modern equivalent in English today? Of the sixty Bible versions available in English today, two stand out. The New American Bible is the officially approved Bible for usage in Catholic liturgies in the United States. The second is the Revised Standard Version Second Catholic Edition (RSV2CE). In my opinion, this Bible (along with its optional overall presentations, more on that a bit later) best represents the ancient Bible, as described above. Let's briefly explore the justification for these selections:

Like the New American Bible, the translation type of the RSV2CE is a literal equivalence rather than a dynamic "translation." There are two fundamental ways of translating the Bible. One is a literal way. The other is a dynamic way. The literal way translates word for word. It painstakingly finds the exact word replacement in the vocabulary of the new language. As such, this kind of translation is highly faithful to the accuracy of the original texts. The other approach is called a dynamic translation. It is less interested in the exact equivalence of the words from one language into another in favor of conveying the meaning behind the original texts. It basically "translates meanings." What are the pros and cons of these translating approaches?

On the one hand, the literal approach, at times, may be less understood upfront, requiring further study to figure out the nuances of ancient Greek, Hebrew, or Latin terms. But only the literal approach preserves the subtle cues of words, which are the irreplaceable starting points to arrive at an accurate idea of the author's word choices and intentions.

On the other hand, the dynamic translation is generally more quickly understood in everyday language. A person can more easily breeze through reading this kind of translation. But the drawback is obvious: the work that would have been invested by the reader of the literal translation is already digested and expressed by the dynamic translator. At first, this seems wonderful. It saves time. However, the practical result is that a dynamic translation may be prone to persuasion according to the personal perspectives and subtle interpretations of the translator. As such, the dynamic translation may result in representing the translator's ideas more than the original author's.

So, at the expense of ease and understanding, the dynamic translation may not accurately convey the original intent of the inspired writer. For example, in Titus 1:7, Paul indicates the moral and spiritual maturity required of anyone appointed a bishop. The foundational word *episkopos* is used in Greek. A literal translation uses the equivalent English word: "bishop." But dynamic translations, avoiding an exact word translation, favor attempts at possible word meanings, such as "Church leader," "overseer," "elder," "Church official," or "minister." A literal, word-for-word translation will always present a more faithful and precise representation of the original text. Both the New American Bible (NAB) and the RSV2CE provide literal translations.

There are various editions of the RSV: There's the Revised Standard Version (RSV) that stands alone, welcomed by protestants. There is the NRSV that filters the scriptures and adopts "gender-inclusive language." I would not recommend this because it changes the words of revealed scripture. There's the "RSV2," designed to update the English to modern usage. This version replaces archaic terms (pronouns and their accompanying verb forms) with the words we use today, making the read more fluent. Examples of such archaic terms might include: "thee," "thou," "thy," "didst," "speaketh," "art," "hast," and more. This updating of old words for new does not alter the meaning of terms. This type of change is a matter of preference.

Besides the literal translation of the RSV2CE, the Catholic Edition (CE) further distinguishes this Bible as ancient. This Catholic version is provisionally approved for liturgical usage, with an imprimatur of the

Catholic Church. It is also the Bible most used in official Catholic Church documents, including the official Catechism of the Catholic Church. It is a popular study Bible used by Catholics, including distinguished Catholic professors who were once protestants. Additionally, the RSV2CE contains the same canon promulgated by Pope Saint Damasus I in AD 382 and by multiple Church councils thereafter. So, every so-called "deuterocanonical book" is included in this thoroughly Catholic Bible.

The RSV2CE also seeks to break away from a strictly Latin-to-English translation (like the Douay-Rheims), choosing instead to reconnect with ancient Hebrew and Greek sources of revelation. In 1943, Pope Pius XII promulgated an encyclical entitled *Divino afflante Spiritu*. (An encyclical is an official letter written by the Pope sent to all Catholic bishops.) Departing from a tight adherence to the old Latin Vulgate, he called for new translations of the Bible into vernacular languages that derive from the original sources of Scripture. While still drawing from the Vulgate, but not depending on it exclusively, he urged the production of new translations that honored the place of the Alexandrian Septuagint during the time of Christ and the Apostles and used by the early Church in liturgies and for evangelistic purposes. He also wanted to draw from the Hebrew scriptures of that same epoch and not from the Hebrew Masoretic text that, years later dropped the deuterocanonical books.

Further, the RSV2CE comes in different overall presentations. Three Bibles use the RSV2CE as the interior scriptural core while adding their own accompanying, distinguishing features. There's The Ignatius Catholic Study Bible (ICSB), which packs the pages with a great number of extras to understand the ancient scriptures and the Catholic Church. This Bible provides an assortment of commentaries, word studies, essays, and prologues. There is also The Great Adventure Catholic Bible (GACB). This Bible focuses on a historical orientation of salvation history so the reader can understand the interconnectedness of the books of the Bible. Then there's the Didache Bible. This Bible is directed toward readers who want to learn the Catholic faith and see how the Bible is related. It heavily cites the official catechism of the Catholic Church.

Welcoming a familiarity with scripture as it was used by the Apostles and early Church may be a challenge for some. But it shouldn't be. Putting aside all reservations and fears, nothing but good would result from hearing, reading, and meditating upon the same literally translated and canonically complete collection of scriptures embraced in ancient times.

Exposure to the Ancient Liturgical Context of Scripture

When we imagine the praiseworthy place of scripture, we sometimes tend to isolate it from critical ancient contexts or limit it to only one context. We close our eyes and see the heroic preaching of Saint Paul and are taken away. We imagine him with a scroll in hand, enlightening his listeners by explaining the fine points of following Christ. Modern preachers try to imitate Paul as they strut the glowing stage of a mega-church with a Bible in hand and, hopefully, courageously bellow hard-to-hear truths.

This manner of scriptural usage is both ancient and worthy of contemporary imitation. It is especially suited for the ears of the uninitiated. Imagine Billy Graham or Pope John Paul II persuading an overflowing stadium to repent. Saint Stephen shines with a wonderful example of this, as he eloquently references the Septuagint just before he's stoned to death. Or, note Saint Peter's sermon immediately after Pentecost. But there's another side to this obvious and dramatic use of scripture. Yes, scripture has its place as an instrument of evangelization. But it also serves to nurture the baptized gathered for the Eucharistic liturgy. This was a primary reason Saint Paul wrote and encouraged the circulation of his doctrine-packed letters.

Decontextualized viewpoints often miss the point of a greater whole. The liturgical context of the New Testament has accompanied and complemented the Eucharistic sacrifice since the beginning of Christianity. In ancient Christianity, wherever there was a pulpit, there was an altar nearby. These two things link inseparably together. They define Christian worship.

Can ancient Christian worship be defined as singing and preaching without the Eucharistic sacrifice and communion? One without the other would be a distortion of the intent and provision of Jesus Christ for his Church —and of verifiable history, too. To define ancient Christian worship exclusively in terms of conveying the Scriptures and preaching would be both historically unsupported and incomplete. For instance, a man who describes an elephant as four calloused living pillars misses the whole. Without a picture of the whole, misrepresentation necessarily ensues. Who would describe birds as feathered creatures that walk but someone who has never seen them fly? Who would define Christian worship only as a gathering of people who believe in Jesus, who sing, listen to the Scriptures, and experience a sermon? By ancient standards, this is not Christian worship, not until the Eucharistic sacrifice completes it.

Let's say you were a faithful member of Saint Paul's community of believers in Corinth. With Paul in town, what would a daydream glimpse of your experience be like? Perhaps you'd walk from the seaport to the spacious home of a well-off Church member for a Sunday morning gathering. Friends of diverse backgrounds happily greet you. You're so eager to see Paul again! Everyone joins in singing a couple of Psalms. Paul reads from the Septuagint and speaks at length of Christ's fulfillment of various prophecies. (Most believers present do not know Hebrew.) Perhaps he comments on a few ideas he recently wrote to another community, or he shares a conversation he had with Peter or Luke. Then, the educational part of the service gives way to the Eucharistic sacrifice, as commanded by Jesus.

Paul holds the bread, blesses it, consecrates it. He holds the cup of wine and then turns it into the Blood of Jesus Christ. Then Communion comes. He distributes the Body and Blood of Christ. Having been baptized and thoroughly believing in the real presence of Jesus in the Eucharist, you receive Communion. Paul encourages all participants to consume the Lord reverently and receive Jesus Christ's union within.

Such a liturgical experience would have been the norm of Christian worship. At that time, they called it the "Breaking of the Bread." The use of scripture would have augmented your eucharistic participation. Paul would leave the next day. So, he takes a moment to emphasize the responsibility of obeying the bishop he leaves in charge of the community. This is a likely description of how things really worked. My goodness! Paul was a bishop who offered a Catholic Mass! Of course, the title "bishop" would go through some fine-tuning. And the terms "Catholic" and "Mass" were just around the corner. Of course, Paul was much more than a bishop, but not excluding the supervisory role of a bishop either.

In the New Testament, Saint Luke indicates that the "Breaking of the Bread" held a prominent place among the early Christian communities. The Christian way of life emphasized a common life of charity that, without hesitation, shared goods and properties for anyone in need. A spirit of learning the ways of Christ and bringing the Gospel to others prevailed. But just as much, focus descended upon the Christian's chief act of worship: the "Breaking of the Bread." (Acts 2:42-47)

Paul demonstrates his familiarity with the "Breaking of the Bread" or Eucharistic liturgy in his first letter to the Corinthians. He shares the theology, command, and habitual practice of the Eucharist passed on to him from the Apostles, originating from Jesus at the Last Supper. He explains the true nature of the bread and wine as the real Body and Blood of Jesus Christ. He underlines the salvific respect owed to Christ's real presence in the Eucharist. (I Cor. 10:16-21; I Cor. 11:27-30)

Tradition reveals that after the Apostle and Evangelist Matthew preached in Judea, he journeyed as a missionary to Ethiopia. Born in Galilee, he readily embraced the challenge of bringing the Gospel to a completely different culture. During his labors, he converted the daughter of King Egippus. Her name was Ephigenia. While she was a young virgin, Matthew had inspired her to live that way of life, especially dedicated to Christ for the sake of the kingdom. It happened that King Egippus died and was replaced by King Hirtacus.

The succeeding king wanted to marry Ephigenia. He, therefore, asked for Matthew's help to persuade the young woman to marry him. Matthew, in return, invited the king to the Christian's Eucharistic liturgy upon the approaching first day of the week. There, Saint Matthew rebuked the king for lusting after the consecrated virgin. King Hirtacus became enraged and ordered his bodyguard to slay Matthew. As Matthew stood at the altar during the Eucharistic liturgy, the king's men rushed upon the Apostle and killed him with drawn knives.

This snapshot of tradition shows not only the martyrdom of Saint Matthew but also the apostolic tradition of offering the same liturgical ritual established by Jesus at the Last Supper. Wherever the Apostles missionized, they rooted this tradition and provided for its continuation by appointing bishops and, through bishops, assigned priests as needed.

About forty years later, Saint Ignatius, the third Bishop of the Christian hub at Antioch, testified of his belief in the Blessed Eucharist. Writing to the Ephesians, Ignatius said:

> Obey the bishop and the priests with an undivided mind, breaking one and the same bread, which is the medicine of immortality, and the antidote to prevent us from dying, but [which causes] that we should live forever in Jesus Christ.

Here, he urges attendance at the Eucharistic liturgy in a unified manner with the bishop and his priests, equating the reception of communion with the inheritance of eternal life. Ignatius confirms in his own way the promise of Christ: "I am the living bread that came down from heaven; whoever eats this bread will live forever." (John 6:51)

Then, while on his way to Rome to be martyred, he sends a letter in advance to the Romans. He can hardly keep back his desire to die for Christ, comparing his martyrdom to the eucharistic sacrifice of Christ:

I plead with you: show me no untimely kindness. Let me be food for the beasts, for they are my way to God. I am God's wheat and shall be ground by their teeth so that I may become Christ's pure bread. Pray to Christ for me that the animals will be the means of making me a sacrificial victim for God.

So, what is Ignatius really saying? He is eager to offer his life like Jesus did as a Eucharistic sacrifice.

Yet, this holy bishop articulates more clearly:

Take note of those who hold heterodox opinions on the grace of Jesus Christ which has come to us, and see how contrary their opinions are to the mind of God… They abstain from the Eucharist and from prayer because they do not confess that the Eucharist is the flesh of our savior Jesus Christ, flesh which suffered for our sins and which the Father, in his goodness, raised up again. They who deny the gift of God are perishing in their disputes. (Smyrnaeans, chapter 6)

Ignatius underlines that the deniers of the Eucharist do not think as God thinks. They shun the gift of the Eucharist and thereby cut themselves off from divine life. Such "believers" are properly called heretics. As such, they pick and choose what they want to believe from the lips of Jesus and leave behind the difficult teachings, just like so many disciples did when Jesus gave his bread of life discourse.

(Note: It may be useful to make a distinction regarding heresy here. There are two kinds of heretics: "material heretics" and "formal heretics." A material heretic is a believer who strays away from the authentic teachings of Christ and his Church out of innocent ignorance. A formal heretic obstinately declares and clings to a doctrinal position opposed to the authentic and official teachings of Christ and his Church. A material heretic is just mistaken but willing to learn. A formal heretic deliberately chooses to believe, assert, and teach a doctrine other than what Jesus and his Church teach. The formal heretic is characterized by the absence of docility to the Church. Material heresy does not always imply sinfulness. Formal heresy does.)

The above teachings of Bishop Ignatius should not be taken lightly. This man was taught by the Apostles, tutored as a devoted disciple of the Apostle John, and appointed the Bishop of Antioch by the Apostle Peter himself. His words represent the authentic sentiments, beliefs, and thoughts of the Apostles.

By the middle of the second century, nearly another forty years after Ignatius, we have an amazing description of the Eucharistic liturgy recorded by Saint Justin Martyr in his "First Apology." He describes in detail the content and order of the "Mass" precisely as it exists today: Its principal day is on the first day of the week. It is presided over by the local Bishop or by a priest assigned by the bishop. It starts with scriptural readings from the Old Testament, the Gospels, and the letters of Saint Paul. A sermon follows the readings. There is a financial collection for the sake of the poor. The consecration of the bread and wine follow, which literally becomes the body and blood of Jesus. This Eucharist is then consumed by the baptized who believe.

This description of the Eucharistic liturgy or "Mass" remains unchanged and constant until today. This description was never challenged or opposed by the Church because it was the common practice of Christians far and wide. Around that time, too, the term "Catholic" Church was commonly used. Almost a thousand and eight hundred years later, Saint Justin's description accurately depicts the Catholic Mass today. The only thing missing is the Nicene Creed, recited by the congregation after the sermon. This would be added a little more than a couple hundred years later to help the Church battle the Arian Heresy. And even then, this creed would simply augment the Apostles Creed already recited by the faithful at large.

As time advanced, liturgical diversification blossomed. While the essential elements of the Mass remained constant, the Church's encounters with varied cultures birthed differences in the way Mass was offered. Each new culture colored the Mass differently. There was the Roman rite of the West, and eventually, no less than twenty-three varied Eastern Rites. Not unusually, a rite could trace its origins back to Apostolic times:

Examples abound. The Roman rite stems from the founders of Christianity in Rome, the Apostles, Peter and Paul. The Slavic Byzantine rites trace back to the founder of Christianity in Ukraine, the Apostle Andrew. The Coptic rite in Egypt comes from the Disciple Mark, once Saint Peter's secretary and the Evangelist of the Gospel. The Ethiopian rite goes back to Saint Matthew. Three rites trace back to the Apostle Thomas as he traveled east to India: the Syro-Malankara rite of Persia, the Chaldean rite of Mesopotamia (founded by the disciples of Saint Thomas), and the Syro-Malabar rite of Southern India. The Armenian rite claims its origins from the Apostles Jude and Nathaniel. The list continues.

When the Roman Empire established the Catholic religion as the official religion of the Empire in AD 381, the diversification of liturgical forms formalized further. Distinct prayers, art, liturgical styles, vestments, theological emphasis, and magnificent architecture flourished. Each rite distinguished itself with its unique charism.

Yet, while the various rites enjoyed their differences, they shared more in common than otherwise. They had ancient roots back to Apostolic times, more than a thousand years before the protestant revolt against Church authority. All the rites shared the same allegiance to the Pope of Rome and observed the Christian liturgy containing the same essential elements. A believer can attend the Roman, Byzantine, or Coptic liturgy and welcome the diversity but experience too the familiar pattern of worship. Of course, All the liturgies flowed from the Hebrew Passover division of scriptural learning first and then the subsequent sacrificial element of worship.

Back to the Roman rite in the West. As this rite advanced in time, it became known as the "Latin rite" besides. This was related to Western culture's shift from Greek to Latin. Inevitably, the main language of the Roman Eucharistic liturgy defaulted to Latin. This is where we get the name change of the Roman liturgy into the well-known term: "Mass."

The ending words of the Latin liturgy are: "*Ite, missa est.*" Eventually, the Western liturgy in English would translate this sentence accordingly: "The Mass is ended, go in peace." That's a very loose translation. More accurately, it means, "Go, it is the dismissal." But the word "*missa*" radically corresponds to the Latin word "*missio,*" which means "mission." The modern translation of the phrase then lacks an important connotation. In theology, the term "*missio*" is employed to describe the sending of the Son of God on his mission to Earth to save us. The comprehensive meaning, therefore, of "*Ite, missa est*" would be this: "Go, you're sent forth to fulfill the same mission of Christ to save the world."

Today, there are more than a billion Catholics. The Mass is available in every language. It's estimated that three hundred and fifty thousand Masses are said every day. The Mass is divided into two parts: the liturgy of the Word and the liturgy of the Eucharist. The liturgy of the word consists of a reading from the Old Testament, the New Testament, a Psalm, and the Gospel. Then there's a sermon, and everyone prays the Nicene Creed in unison. A handful of scripturally based songs or chants are sprinkled throughout the entire service. This closes the liturgy of the word.

Next, the liturgy of the Eucharist takes place. The bread and wine are offered, consecrated, and changed into the Body and Blood of Jesus and then distributed as communion. Only those who are baptized and in the state of grace may approach and receive communion. For instance, a politician known for supporting abortion and unrepentant is properly denied communion. An engaged Catholic who is already living with and having sex with his girlfriend is not permitted to receive communion. Visiting Lutherans, Muslims, or curious Baptists are not allowed to receive communion and the like. Some ending prayers are said. A final blessing is given. Then, the crowd is officially dismissed.

We already suggested a practical step to make the ancient Bible your own by owning and reading an RSV2CE Bible. Yet, another practical step could be taken to connect or reconnect with ancient Christianity. Exposure to the ancient liturgical context of scripture would be a wonderful step. Witnessing the original context of scripture may enrich your understanding and appreciation of how scripture was used by the early Church. This may be done simply by attending any of the rites' Catholic liturgies.

How to Read the Bible

When reading any book, the reader's inner disposition defines prolificacy. This implies that the more the reader invests with the inner powers of the soul, the richer the outcome. When intellectual hunger rivets the reading experience, better understanding results. For instance, a despairing man entrapped in mountainous debt will have a welcoming mind to benefit from reading a book devoted to getting out of debt. We're describing a psychological state of mind. It applies in both the natural and supernatural domains.

How hungry am I to know God? How deeply do I believe in God? How desperate am I to discover God? How determined am I to love God? How ready am I to do whatever he asks? The answers to these questions suggest a true psychological inclination. The answers signal either a resistant or open heart. When open, a fertile soul is laid bare before God, ready to receive. Such a disposition determines how much a believer will get out of each page and chapter. When the soul pants for God and surrenders to His voice, the Bible truly springs to life and speaks.

Accordingly, faith and prayer are the necessary preconditions for fruitful Bible reading. I pray a little and read a little; I pray a little more and read a little more. Reading the Bible is not like reading Huckleberry Finn, driven by the curiosity and entertainment of the moment, even if such a reading modality may default at times.

Bible reading should neither be reduced to the mere hunt for data, like scanning a textbook. Granted, sometimes, when researching, this is needed. But it shouldn't replace slow, prayerful, heartfelt reading. Bible reading tries to avoid filling the brain, leaving the heart empty and love undone. Most importantly, cradling the Bible is like reading a personal letter from God to me. Remember, God is the primary author of scripture. And to whom does he write? But to me! He writes to help me conform to the truth, both in thought and action. I read then as a child, admitting my ignorance and waiting to learn.

These things describe the psychological and spiritual disposition needed to read the Bible. But there is another side to the coin. My readiness to surrender to God is only the first step to reading. The second step is God taking over and personally speaking to me. I start with seeking and finish with passive receiving. God speaks when I read. That's why I need to pause at times. Otherwise, I may miss him speaking. The Bible is not merely words written thousands of years ago that I try to figure out. The Bible is the instrument used by God to speak to me here and now as I read. So, periodically, pause, pray, and listen. It takes faith to read the Bible and a commitment to do as Jesus whispers within.

Much can be gleaned from the account of the Apostle Philip and the baptism of the Ethiopian eunuch. The Evangelist, Luke, records this just before the conversion and baptism of the Apostle Paul. The short story confirms what we just said and introduces the occasional challenges surrounding the interpretation of the Bible.

> Then, the angel of the Lord spoke to Philip, 'Get up and head south on the road that goes down from Jerusalem to Gaza, the desert route.' So, he got up and set out. Now there was an Ethiopian eunuch, a court official of the Candace, that is, the queen of the Ethiopians, in charge of her entire treasury, who had come to Jerusalem to worship, and was returning home. Seated in his chariot, he was reading the prophet Isaiah. The Spirit said to Philip, 'Go and join up with that chariot.' Philip ran up and heard him reading Isaiah the prophet and said, 'Do you understand what you are reading?' He replied, 'How can I, unless someone instruct me?' So, he invited Philip to get in and sit with him... (Acts 8:26-31)

After they had read of the prophesied passion of the Messiah:

…the eunuch said in reply, 'I beg you. About whom is the prophet saying this? About himself or about someone else?' Then Philip opened his mouth, and, beginning with this scripture passage, he proclaimed Jesus to him. As they traveled along the road, they came to some water, and the eunuch said, 'Look, there is water. What is to prevent my being baptized?' Then he ordered the chariot to stop, and Philip and the eunuch both went down into the water, and he baptized him. When they came out of the water, the Spirit of the Lord snatched Philip away, and the eunuch saw him no more but continued on his way rejoicing." (See: Acts 8:34-39)

There are a few lessons here. Reading with the faith of a child, we instantly believe in angels, God speaking to a man, and God miraculously whirling a man away to deliver him elsewhere where the proclamation of the Gospel is wanting. We need no Biblical scholar to convince us that everything is an analogy, that the angel was probably just a charitable traveler, or that snatching Philip away really means he skipped away quickly without notice. Reading with faith is better than an overreliance on shoddy, faithless Biblical "scholarship."

Further, the eunuch teaches something about acting on the word of God and interpreting the Bible. His heart was ready. Once Philip explained the purpose and need for baptism, the eunuch wasted no time acting on the revelation of God. Philip fulfilled the command of Christ to go forth and baptize. The eunuch commanded the chariot to stop. He did not need to consult a dozen books written by scholars with PhDs. It was enough to listen to the Apostle sitting next to him. Faith and determination were enough.

What does this story tell us about how to interpret the Bible? It shows the humility of begging for help, not so much from God directly, but from an Apostle of Jesus Christ. Of course, these things are not opposed to each other; they go together. This story shows that a reliable interpretation of scripture traces back to the Apostles. A good interpretation does not rest upon the latest intellectual dance of a contemporary professor with academic degrees dangling on his office wall. Truly, the best interpretation is not the most innovative but the most ancient. What did the Apostles say of this or that passage, or what did those taught directly by the Apostles say? The ancient path is always a dependable wellspring of good Biblical interpretation. How did the first Christians and early Church understand and live this or that passage of the Gospels or Paul's letters?

The Church used ancient confirmations to help weed out apocrypha and canonize the Bible. The Church applied this same principle when interpreting the Bible and still does. It considers the beliefs, thoughts, and practices of the Apostolic Fathers and the earliest Christians to help discern scriptural passages. Ancient evidence often clarifies revelation.

The Apostle Philip taught the Gospel throughout Greece, Syria, and Turkey. He was originally from Bethsaida, near the Sea of Galilee, Jesus's backyard, so to speak. He "studied" as an Apostle, living with Jesus for three years. Philip was taught by God himself and appointed as a teacher, along with the rest of the Apostles. The Apostles, in return, taught the next generation of disciples, called the "Apostolic Fathers." For instance, the Apostle John taught Saint Polycarp of Smyrna, who taught the great Saint Irenaeus; the Apostles Peter and Paul taught the Saints Linus, Cletus, and Clement; the Apostle Peter taught Saint Ignatius of Antioch. The Apostle Paul taught Luke, Timothy, and Titus. The Apostle Peter taught Mark. And so on.

The Apostles were the first set of Bishops (official teachers) in the history of the Catholic Church. They passed on their authoritative teaching assignments, just as Saint Paul had instructed Saint Timothy: "What you have heard from me before many witnesses entrust to faithful men who will be able to teach others also." (II Timothy 2:2) Many men were handed the faith from the Apostles. This citation shows Paul's vision of passing on teaching authority until the end of time. The other Apostles saw the spread of the faith in the same way.

Besides the principle of antiquity, the story of Philip and the eunuch suggests that the interpretation of the Bible links to a wellspring of (not only ancient but) authoritative teaching. Jesus designed a teaching and clarifying apparatus in his Church to preserve divine revelation. The Apostles held the paramount positions to teach. They and their successors carried on this authoritative teaching role anointed by Jesus Christ himself.

This does not mean that the Apostles and their successors were the smartest teachers, but that they were authorized by God to officially teach all that has to do with the revelation of Jesus Christ. Jesus didn't teach like the scribes by copious quotations but by divine authority. He bestowed this mission upon the Apostles, sent them to teach, and guaranteed this same mission to the Apostle's successors: "Whoever listens to you listens to me. Whoever rejects you rejects me…." (Luke 10:16) This is teaching authority granted to twelve uneducated men! Of course, this underlines the special place of Saint Paul, made an Apostolic teacher, but gifted with a superb education too.

(Note: Catholics use the term magisterial teachings or magisterium. These terms derive from the Latin *magister*, meaning "teacher." This term distinguishes the authoritative teachings of the Apostles and their successors, including the Pope and the bishops in union with him throughout the world, back to Apostolic times. Why is this term significant? It helps make the distinction that not everything taught by a bishop, saint, or Pope may be magisterial. Therefore, such a private teaching would be unofficial and perhaps false besides, disconnected from the revelation given by Jesus Christ. If a bishop wanders away on his own, for instance, and teaches that the sin of sodomy is a sexual virtue, such would be a heretical and not a magisterial teaching. Remember, two-thirds of the bishops at one time were followers and teachers of the Arian heresy, propagating that Jesus was not God. Those renegade bishops did not represent the magisterial teachings of the Church.)

Applying this to Biblical interpretation, the magisterium balances between accommodating private inspiration and establishing protective parameters to help avoid heresy. The premise here is that the Bible is produced by the Church as a teaching and worshipping instrument. As the Church made the Bible, the Church accordingly retains the responsibility of assuring the correct usage and understanding of its content. Consider Paul's instructions to Timothy. Paul explains that the Church, not the Bible, is "the pillar and foundation of truth." (I Timothy 3:15)

Consequentially, the Church's magisterium has the God-given authority to secure the proper understanding of the Bible. Ponder this: When Paul wrote those words to Timothy, his letter was just a letter. The Church assumed the authority to declare that Paul's letter was indeed an authentic canonical book of the Bible. If the Church possesses the authority to say what's in the Bible, it certainly has the authority to say how Biblical content should be understood. The canonization of the Bible by Church authority is a radical declaration of Biblical interpretation. The Bible is the Church's tool, yielded in the hands of the Church.

How does this play out on the practical level? Due to the multi-layered meanings of scripture, the Church is careful to accommodate multiple possible meanings of this or that passage. The Church does not exclude possible meanings as much as possible. Private inspirations and insights flow from God at work in a soul, truly communicating for the spiritual benefit of the reader. Nonetheless, the Church, at the same time, establishes parameters that guide how this or that passage should be understood. Note how Philip did this with the eunuch. Philip did not say: "Whatever you feel God is saying, that is the truth."

The Church's guidance is not a dictatorial or prohibitive mechanism of control that makes no room for private inspiration. It is the fulfillment of a responsibility laid upon the Apostles and their successors to preserve the deposit of faith. Whenever private inspiration and divinely revealed truths clash, Magisterial teachings intervene and prevail.

Perhaps an example may help. In the story of Genesis, God creates Adam and Eve. There are multi-layered possible meanings that surround the story. The story may be used by God to reach into the reader deeply and bring forth a subjective, personal meaning, perhaps about marriage, perhaps about God's creative purpose in one's own life. The Church encourages such possible private graces. Nonetheless, to protect from heresy, the Church steps in and establishes a few parameters that limit interpretations. Such parameters are like the protective walls that wrap around a bumper-car platform.

In this case, the magisterium indicates that Adam and Eve were truly two distinct individual persons and not analogical representations of two groups of people. Nor were they genetic productions achieved by the surgical hands of aliens from another galaxy. Besides, at the moment of their enlivening, Adam and Eve were fully human, with created human souls infused in them by God's creative power. Additionally, as the first parents of the human race, they sinned, causing the need for redemption for the human race. There's more, but this should be enough to demonstrate how magisterial teachings work when helping to interpret the Bible. While enjoying personal inspiration in the soul, we at the same time respect the objective order of God's revelation through Jesus Christ and his Church.

In summary, the Church, of course, allows for God's personal, mysterious inspiration and communication within the soul. How wondrous is God's work in the soul of the just man! At the same time, through magisterial authority, the Church guards against heresy by establishing interpretation parameters. Still, there are three significant, additional principles to keep in mind when interpreting the Bible.

The first principle is that God does not (cannot) contradict himself. It seems so obvious to say, yet it's indispensable to keep in mind when interpreting the Bible. I may find passages that seem contradictory to one another. But such is only apparent. It's contrary to the divine nature to reveal and hold firm to contradictory assertions. Such a stance implies an imperfection (an intellectual mistake or void of knowledge) in God. But God is perfect. Mindful of this, the efforts of interpreting then must be oriented toward finding how apparent contradictory statements are both true and complementary.

This principle of non-self-contradiction has another application. Sometimes, scriptural and traditional revelation and authoritative magisterial teaching may all match perfectly. They may consistently and harmoniously reveal the same truth. For instance, the Old and New Testament, the beliefs and lifestyle of the early Christians, and the official teachings of the Church affirm that adultery is sinful. However, a prayerful man may sincerely feel God urging him to leave his wife and enjoy sexual intercourse with the neighbor. In this case, the objective order of divine revelation and the subjective order of personal inspiration oppose each other. Which revelation is true? Could both be true?

Based on the principle that God does not contradict himself, only one can be true, precisely because the two "inspirations" here are diametrically opposed to each other. In this case, truth rests in the objective, not the subjective order. Otherwise, God's purpose and design of rooting divine revelation in the objective order becomes empty and pointless. Moral and doctrinal truth disappear if defined by feelings opposed to objective revelation. Of course, personal feelings may complement divine revelation, but when such feelings lead in the opposite direction, they cannot be trusted as God's truth.

Further, the principle of personal, subjective inspiration has become so exalted that Christ's revelation of the truth has little value. Today, sadly, the rush of emotions even trumps the verifiable facts of history. A tyranny of feelings now imprisons truth. The greater and more intense the feeling, the less need for the mission and revelation of Christ, rooted in history and preserved by Church authority. And the consequences? A man feels like a woman, so he is a woman. A preacher feels that homosexual acts such as sodomy are virtuous acts of love, so they are. A congregation feels that the Catholic Church never really canonized the Bible, so history is denied. The logical outcome of making private inspiration supreme is a million versions of Christianity, none of which are the true Church established by Christ historically.

The second helpful principle is that all scripture is equally inspired. There's not one passage of scripture more inspired than another. Neither is there a gradation of inspired passages as if there was a scale of inspiration. The consequence follows that apparent scriptural contradictions can't be solved by asserting the inspiration of one passage over another. A unity and harmony of the whole of scripture must be perused as the only possible solution to apparent contradictions.

The third principle expands upon the two just mentioned. When interpreting the Bible, the truth lies in the whole of God's revelation to men. This means that scripture, magisterial teachings, and early Church traditions match up in a complementary way. This is so because scripture alone does not represent Christ's full revelation. Since Jesus instituted the Church as the foundation of truth, the earliest traditions of the Church and magisterial teachings must also complement the written words contained in scripture. Accordingly, uniformity of all these ancient fonts would assure a completely reliable interpretation of Scripture.

With that said, it's beneficial to demonstrate how these principles work together. Take, for instance, our long-standing belief in the Holy Trinity: of three divine persons in one God. We start by underlining that this doctrine is introduced but not completely spelled out in the New Testament. The term "Trinity" is neither mentioned in the Gospels nor the epistles. We should demonstrate then how scripture, tradition, and magisterial teaching harmoniously merge to definitively declare this divinely revealed mystery.

We start by simply stating the Trinitarian doctrine: In the unity or oneness of God, there are three divine persons: the Father, the Son, and the Holy Spirit. The ancient Athanasian Creed underlines both the distinction of persons and the oneness of God at the same time: "The Father is God, the Son is God, and the Holy Spirit is God, and yet there are not three Gods but one God." Within the Trinity, the Son is begotten of the Father by an eternal generation, and the Holy Spirit proceeds by an eternal procession from the Father and the Son. Accordingly, each divine person is distinct but uncreated, co-eternal, co-equal, omnipotent, and a full possessor of all the divine attributes inseparable from the very essence of God.

The Trinitarian doctrine is the dogmatic foundation of Christianity. So much so that the deniers of this doctrine are both heretics and no longer Christian. In one way or another, the fundamental Christian teachings flow from the Trinitarian doctrine: for example, creation, the incarnation, the divine person of Christ, our redemption, and so forth. These doctrines all begin with the Trinity. Further, this doctrine is so mysterious and detached from man's limited ingenuity it presupposes divine revelation. It's thus a truth so profound and sublime that we couldn't arrive at knowing it unless by God's revelation to us. Consider that Aristotle could figure out that God exists, manifesting reason at its best performance. Yet, that there are three divine persons in God is impossible to know by the powers of human reason alone.

The Trinitarian revelation is so unexpectedly transcendent that Jesus only made it known to his Apostles step by step. He first gradually taught the Apostles about his own identity as the eternal Son of God the Father. Then, as his ministry drew to a close, Jesus promised that the Father would send another, the Holy Spirit, in his place. Finally, after his resurrection, Jesus revealed the Trinitarian doctrine explicitly. Unleashing his Church upon the world, he spelled out the truth:

> All power in heaven and on earth has been given to me. Go, therefore, and make disciples of all nations, baptizing them in the name [singular] of the Father, and of the Son, and of the Holy Spirit, teaching them to observe all that I have commanded you. And behold, I am with you always, until the end of the age. (Matthew 28:19-20)

Jesus's commission reveals the clearest expression in the New Testament of Trinitarian belief. From the terms "Father" and "Son," distinct and mutually exclusive persons are clearly iterated. Joining the "Holy Spirit" in the same connected context strongly suggests his divine personhood besides.

Yet, elsewhere in scripture, hints are given of the mystery. Jesus is in the Father, and the Father in him. He who sees the Father sees the Son, and he who sees the Son sees the Father. Just as much, Jesus suggests the personhood of the Holy Spirit by inferences. He attributes to the Holy Spirit only what is attributed to a person: "The Holy Spirit shall teach you in the same hour what you must say." (Matthew 10:20; Luke 24:49) "… When he comes, the Spirit of truth, he will guide you to all truth. He will not speak on his own, but he will speak what he hears and will declare to you the things that are coming." (John 16:13) Thus, the Holy Spirit will speak what the Father speaks, and what the Son speaks, and will prophesy. Christ compares the Holy Spirit's presence among the Apostles to his own: "And I will ask the Father, and he will give you another Advocate to be with you always, the Spirit of truth, which the world cannot accept…." (John 14:16-17) Christ himself is the first Advocate or teacher; the Holy Spirit is the second, who will teach again all that Jesus taught exactly when it will be needed. The Apostles will not be left as orphans. (John 14:18)

These scriptural passages and more reveal the Trinitarian doctrine in its rudimentary form. Continuing onward from these revelations, the early Church bursts forth with Trinitarian belief. Familiarity with the mind and sentiments of the early Church is the next step to confirm a proper Biblical interpretation.

The Church's fixed usage of the formula of baptism is a good starting place. Following the command of Christ, baptizing in the name of the Father, Son, and Holy Spirit was instituted from the very day of Pentecost.

Baptism was seen as an act of repentance and supernatural regeneration. Further, it was exercised as a formal renunciation of Satan and his works. By baptism, the idolatry of paganism was rejected, and a solemn consecration to the one true God was formalized. This act of consecration invoked the Father, Son, and Holy Spirit. Any supposition that would have regarded baptism as a consecration to three separate gods or to one God plus two created beings would have been manifestly absurd after all that Jesus Christ had taught.

In AD 40, the Didache teaches how to go about baptizing:

> After the foregoing instructions, baptize in the name of the Father, and of the Son, and of the Holy Spirit, in living [running] water…. If you have neither, pour water three times on the head, in the name of the Father, and of the Son, and of the Holy Spirit.

Saint Hippolytus would summarize the early Church's understanding of baptism accordingly:

> He who descends into this laver of regeneration with faith forsakes the Evil One and engages himself to Christ, renounces the enemy, and confesses that Christ is God…he returns from the fount a son of God and a coheir of Christ. To whom with all the holy, the good and life-giving Spirit be glory and power, now and always, forever and forever. Amen.

Soon, the baptismal formula would give rise to similar incorporations into creeds, prayers, and doxologies, and eventually, the usage of the sign of the cross as an expression of faith. Long before the Council of Nicaea, phrases abounded, like: "Glory to the Father, through the Son, in the Holy Spirit." Or again: "Glory be to the Father and to the Son, and to [with] the Holy Spirit." The martyrdom narrative of Saint John's student, Saint Polycarp, included: "With Whom to Thee and the Holy Spirit be glory now and for the ages to come." Saint Basil tells us that it was an immemorial custom among Christians when they lit the evening lamp to give thanks to God with a short prayer: "We praise the Father, and the Son, and the Holy Spirit of God." These are just small samples of the Trinitarian beliefs of the early Christians, all stemming from the baptismal formula taught by Christ.

As time advanced, more and more usages of baptismal formula derivations spread. But besides this, theological penetration emerged. Trinitarian references are found in the writings of Ignatius in AD 110, Justin Martyr in AD 151, and Saint Irenaeus in AD 189. It was Theophilus of Antioch in AD 181 who first employed the term Trinity to identify the three divine persons. The term came into common usage. Tertullian picked up on this and coined the Latin *Trinitas* in AD 216.

Origen taught of the Trinity in AD 225. In AD 260, his brilliant student, Bishop Gregory Thaumaturgus, taught:

There is, therefore, nothing created, nothing subject to another in the Trinity: nor is there aught that has been added as though it had once not existed, but had entered afterward: therefore, the Father has never been without the Son, nor the Son without the Spirit: and this same Trinity is immutable and unalterable forever.

Though more examples can be shared of the early Church's belief in the Trinity, this small selection of ancient sources should be sufficient to demonstrate that Trinitarian belief was firmly embedded in Christianity. Next would come the crowning capstone of magisterial teaching on the matter.

In AD 381, only a year before the universal, papal canonization of the Bible, a Church council met in Constantinople. Among other orders of business at hand, including the condemnation of Arianism, Macedonianism, and Apollinarianism, this council produced a formal statement on the doctrine of the Trinity. After beholding the scriptural basis of the doctrine and the long-standing traditions of the ancient Church, it formally added an enlargement to the Nicene Creed. In the face of heresies, it was deemed best to add an emphasis regarding the divinity of the Holy Spirit. Accordingly, the Nicene Creed, with the addition, would eventually be called the Nicaeno-Constantinopolitanum Creed. This creed is still prayed by multiple Catholic rites throughout the world every Sunday, just before the liturgy of the Eucharist.

The Church's official doctrinal clarification was approved by Pope Damasus I and inserted into the Nicene Creed in AD 381. Accordingly, the Council expanded the third article of the Nicene Creed that dealt with the Holy Spirit: "I believe in the Holy Spirit, the Lord, the Giver of life, Who proceeds from the Father, With the Father and the Son he is worshipped and glorified." As such, the Council gave the first universal, formal declaration of the doctrine of the Holy Trinity. It aimed at distinguishing the three persons and confirming the divinity of each.

In summary, the above paragraphs show an aspect of Biblical interpretation. First, complementary Bible passages are identified. Second, Complementary early Church practices and teachings are additionally identified. Third, the magisterial teachings of the Church confirm the complementarity of scripture and the praxis of ancient Christianity. Notice how everything finds its roots in the ancient. This age-old method of preserving the deposit of faith handed down by Jesus Christ through his Apostles faithfully guards God's revelation to man unto the end of time.

CHAPTER SIXTEEN

The State of Today's Church

Historical Note: Founding and Development

Step by step, we strolled the bumpy cobblestones of ancient Bible context. Arriving at the present, we shall now weigh the consequences of our journey. Adept investigators impartially follow a string of evidence to wherever it may lead. Having pieced together the "evidence" of Bible context, where does that lead us? What is the conclusion?

Without a prior deduction about scripture, we straightforwardly dove into reality thousands of years ago and excavated the contextual surroundings of the Bible. Looking through the lens of the ancient, the birth and meaning of the Bible came into sharper focus.

Sometimes, contemporary methodologies blunder with an opposite approach. A pre-determined stance is used in a deliberately destructive manner to erase the inconveniences of history. Such is the "cancel culture" craze of our age. The past is seized and twisted to isolate the present and hijack the future. History is rewritten to manipulate an ideologically preferred world.

Unfortunately, the history of the Bible is often subject to a similar kind of historical and theological filtration. Ignorant preachers sometimes undervalue the rich insights that flow from verifiable Church history. Real history is a marvelous educator.

The Bible's historic account begins with the popular and widely used forty-six-book Septuagint of Jesus's time. The account includes Jesus's founding of an authoritative Church and the appointment of the Apostle Peter as its head. Little makes sense without this key premise. The true account of the Bible next includes the explosion of the oral Gospel far and

185

wide. Converts of sound character were educated and appointed bishops throughout the Roman Empire and beyond –to protect all that Jesus had revealed. Then, six Apostles and two disciples recorded in writing the essentials of what Jesus had revealed.

The early Church (soon called "Christian" and soon afterward called "Catholic") shared these writings in the Eucharistic liturgy initiated by Jesus at the Last Supper and subsequently passed on to every Catholic community. With the help of these Gospels and letters, local bishops guarded against apocrypha and discerned what was genuinely handed down from Jesus and the Apostles. The Church assumed the authority to determine the Old Testament canon, honoring and confirming the list of books that had been commonly used by Jesus and the Apostles. Finally, a successor of Saint Peter, still exercising the chief Apostle's authority, Pope Saint Damasus I, declared the full content of the seventy-three-book Bible in AD 382. Many other Church councils and Popes thereafter confirmed the same. As the Church preceded the Bible, created the Bible, and author-itatively used the Bible, it continuously exercised its authority to interpret the Bible: its own instrument for teaching and worshipping. These high points abbreviate the Bible's authentic, historic account.

The early history of the Bible then establishes a groundbreaking, inevitable conclusion. Following the evidence of ancient Bible context, we are led to the doorsteps of the Catholic Church. The way the Bible was birthed and used in ancient times undeniably confirms the Catholic Church (including all its varied ancient rites) as the one Church founded by Jesus Christ and passed on to the ages from the Apostles.

Among Protestants, today's general persuasion is that the tighter a believer grasps the Bible, the weaker his link with the Catholic Church. Unfortunately, from a subjective or psychological perspective, this is often true. Various life experiences may have caused a Catholic to leave the Church and paradoxically discover the Bible.

A believer may have suffered injury from a Church-related trauma. A Catholic may have experienced profound spiritual deprivation without the support of knowledgeable and genuinely loving Catholics coming to his aid. A needy Catholic soul may have stumbled upon sincere but erroneous interpretations of Biblical passages from trusted non-Catholic believers.

Yet, our present comprehensive study brings to light a markedly different insight. From a historical perspective, the more thoroughly the ancient context of the Bible is understood, the more the Catholic Church stands out as both the practical and authoritative parent of scripture. The Protestant ought to ponder the opened pages of scripture unfurled in his lap. Here rests a book made by the Catholic Church yet retained by Protestants, albeit after a handful of unauthorized tweaks. It may be a challenging historical fact, but the truth is always worthy of reflection.

Nonetheless, the assertion that Jesus founded the Catholic Church, and no other, begs for critical distinctions. Perhaps this image may help: There's a profound difference between a newborn and that same human being eighty years later. But the difference relates to development, deterioration, and appearance, not to the essential identity of the being. In this case, though the baby and old man look different, they are fundamentally the same person. A singular continuity persists.

The same happens with the Church. Jesus founded and structured a primitive Church with twelve men at Caesarea Philippi. That Church secondarily changed throughout the centuries but primarily remained the same. Admittedly, the institutional Catholic Church appears very different than the early Church of the first century. But it persists as the same Church founded two thousand years ago. In view of his extremely short ministry, mission to save souls until the end of time, and intent to involve man in the dissemination of salvation, Christ established a Church that would last. He promised: "And so I say to you, you are Peter, and upon this rock I will build my Church, and the gates of hell shall not prevail against it." (Matthew 16:18) As such, Jesus affirmed that the Church he built would not be conquered by the demonic kingdom.

Another critical distinction is that Christ founded his Church in stages. Although not explicitly identified and categorized as such, the Gospels and Acts of the Apostles suggest these progressive steps, especially when Jesus periodically withdraws from the public and teaches the Apostles in seclusion:

Jesus recruits twelve leaders, trains them to minister, teaches them to teach, organizes them, and appoints one as the head, empowers them to work miracles, cast out demons, forgive sins, and turn bread into the sacrificed lamb of the New Covenant. Jesus commissions his Apostles to baptize unto the ends of the earth. He then introduces the Holy Spirit to work through his Church to bring salvation to the world. The Spirit comes and enlivens the Church, analogous to an infused soul enlivening a body. Many say that the Church was born on Pentecost. True, but the complete picture includes the steps of founding the Church up until the moment of birth. The developing stages of a fetus in the womb always precede the moment of delivery. Similarly, the Church experienced a period of gestation. At last, the Church emerges as an organic perfection of the Old Covenant, by a structured, authoritative, and visible New Covenant —with its own new kind of sacrificial rite and communion.

It only takes a patient reading of the Gospels to see Jesus instituting his Church –in slow motion. Some eager readers search the scriptures for a buzz phrase about "founding a Church." They desperately hunger for a quote. Not finding things so tightly described, they conclude that Jesus did not institute a Church. Yet, the answers to our questions hide in plain sight. From one perspective, the Gospels in their entirety are about founding the Church. It's all there, unlabeled. Then, when the explicit passage of Matthew 16:18 comes along, it is dismissively scorned as not possibly meaning what it says. Sadly, we're not really reading. We're narrow-mindedly flipping through pages, looking for what we want to see, doubting it's there anyway. Our paradigms, psyches, and prejudices, at times, can't handle the truth.

Let's now jump ahead to the transformation of the embryonic Church to the colossal Catholic institution. The Catholic Church of today rises from three fundamental causes: God, man, and Satan.

(Note: Alarm bells! Some may immediately object that Satan exercises any causality regarding Church development. A further distinction may help. Is there a way in which you can say that Satan exerted an influence in making you who you are today? The answer is yes. Demonic temptations and subsequent sins influence the way you feel, think, desire, and seek. The inclinations and bad habits that lodge in the soul from demonic temptations may take a long time to dig up and root out. The opposite is true, too. Victory over a demonic temptation may set the stage for a strengthening of virtue that may last a long time. Unless the devil's hand is discovered, confronted, and renounced, demonic influences subtly leave their scars carved into the modality of human nature. In these cases, demonic activity does not work as an intrinsic, constitutive cause but as an external influence that persuades ungodly human choices. His influence, then, is an efficient cause that acts from outside the human person and upon the human person. Isn't this what temptation is all about? Just as the devil can exert an influence in progressively forming a person, similarly, he does the same with institutions, including the Church. It's certainly granted here that Satan cannot corrupt the divine dimension of the Church. The historic development of the Church then proceeds from God's supernatural power, man's cooperation or non-cooperation with grace, and the devil's cunning machinations to destroy the Church by drawing man into error and sin.)

Each of these three causes contributes toward either shaping or disfiguring the Church in its own way. The claim of Satanic influence contradicts nothing said above. It doesn't negate the divine founding and divine governance of the Church. It merely helps to partially explain evil developments in an infiltrated Church. What God creates is good. What Jesus founds is good. But wherever free will is given the chance, varying degrees of corruption may follow.

The divine presence rests at the heart of the Church. Jesus Christ acts when and how he wills through the members of his mystical body. He continuously inspires and develops the Church. The Holy Spirit does the same. This is the supernatural side of the Church, stirring up repentance, conversions, the acceptance of Jesus Christ, miracles, sacramental grace, and growth in personal holiness. The Church's nourishment by the consumption of the Body and Blood of Christ is a sign of the supernatural modality of the Church. The regenerative waters of baptism, too, sing of the supernatural power of God in the Church. The infinite knowledge of God, His eternal designs, and His all-powerful hand have always endured as the primary catalyst of Church development.

There are many signs of the supernatural at work in the Church. Certainly, martyrdom is one. Up until the Edit of Milan in AD 313, rivers of sacrificed blood flowed from the Christians who had testified to Christ before the eleven Emperors who had vowed to exterminate Christianity. Such extraordinary sacrificial love only flows from God. Then there were the doctrinal heroes who had combatted thirty-four major heresies that tried to destroy the revelation of Christ. Here, again, is the supernatural at work. God's intervention in holy lives, the gifted minds of decent theologians, and the authoritative structure of the Church all combined to preserve the truth revealed by Jesus.

(Note: Pause and appreciate God's providential sovereignty, preserving true Christian doctrine during those first years of Christianity. Each heresy distorted Christianity in its own way. Consider the following heretical teachings during those early years of Christianity: there were two different gods, an evil god and a good god; material creation was evil; Jesus was not God; Jesus was two persons, one divine and the other human, each superficially united; Jesus was neither a true human; Jesus had no human soul; there was no Trinity; the Holy Spirit was not God; Jesus was born only a man and became god later; Jesus's physical body was an illusion; Jesus had only one, unique, mixed divine and human nature; Jesus had two natures but only one will; the Father and Son were not two distinct divine persons; Jesus was a unique creature, something like an angel; each person in the Trinity was not a distinct person, but a manifestation of the one God; secret knowledge was required to be saved; a person can be saved through his own natural efforts, without the help of God's grace; private prophesies superseded the doctrines proclaimed by the Apostles;

and the list continues. The supernatural interests of God, working through the divinely instituted teaching structure of his Church, conquered each of these innovations. The preservation of the true revelation of Jesus Christ in the face of so many doctrinal wars is no doubt a sign of God's supernatural power at work in his Church.)

(Additional note: Protestants tend to focus on an alleged doctrinal corruption of the Catholic Church. Notice that the key doctrinal errors of Christianity's toddler years are listed here. For the most part, Protestants still believe that Jesus was True God and True man, that there are three divine persons in one God, that all material creation was created good, and that a person cannot save himself without the help of God's grace. As such, in these cases, Protestants still believe in Catholic doctrines. Through bitter fights against heretics long ago, the Catholic Church preserved such divinely revealed truths. But of course, what about the doctrines like purgatory, Marian devotion, or the intercessory prayers of the saints in heaven? Because the scope of this book is limited, the reader is encouraged to pursue a renewed study of such matters, mindful of the principles of interpretation presented in the previous chapter of this book.)

Modern Catholicism also rises from man as a cause. This is not the divine but the human side of the Church. There is both good and bad in this, depending on a believer's degree of surrender to God or slavery to sin. Man's cooperation with God may result in lasting positive developments in the Church for the salvation of many. However, man's sinful predispositions may profoundly wound members of the Church and mislead vulnerable souls to eternal damnation. Man, either builds up the Church or tears it down!

In the best-case scenarios, wonderful personal gifts benefit everybody. Saint Paul's instructions on the identification and use of gifts is an example of how the Holy Spirit builds up the Church by man's cooperation. God is the source of the gifts. God individualizes the gifts according to their suitability for the user. The gifts also need man's cooperation with God. They are exercised in a complementary manner for the good of the body of believers. (I Corinthians, chapters 12-14)

It might be added here that God always remains the master of the gifts. Each person's gift is like a tool in the hands of the Holy Spirit. Once the tool surrenders to God's usage, the gift flourishes and does much good. Not all tools in a toolbox are equally applicable to the purpose of the worker. For one task, a hammer may be needed; for another task, a screwdriver or saw may be the opportune tool to weld in hand. God takes up a gifted soul in a similar way. He sees the work at hand and applies the proper tool.

Much good flows from man's cooperation with the inner grace of God to love. Examples of this might be St. Patrick's prayers and work for the conversion of Ireland or St. Boniface's conversion of Germany. Perhaps other examples might include the architects of Notre Dame in Paris, the writers of Gregorian chants, the compassionate founders of the six thousand Catholic hospitals globally, or the priests who serve at the million Catholic parishes and missionary outposts worldwide. God inspires such souls to spread the Gospel, each according to his temperament, talent, or vision. Each soul hopefully responds positively and constructively to the prompting of the Holy Spirit.

At the same time, great evil arises through the heresies and sinful vices of Church members. Examples abound: A husband may cheat on his wife and inflict untold damage on his children that will last for a lifetime. A bishop may fund a social program that promotes abortion, ultimately causing the murder of countless babies. A Mother may fail to practice her faith and cause her children to become agnostics, ultimately resulting in their eternal damnation. A preacher may fail to preach the Gospel, causing lukewarmness and ignorance. A priest may sexually abuse a child, causing the priest to lose his soul and many others to reject the Church. A Cardinal may maliciously elect a fellow Cardinal, the Pope-elect, who colludes with Satan, causing millions to abandon the Church. Such sinful human choices wound the Church and scandalously position it as an occasion of evil. Do you see the interconnectedness of a believer's good or bad acts with the rest of the members of the mystical body of Christ?

(Note: God governs his creation in two ways: either through his "active will" or his "permissive will." He exercises his active will when he directly wills, like when he creates, bestows personal existence, or calls a soul to a specific mission. The active will represents God's personal choice in the matter. Yet, he does not interfere with man's free choice. God exercises his permissive will when he allows sinful choices and behavior to take place. This is how some angels became devils and how Adam and Eve sinned, for instance. The freedom to choose between good or evil is granted to us. Why? God is interested that man enjoys His divine love. But love implies free choice. So great is our possession of God's love that he allows sin and its terrible consequences as possible choices. No free choice, no genuine love. Nonetheless, when we choose evil, God mitigates the gravity of consequences by his interventions to bring good out of evil. This simple distinction of God's active or permissive will applies to the situation when cardinals elect an evil Pope: such as Pope Benedict IX, who lived a disgraceful life of bribery, rape, murder, and sodomy. Accordingly, the election of such a man may be attributed to the permissive will of God, allowing man to choose a sinful man to spread further corruption. However, the governance of an evil Pope is a sign of God allowing man to make sinful choices and does not prove that Christ did not establish the papacy. If personal holiness was required for a man to exercise divinely instituted authority to govern, then nobody on earth could ever shoulder such responsibility.)

It should not be overlooked that the Church is made up not only of God and the saintly but of sinners, too. Good and evil contend in the depths of every human heart. Logically, then, the whole tends to assume and manifest the characteristics of the parts. The Church, therefore, also suffers a similar inner conflict. No wonder the extremes of both good and evil flourish within the Catholic Church. On one hand, you can find holy souls. On the other hand, you can find vast numbers of people who have no interest in God whatsoever. Yet, there is a hideous power that hides deep within Catholicism that is immeasurably worse than the moral frailty of human beings.

We underlined three fundamental causes of modern Catholicism. The first is nothing less than God's supernatural power, especially noted in the continuous miracles of the sacraments. The second is either the positive or negative response of man to God's freely offered graces for the good of the salvation of souls. The third cause of the modern Catholic Church is Satan and his minions. Minions are defined here as servile followers, sometimes virtual, sometimes formally vowed, servants of the principal creature turned evil, named Satan, also named Lucifer. Such minions are both demons from the underworld kingdom of Satan and earthbound human collaborators —even cardinals, bishops, and priests-- who have pledged their allegiance.

The Church, as infiltrated by the demonic, is seldom talked about, but it stretches back to ancient times. Both Jesus and his Apostles indicated this hideous reality of the devil in the Church. They did not want the innocent and vulnerable members of the Church to be naive about something so threatening to salvation.

Such iniquity should not be too surprising. Precisely because Christ established the Church as the ark of salvation (like Noah's ark during the great deluge), it has always been a perpetual target for destruction by the kingdom of Satan. History unveils the devil at work to topple the Church: bloody persecutions, rampant heresies, schisms, corrupting links with political kingdoms that weaken the spiritual message and supremacy of Christ, and especially since the reformation, a continuous cascade of doctrinal fragmentation. In our own age, the devil has stirred up unbridled sexual immorality like oral sex, sodomy, acts of pedophilia, adultery, and the like among the bishops and clergy unparalleled since the beginning of Christianity.

With a down-to-earth parable, Jesus introduces the idea of demonic interweaving within his Church:

> The kingdom of heaven may be likened to a man who sowed good seed in his field. While everyone was asleep his enemy came and sowed weeds all through the wheat, and then went off. When the crop grew and bore fruit, the weeds appeared as well. The slaves of the householder came to him and said, 'Master, did you not sow good seed in your field? Where have the weeds come from?' He answered, 'An enemy has done this.' His slaves said to him, 'Do you want us to go and pull them up?' He replied, 'No, if you pull up the weeds, you might uproot the wheat along with them. Let them grow together until harvest; then, at harvest time, I will say to the harvesters, 'First collect the weeds and tie them in bundles for burning; but gather the wheat into my barn.' (Matthew 13:24-30)

A bit later, Jesus explains the deeper meaning of this parable to the Apostles, his original group of "bishops-in-training." (Matthew 13:36-43) As he was accustomed to do, Jesus employed an unforgettable image to get his point across. His listeners, acquainted with planting and harvesting, perhaps had a head start tackling the meaning. They likely nodded their heads in agreement, at least regarding the farming content of Jesus's words. There's a prominent weed in the Middle East called the "darnold." Darnold thrives in the agricultural conditions most suitable for the growth of wheat. Growing side by side, wheat and darnold appear almost identical to each other. This poses a serious problem, especially if the plants take root around the same time.

The way around the problem is to patiently wait until the plants mature to the point of harvest. Jesus voiced what the local farmers already knew. At the point of harvest, the ears of wheat turn a rich golden brown; the darnold turns black. At last, the good and bad, the gold and black, were distinguishable. At harvest time, the uprooting of the wheat was no longer a problem. But the separation was vital precisely because the darnold was poisonous! The separation was a tedious process but entirely necessary to save the wheat.

What a rich explanation of the holy and the demonically manipulated living side by side within the Church! The simple parable hid a profound mystery. On the one hand, the wheat, the holy members, truly loved one another and respected the authentic teachings of Christ. They hungered for the revealed truth from the lips of Jesus. They lived their faith relationship with Jesus Christ.

On the other hand, the darnold, the children of the devil, appearing identical to the other Church members in the pews, are anything but. They believe entirely differently than the official teachings of Christ's Church. They do not believe in the real presence of Jesus in the Eucharist. Half of the age-old doctrines they deny. Comfortable with their lukewarmness, the other half of the Church teachings they neither know nor care to know. They follow an entirely different set of morals. They practice abortion, contraception, lust, drunkenness, theft, homosexual sex, sex before marriage, divorce and remarriage, and the like. They call sin, virtue, and virtue, sin. Their lifestyles focus on false "sins," like not manifesting politically correct language, not welcoming "homosexual marriages," or not embracing all religions equally, and the like. And their hearts, shriveled from a deprivation of prayer, are far from the Lord, without the smallest spark of an intimate relationship with Jesus.

As such, the holy and unholy live indistinguishably together, side by side, until the harvest. When that season dawns, the separation of the holy children and the evil minions shall be manifest. Suddenly, it will be clear who is on which side. The Apostle Paul describes this time of harvest, this moment of separation, as the "apostasy." This separation will ultimately, conspicuously result in two opposing bodies: the wheat and the darnold!

The black darnold will morph into a false Church that believes entirely differently than the original Church of Christ. The golden wheat, the true Church, will endure underground. This open division will soon unravel into a persecution of the true Church. The betrayal of this ancient-magisterial-believing remnant will follow. The saints of Christ will be hunted down. They shall glorify Christ with the shedding of blood, like the Lamb of God himself. This will be the last breath of the mystical body of Christ —until Christ's miraculous intervention!

Indeed, this Great Apostasy is already in motion. The crack of division stretches mortally, renting the whole into two conflicting bodies. Today's Catholic Church is already in a state of (invisible) *de facto* schism. Distinguished from historical schisms whereby heretics leave the Church to start another, today, modern heretics burrow into the Church, rise to positions of power, and vow to change the Church from within. They appropriate a

Catholic identity while believing otherwise. They master the power of a global hierarchical structure to build their own church from within.

(Note: A schism is a division between two opposed and irreconcilable sides. Caused by significant differences of doctrine, opinion, or beliefs, a formal split comes about, resulting in two opposing groups that were once religiously united. Often, newborn churches stem from the schism of a church split into two halves.)

Still, there are further examples of the mixture of the good and bad in the Church, as scripture warns: Jesus alerts Peter of Satan's interest to tear apart the Church. "Simon, Simon, listen! Satan has demanded to sift all of you like wheat." (Luke 22:31) Jesus adds that the assault of the devil would furthermore lash out against them: "Remember the word that I said to you, 'Servants are not greater than their master.' If they persecuted me, they will persecute you." (John 15:20) This persecution may be from an enemy exterior to the Church, or from corrupted Church members working to destroy from within.

The Last Supper equally offers a glimpse of what is to come regarding the destiny of the Church. Like Christ, his Church will be betrayed, too. Identifying the betrayer, Jesus dipped and gave a morsel of food to Judas. "After he took the morsel, Satan entered him." (John 13:27) If an Apostle can be taken over by Satan, so too can any Cardinal, bishop, or priest. Judas betrayed Christ with a kiss. So, too, a multitude of bishops betray Christ with unending streams of empty ritual kisses.

Following his betrayal and passion, Jesus hung on the cross, hardly recognizable: "Just as there were many who were astonished at him —so marred was his appearance, beyond human semblance, and his form beyond that of mortals." (Isaiah 52:14) So too, the Church walks in the same footsteps as the Master, betrayed, humiliated, beaten, scourged, nailed to a cross, and crucified. Indeed, the climactic, Satanic onslaught and bleeding out of the Church on the cross is upon us. Sadly, the Catholic Church today is hardly recognizable as Christ's ancient and holy Church.

The Apostles were keenly knowledgeable of demonic forces aligned against the Church. Saint Peter forewarned believers to beware: "Be sober and vigilant. Your opponent, the devil, is prowling around like a roaring lion looking for [someone] to devour. Resist him, steadfast in faith, knowing that your fellow believers throughout the world undergo the same sufferings." (I Peter 5:8-9)

The Apostle Paul had his own way of expressing the same:

Finally, draw your strength from the Lord and from his mighty power. Put on the armor of God so that you may be able to stand firm against the tactics of the devil. For our struggle is not with flesh and blood but with the principalities, with the powers, with the world rulers of this present darkness, with the evil spirits in the heavens. (Ephesians 6:10-12)

Further, the Apostle John, in his Apocalypse, traces the encroachment of evil into the Church. His vision certainly harmonizes with Christ's parable of the wheat and the weeds, where the devil sows evil in the bosom of the Church. Truly, John saw churches that had been corrupted from within by the hand of the evil one. John reveals an impenetrable mystery of evil from without and within the Church. He does not trumpet an easy victory. Rather, he sees something evil lurking in the Church, the Great Apostasy, but a holy remnant too, chased, purified, and slaughtered gloriously for Christ.

We scrutinized ancient Bible context. This inevitably traced to the newborn Church as the cause of scripture. Equally, it unveiled the Catholic Church as the Church founded by Jesus Christ. The above section then detailed how the Church was founded and how it was subject to both good developments and evil temptations throughout the past two thousand years. Lastly, we beheld the suffering Church foretold by Jesus and his Apostles.

The Crucifixion of the Catholic Church: The Great Apostasy

The next two sections are set apart from the general content of ancient Bible context. They expose unfiltered, hard-to-digest, contemporary Church history. The theology admittedly is speculative. However, the supporting history is factual and accessible to the average researcher, though the facts are often not easily ferreted. The two sections together represent my interpretation of recent Church history –precisely as the time period of entering the foretold Great Apostasy in scripture. Intending to comment on the state of the Church, I equate today's ongoing "crucifixion of the Catholic Church" with this prophesied Great Apostasy.

This conclusion rests on three given premises: The first is that the Catholic Church is the one and only Church founded by Jesus Christ. The second is that the New Testament's references about apostasy in general and the Great Apostasy in particular accordingly apply to the Catholic Church. The third premise is that historical context can be a reliable indicator to help discover the meaning of scripture. As the general content of Ancient Bible Context adequately substantiates these premises, avoiding the redundancy of proving them again, we move ahead.

Mindful of the pertinent parameters of magisterial teachings, this present section states my viewpoint and indulges in my opinion. My intent is not to explain the book of Apocalypse. I dare not presume to grasp the depths of that multi-layered, mysterious vision. But I possibly have a modest contribution to make, based upon historical hindsight. Theologically speaking, I believe that today's Catholic Church is experiencing the unfolding of the Great Apostasy foretold by Saint Paul in his second letter to the Thessalonians. The Church is entering into the fulfillment of that prophesy. (See: II Thessalonians 2:3-12) After considering the scriptural basis of the Great Apostasy, the next section will offer a historical chronology that I believe supports my stance.

As I attempt to encapsulate the condition of today's Catholic Church, I'm drawn to Saint Paul's teaching on the Great Apostasy. It's the reading of recent Church history that led me to scripture for understanding. Yet, in return, this led to understanding scripture better. The prophecy and history fit together like a hand in a glove. There is a significant degree of complementarity between the escalating desecrations plaguing the Catholic Church and the scriptural account of the Great Apostasy.

We start with the account of the Great Apostasy in the second letter of the Apostle Paul to the Thessalonians:

Let no one deceive you in any way. For unless the apostasy comes first and the lawless one is revealed, the one doomed to perdition, who opposes and exalts himself above every so-called god and object of worship, so as to seat himself in the temple of God, claiming that he is a god—do you not recall that while I was still with you, I told you these things? And now you know what is restraining, that he may be revealed in his time. For the mystery of lawlessness is already at work. But the one who restrains is to do so only for the present until he is removed from the scene. And then the lawless one will be revealed, whom the Lord [Jesus] will kill with the breath of his mouth and render powerless by the manifestation of his coming, the one whose coming springs from the power of Satan in every mighty deed and in signs and wonders that lie, and in every wicked deceit for those who are perishing because they have not accepted the love of truth so that they may be saved. Therefore, God is sending them a deceiving power so that they may believe the lie, that all who have not believed the truth but have approved wrongdoing may be condemned. (II Thessalonians 2:3-12)

Apostasy is defined as the abandonment or renunciation of the faith. It's worse than heresy because it surpasses the misinterpretation or propagation of erroneous teachings. A person may embrace a heresy plainly out of ignorance or, worse, stubbornly cling to doctrinal error, clearly knowing that the Church officially teaches otherwise. But apostasy is the wholesale repudiation of Christ and everything having to do with him. It's a "falling away" or "defection from the truth" originally revealed by Christ.

This is not to say that the believers in the time of the Great Apostasy will have no beliefs. They will. Unless they turn to atheism, their "Christian beliefs" will be corrupt and false, not corresponding to the truths that Jesus revealed. For instance, such "end time" Christians may believe that Judas Iscariot reigns gloriously in heaven and that Jesus is not divine. They may hold that Jesus did not establish a Church, that eternal hell does not exist, and that sex before marriage is fine. The content of their faith will be totally foreign to what Jesus taught.

Jesus clarifies the characteristics of the upcoming Great Apostasy. The Great Apostasy immediately precedes the return of Christ. In its wake, the world is left drained of the authentic faith Jesus once revealed. Only the slightest residue of that faith is left. "But when the Son of Man comes, will he find faith on earth?" (Luke 18:8) Two thousand years after he walked the earth and preached, how much of what Jesus taught will be believed by the average Catholic in the pew?

Further describing the Great Apostasy, Jesus speaks not only of a faithless world but the disappearance of love, too. He prophesied that "many will fall away" and "most people's love will grow cold." (Matthew 24:10,12) Genuine Christian love will hardly be understood or practiced. A corrupt Church will define love differently. A false love, detached from its ancient Christian anchor, will be taught. Extreme selfishness shall reign. Jesus taught that love included following his teachings, living the Ten Commandments, doing the will of his Father, and self-sacrifice. Today, "Catholic apostates" secretly nurture a modern kind of "spirituality" for its clergy that enjoys sodomy and oral sex in hidden debauchery among themselves. They call this "love." And then, such lost souls venture into the sanctuary on Sundays and pretend holiness.

Jesus warned against false prophets, who are really wolves disguised as sheep. He warned against ministers who prophesy, throw out demons, and perform miracles but who do not really love by doing the will of his Father in heaven. Such Christians will one day die, and Jesus will say to them, "I never knew you. Depart from me, you evildoers." (Matthew 7:23) This describes a multitude of hell-bound bishops and priests during the thick of the Great Apostasy.

Jesus adds that the atmosphere of the Great Apostasy, immediately before his return, includes false prophets, wars, and rumors of wars, famines, earthquakes, persecutions, and martyrdoms. Paradoxically, the Gospel will be preached throughout the whole world, while all nations will nonetheless hate Christians. There will be a great desolating abomination of the holy place and a tribulation that blankets the world in unprecedented fear. Apostasy will flourish and reach its apex in this kind of chaotic environment. Then the sign of the Son of Man will appear in heaven.

While Luke notes Jesus's words regarding the abandonment of the faith and Matthew the vanishing of Christian love, the Apostles Jude, Peter, and Paul add further applicable teachings regarding the Great Apostasy. Jesus had obviously taught much on the theme.

Saint Jude (not Judas Iscariot) underlines that apostasy comes about in a subtle manner. (Jude 1:4) In the context of guarding the faith originally handed on from Christ, he warns that apostate teachers enter the Church to teach in a stealthy manner. Trying to catch the nuance of the Greek word *pareisedysan*, various Bible translations end up with "invade," "creep," "intrude," "secretly enter," or "infiltrate." So, the teachers that will stir up the Great Apostasy will excel with a subtle modality, as if their lies will resonate as a refined art.

Saint Peter echoes the same nuance. He teaches that "there will be false teachers among you [within the Church], who will introduce destructive heresies and even deny the Master who ransomed them…." (II Peter 2:1) In this passage, the Greek word *pareisaxousin* is translated as "will introduce." However, this term connotes something introduced sneakily and secretly. Many Bible translations reflect the full, nuanced meaning, respecting the subtlety of the Greek. It's enough to underline the agreement of the Apostles Jude and Peter on the manner in which the Great Apostasy will seduce the world. For many Church members, weak in knowledge of the faith, the Great Apostasy will creep into their souls in a practically imperceptible manner. Not capable of discerning the truth, they will swallow the lie.

Jesus substantiates the diabolical refinements of the false teachers during the spiritual scourge of the Great Apostasy. "For there will arise false Christs and false prophets, and they will perform signs and wonders so great as to deceive, if that were possible, even the elect." (Matthew 24:24) Accordingly, the Christians who are ignorant of the original revelation of Jesus Christ will have little chance of escaping the deception of the Great Apostasy.

Further, Saint Paul clarifies a fine point about the nature of the apostate. He describes such a man as deceitful and a false apostle. He's essentially an imposter who masquerades as an apostle, a phony minister within the Church. (II Corinthians 11:13-15) Such apostates are outwardly pleasing and, at first sight, seemingly orthodox, yet they teach and lead astray with a forked tongue. The worst forms of wickedness are perversions of the truth. Half of what the false prophets say is true, the other half is a toxic lie. Lukewarm listeners can't discern one from the other.

At the time of the Great Apostasy, a charming but deceitful bishop within the Church would accordingly, masterfully, diabolically lead most Church members away from Christ unto their eternal damnation. Perhaps historically, the great heretic Arius reflects a type of leader of the Great Apostasy. It will come through the "giftedness" of a ranking minister who fools most believers. Saint Paul lays out the order of events as the Great Apostasy unfolds:

First, the beginning of the evil to come is already present during the age in which Paul writes. Satan already has his foot in the door of the Church from Apostolic times onward. This explains the widespread diffusion of heresies from the earliest years of Christianity and the bloody persecutions. The Great Apostasy will manifest an organic link to Satan's persuasion of early theological errors that once contested to corrupt Christianity from the beginning. Arianism is a good example of this. It never really died. It shape-shifted. It again spreads like cancer.

Second, someone restrains the full force of the apostasy and the "lawless one," the Antichrist, from appearing and ruling. Yet, this person who mightily counteracts the worst of evils to befall the Church can only hold back the deluge of apostasy temporarily.

Third, as this "restrainer" is removed, two catastrophes unravel: the Great Apostasy takes place, whereby the Church suffers a colossal denial of the faith, and the Antichrist appears on the scene and works his deceitful signs and wonders, bringing the whole world beneath his rule.

Meanwhile, the leader of the Great Apostasy, the "Second Beast," the "False Prophet," labors with deceptions and signs to win over every Church member to follow the Anti-Christ. Consider the relationship between the leader of the Great Apostasy and the Antichrist, Just as John the Baptist led his *ekklesia* to Christ. Similarly, the False Prophet leads Christ's *ekklesia* to the Antichrist.

Fourth, because of their denial of the truth and acceptance of sin, in his justice, God punishes the apostatized by letting them suffer from the consequences of their comfortable and preferred ignorance and unopposed sinful ways. The time of mercy bends to the time of God's justice. The superficial believers lacked enough interest in their faith even to make the effort to understand it. Jesus, accordingly, lets them live by the deception of the Great Apostasy and its demonic consequences.

Fifth, Jesus Christ returns in glory, rendering the leader of the apostasy and the Antichrist powerless. Both are thrown into hell.

The Greek term *apostasia* suggests a "withdrawal," as does the Latin term *discessio*. The Great Apostasy, then, is a type of stepping away from the Church by a majority of members. But this can be viewed in two ways: either a large body of apostates exit the Church or a large body of apostates usurp the Church, claiming it as their own, like the mutiny of a great ship. These two differing theological opinions are found among ancient theologians.

In the first case, the apostates would leave and abandon Christianity entirely or establish their own false Church, building from scratch. Like with past heresies, the remaining magisterial believers would retain the properties, governing apparatus, and priestly and sacramental structures of the Church. For the most part, something similar happened during the protestant revolution. In that case, it was the heretics who left the Church. This is the way many people imagine the Great Apostasy.

In the second case, the apostates would remain firmly in control of the Church. The corruption would run so pervasively within the body that the Church itself would morph into an apostate Church. Every leverage of Church policy, regulation, and government would remain in the hands of the apostate bishops. Most cardinals, bishops, priests, and laity would be so thoroughly deceived that the inner beliefs and faith of the majority would fall away from the ancient, magisterial teachings. As such, a new non-Christian faith would replace the old.

Thus, a false Church would rise, claiming to be the official Catholic Church. The ignorant would be fooled. A small exodus from the Church would soon ensue. This small number of "resisters" would continue as the authentic, magisterial Church founded by Jesus Christ. These believers would "leave the Church" and continue to practice the true Catholic faith as an underground remnant Church.

Today's Catholic Church manifests signs of both kinds of apostasy underway. On the one hand, apostates leave the Church wounded by this or that scandal or hard doctrine. These souls either lose their faith in God or believe hardly anything rooted in the magisterial teachings of the Church. On the other hand, apostates remain in the Church, often occupying power positions and propagating many innovative heresies, decidedly corrupting the believers from within. More so, many such apostates deliberately remain in the Church, which no longer disciplines them precisely as a strategy to force the Church to change.

Paul links the Great Apostasy and the reign of the Antichrist to the removal of someone called the "restrainer." The term in Greek is *katechon*, meaning "the one [or thing] holding back." The idea here is that upon the removal of the *katechon*, all hell breaks loose. The full force of the apostasy explodes, and lawlessness welcomes the charming, wonder-working, peace-giving, unbound-by-laws Antichrist, who appears on the scene as a type of savior. While difficult to interpret, the Greek term *katechon* suggests a person or entity that functions as a type of gatekeeper, enforcer, or protector of the law itself. Its (or his) presence holds back lawlessness. Remove it, and chaos gushes through the Church and the world.

Having revealed the prophetic foundation of the Great Apostasy and touched upon its general meaning, we now shift from ancient scripture to recent history. We'll focus on a roughly three-hundred-year window of people and events in the Catholic Church up to the present. As the scope of history is broad, we'll narrow our selection to Satanic interventions directly or by minions to infiltrate and rule the Catholic Church. Unfortunately, an overabundance of material had to be reduced and abbreviated. Still, the selection of materials adequately captures the horrifying story.

Let's trace the demonic at work to bring about the Great Apostasy. Understanding Lucifer's objective may serve as a key to interpreting his ancient resolve to apostatize the Church. Lucifer was the highest angel of the highest order of angels. He accordingly led the highest creaturely act of heavenly worship. Yet, this most exalted and perfect creature wanted to be God and be called God. He rejected God by pride and envy, taking a third of the angels in heaven with him into hell, specially made for him and his followers. "I watched Satan fall from heaven like lightning." (Luke 10:18) Lucifer thought it better to reign as the master of hell than to be a mere servant in heaven. Once the incarnation of the Son of God came about, Lucifer attempted an extreme act of retaliation.

He would persuade Jesus Christ to worship him. Notice Lucifer's audacious bid to bring this about when he tempts Jesus: "All these I shall give to you if you will prostrate yourself and worship me." (Matthew 4:9) Having failed at that, Lucifer then set his target upon the Church, Christ's beloved ark of salvation for the whole world. There were certainly weaknesses therein to exploit. From the moment of Saint Peter's appointment as the first Pope, Lucifer strategized to rule the Church from the peak of its highest authority, the papal throne. He also planned that the Church's worship would suffer corruption. The Great Apostasy would include Satan's orientation of the Holy Mass to the perverted worship of himself. Christ's vessel of salvation would be manipulated into Lucifer's vessel of damnation.

Escalating Desecrations Toward the Great Apostasy

This section shows snapshots of selected historic developments in recent Church history. Each dated entry notes an event that pertains to Satan strategically maneuvering the Church toward the Great Apostasy. The selections offer glimpses, each wanting for exhaustive development. A great amount of dated material has been entirely omitted for the lack of space. Yet, there is enough information here to share a sketch of Lucifer's progressive conquest of Christ's Church.

AD 1226: Shortly before his death, a remarkably holy mystic and miracle worker named Saint Francis of Assisi prophesied about a man of iniquity to rule the Church eight hundred years in the future. That date has arrived. Of course, Francis's words were an incomprehensible mystery at the time of their utterance. Yet, they were spoken and passed on to us for our sober reflection.

Saint Francis warned of an imposter Pope who "tyrannically usurps the papacy." "Someone who is not canonically elected and infected with heretical wickedness, at the turning point of the tribulation, is raised to the papacy. He will make a refined effort to give many the death of his error to drink." Saint Francis further indicated that this would take place during a time of schism, apostasy, great confusion, and pervasive temptation. The sanctity of life would be disdained. Preachers would be silent about the truth. The zealous would be persecuted and martyred. Perhaps Saint Francis's prophecy points to the diabolically persuaded Pope who would lead the Great Apostasy.

AD 1738: Pope Clement XII issued the first prohibition of Catholics joining the Freemasons. Over the next 169 years, from AD 1738 to AD 1907, eleven Popes, by means of weighty Church documents (including encyclicals, constitutions, and papal bulls), consistently condemned Freemasonry and penalized Catholics with excommunication for joining any such secret society. These Popes demonstrated an impenetrable unity of purpose, vision, and action regarding the Catholic Church's opposition to Freemasonry.

The many, varied heresies of historic epochs, such as Gnosticism, Pelagianism, Arianism, Nestorianism, and the like, each claimed a destructive moment in the timeline of history. But any heresy of the past pales compared to today's Masonry. For Masonry is the totality of all heresies. Every heresy against Christianity is welcomed. Masonry accepts all and orients all toward the long-term goal of destroying the Catholic Church, the civil state, and the entire moral order.

Only the recognition of demonic evil and the collaboration of men with the devil can possibly explain the heartbeat of Masonry. The ultimate, veiled goal of Masonry is the preparation of the governing seat for the reign of the Antichrist. An accurate perception of Masonry requires a glimpse into the intellect of Satan, who labors to rule the world and bring all souls to hell. Masonry is a human societal tool he uses. Popes accordingly referred to Masonry as the Abyss of all Errors and the Synagogue of Satan.

The goal is reached by plans that outlive members. Besides, layers of membership protect the hidden purposes of the highest levels of dedication. The naïve, surface membership knows little, unwittingly protecting the inner evil core, enabling the rulers to commit outrageous perversions as needed. For example, most Masons are very good people who have no idea of the true nature and intent of the hard-core leadership.

This leadership, distancing itself from a personal, loving relationship with Jesus Christ and his authentic Church, promotes any heresy: pantheism, naturalism, Pelagianism, indifferentism, paganism, Satanism, atheism, modernism, liberalism, communism, rationalism, socialism, syncretism, and the like. Of course, Pope Leo XIII made the correct conclusion: "Let us remember that Christianity and Freemasonry are essentially incompatible, to such an extent, that to be united with one means being divorced from the other." (Pope Leo XIII, 1892)

In a chess match, the opening moves are about planning and positioning. Similarly, Satan's "chess match" to take over the Catholic Church in modern times opened with recruiting human minions and positioning those collaborators for the early tasks at hand.

AD 1822: Written by "Tigrotto," *The Permanent Instruction of the Alta Vendita* is a two-thousand and eight-hundred-word Freemasonic internal document regarding the subversion of the papacy. It's a clear-cut plan to achieve it. It laid out a practical course of action to secure a Pope, even by the standard practice of traditional papal election, who is imbued with the ideals and principles of Freemasonry and thus entirely controllable unto the internal apostasy of the Catholic Church. Tigrotto was fond of emphasizing his calls to action: "Catholicism must be destroyed throughout the whole world." He believed this could be done by focusing on the correct choke point: "Let us conspire only against Rome!"

His plan recognizes that the blood of the martyrs is the seed of Christianity. It acknowledges that the ultimate vision of Voltaire and the French Revolution, the eternal destruction of Catholicism, although most worthy, is impossible by external force. Raised on the ruins of Rome, time and again, Christianity would only resurrect again, unconquered. So, a different methodology is required. The document goes on to outline the usurpation of the papacy by an insidious inner infiltration of the Church.

The plan explains how the voting body, the cardinals, must vote for a Pope, guided by their very own welcomed and habitual Masonic ways of thinking, wanting a man who may best represent their own way of thinking. To foment such a body of "cardinal voters," it will be necessary to start with the infiltration of the "nurseries" from where the bishops and cardinals arise. The simple churches, social structures, schools, and seminaries must be infiltrated, and the ideals and principles of Freemasonry must be gently planted. In such a manner, high churchmen, from the youngest ages, will be cultivated in the values of Freemasonry, emphasizing the natural, not the supernatural. Then, when the crop has matured, perhaps in a hundred years or more, the cardinals will simply elect one of their own.

The multi-generational nature of this plan was explained: This plan will require patience, yet, in our ranks, the soldier dies, but the war continues with new recruits. We can outlast the passage of time and endure with an unbroken effort. Eventually, the entire body of papal voters will be "corrupt," as the Church says, but ripened as far as Masonic thinking goes.

October, AD 1917: The communists launched the Russian revolution in Petrograd. They killed the Royal family. Over the next handful of years, they confiscated almost six hundred monasteries; widespread executions of monks and nuns accompanied the theft. Twenty-eight bishops were executed, along with 6,775 priests. The experiment of the French Revolution paved the way for the strategy of controlling a population precisely by a reign of bloody terror against the Church. Paralyzing fear was provoked to check resistance.

Jesus taught his Apostles how to identify and judge evil. He explained that evil essentially flows from the heart: "But the things that come out of the mouth come from the heart, and they defile. For from the heart come evil thoughts, murder, adultery, unchastity, theft, false witness, blasphemy." (Matthew 15:18-19)

Understanding communism starts with the heart of Karl Marx, the "Destroyer," the father of the communist way of life: "Thus heaven I forfeited, I know it full well; my soul once true to God, is chosen for hell." And from another poem by Karl Marx: "Look now my blood dark sword shall stab, unerringly within thy soul, the hellish vapors rise and fill the [my] brain till I go mad and my heart is utterly changed...." Marx felt drawn to his favorite character and line of Faust: "All must be destroyed; everything that exists deserves to perish." Marx's heart longed for the "forcible overthrow of all existing social conditions." Judging by the fruits of such a diabolically led heart, it's not surprising that communism brought about the murder of one hundred million people. Marx's biographers, even his father, judged that demons possessed the broken man's thoughts.

The Church consistently condemned communism for a multitude of reasons: It taught that God does not exist, that there is no immortal soul, that man is the end of all things, that man himself is the real God, and that the entire meaning of life is to create a naturalistic paradise on earth, achieved by man alone, for man. Communism also taught that the moral leash of the traditional family (the foundation of civil society) held back human progress and should be abolished. It also taught man that union with the State was the measure of the goodness or badness of everything. For instance, history, art, business, philosophy, education, science, and social activities were only considered good as much as they conformed to the thinking and preferences of the State.

Political analysts tend to define communism in terms of an economic philosophy. But that philosophy is only one aspect of a wider picture. Communism anchors its recruits to a comprehensive ethical system of thought and practice that represents more a religion than a monetary point of view. A person is not yet a true communist until he embraces the whole way of life, beginning with denouncing God himself. Even worse, a true communist embraces a revolutionary intent of life. The perfecting of humanity, the "salvation" of the global population, depends upon the forcible "conversion" of the race to the communist way of life.

Accordingly, Christianity and communism cannot peacefully co-exist. Christianity must convert the communists; the communists strive to defeat their paramount enemy, the Catholic Church. In AD 1937, the encyclical *Divini Redemptoris* called communism "a Satanic scourge right out of the pit of hell, orchestrated by the sons of darkness." Examples of the struggle abound. Throughout the years, wherever communism spread, it went after the Catholic Church heavy-handedly.

Consider the Spanish Civil War from AD 1936 – AD 1939, which was essentially an attempt by communism to seize the country. Countless monasteries, convents, and churches were either desecrated or burnt to the ground. Thirteen bishops were assassinated; 6,832 priests and seminarians were hunted down and executed; 2,647 monks and nuns were murdered as well. Typically, communism uses the guise of a "civil war" as a convenient form of propaganda to advance its ends.

Besides marking the birth year of communist rule in Russia, AD 1917 also set the stage for heaven's counter-offensive. That same year, the Blessed Virgin Mary appeared to three shepherd children in Portugal. Lucia dos Santos was ten years old. She experienced the visitor from heaven with her two younger cousins, Francisco and Jacinto Marto. The Virgin Mary warned the children that if the sinful world did not amend its ways, a terrible chastisement would fall upon mankind. She asked the children to pray and do penance and to appeal to humanity to do the same, to repent and amend its ways.

She had revealed three secrets to these children. The children were shown a vision of hell (to prove that it really existed) and told that if men did not repent, a second and worse war (World War II) would come and that Russia (communism) would spread her errors throughout the world. If the world continued with its sins, a third secret would transpire. The sensitive content of this secret was not revealed to anyone for a very long time.

To prove the truth of the visits and draw attention to the weight of the messages that called for prayer and penance, on October 13, AD 1917, the Blessed Mother worked the "Miracle of the Sun." There were seventy thousand people gathered, including many skeptics and atheist journalists hoping to publish anything negative about God and the Church. A miracle had been promised. The non-believers were expecting to witness an elaborate fraud.

It had rained in the fields all night and throughout the morning. Beneath a sea of umbrellas, everyone was miserably drenched. Mud puddles flourished. The Blessed Mother appeared. Suddenly, the sun began to spin and flash an array of colors. It then danced around in the sky. Suddenly, as if jerked from its fixed position in the heavens, it fell and plunged to earth. Everyone was terrified! The crowd filled with panic and screams. They believed the end of the world had arrived.

Many ran; others fell on their knees and confessed their sins, even publicly, and repented. Before the sun hit the world, it abruptly stopped and rose back to its normal place and proper brightness. Both the soaked fields and peoples' wet clothes were now completely dry and clean of mud splashes. Converted journalists had recorded this historic event in their newspapers the next day and beyond. People saw the event from twenty-five miles distance. This miracle represented the greatest number of people in modern times to witness a miracle while all gathered at the same place and time. Yet, there was a greater miracle worked in history with a much bigger crowd of witnesses: the parting of the Red Sea by Moses.

It so happened that Francisco and Jacinto died very young of the Spanish Flu immediately following World War I, in 1919 and 1920, respectively. Lucia eventually became a nun. Because of a serious illness, the bishop asked Lucia to write the third secret, just in case she might die. The Blessed Mother appeared to her and confirmed that this should be done. So, in AD 1944, the third secret was written by Lucia.

In four pages, sixty-two lines, she wrote a visual description of what she saw. This was put into a sealed envelope. Then, only after a great demonic attack that prevented her writing, on one page, she finally wrote the exact words spoken by the Blessed Mother in twenty-five lines. This was sealed in a separate envelope. The visual description lacks a clear portrayal of meaning without the succinct and explosive explanatory words.

After the time of the writing, the Blessed Virgin told Lucia that this secret ought to be revealed to the world no later than the year AD 1960. Throughout the following years, the advocates of the Fatima message grew into a global Catholic multitude. More than once, Lucia was asked: why did the Blessed Mother say to reveal the secret no later than AD 1960? Lucia consistently responded that, "It would be clearer then." Hence, the environment, mentality, and happenings of the times would clarify and help make the secret better understood. The whole Catholic world patiently waited for the dated release of the third secret of Fatima.

It should be added here that the small scrap of paper became a hot potato. No member of the hierarchy wanted to shoulder the responsibility of reading the secret. The local bishop in Portugal had inserted the sealed envelopes into his own official envelope without reading anything. Eventually, Pope Pius XII asked for the letter. He received it but did not read it. He thought it best to simply follow the instructions of the Blessed Mother and wait until the year AD 1960. By AD 1957, it sat still unopened in a safe in the papal apartment in the Vatican. However, Pope Pius XII died on October 9, AD 1958. Pope John XXIII inherited the chair of Saint Peter and the task of dealing with the third secret of Fatima.

AD 1929: Meanwhile, communism advanced with a strategy of subverting the Catholic Church. After twelve years of stabilizing the communist way of life in Russia, instructions were passed on from the Kremlin to communist agents in the United States. Remember, communist rule was (and still is) about world domination! The outright, bloody slaughter of Christians gave way to a more calculated strategy for America. The refined plan benefited from the analysis of William Foster, a communist who ran for the presidency under the communist party in America. He concluded that three things blocked the development of communism in the United States. These were solid Christian morality, strong family values, and fervent patriotism.

The communists concluded that the best way to break down these obstacles gradually was by the covert insertion of homosexuality and radical feminism into American society. So, communism infiltrated schools, institutions, and labor unions to nurture an immoral "gay" subculture and teach a communist way of thinking and believing among the general population. Thanks to the highly successful experience of Bella Dodd, a communist agent who helped work out the details of this strategy, we understand the nature of this infiltration. After decades of undercover work, Mrs. Dodd was expelled from the Party in AD 1949. She testified before Congress in AD 1953, and that is where we discover her expertise in destroying the Catholic Church.

The general approach was to "communize" the manner of thinking within social institutions, schools, and universities. Personally, she managed about a thousand infiltrated communist teachers, many in prestigious universities. "It's not surprising that those against God should aim their biggest weapons at our schools…. Eliminating the concept of God from education leaves the student with no basis for determining right from wrong." Instilling immorality promised even better results.

She also managed her own network of one thousand and two hundred bishops and priests. Targeting the seminaries, she learned that her best candidates for communist subversion were the brightest of students. The Kremlin had told her it would be so. You had to be mindful of who had the requisite aptitudes for quick promotions within the hierarchical system. You needed people smart enough to lead double lives and remain intact. Good-looking and sociable personalities would be noticed by bishops, and soon, such excellent men would be placed in power positions as vocation directors, rectors of seminaries, and future bishops. Still, the communists wanted the predatory type.

A homosexual network does not happen by chance. Immorality is enflamed intentionally for the purpose of rooting corruption. Her goal was not so much to make communist members but to form priests trapped in vice, yet in agreement with the communist worldview. This approach drained the supernatural out of Christianity and neutralized opposition to communism. Once the network was in place, it self-perpetuated. Each homosexual protected the other, lifted the other to a higher power in the Church, and filtered out any young seminarian candidate lacking the tendency. A seminarian couldn't report to the bishop that a fellow seminarian was having sex with another, as the bishop may be part of the network. If you wanted to become a priest, you had to remain silent. If you wanted to remain a priest, you had to shut up. Never preach against homosexuality from the pulpit, or your days were numbered. Until finally, the Catholic priesthood in America slowly transformed into a gay profession.

Way back in AD 1953, Bella Dodd was able to confess to Congress that the program was so successful that the communists already had four cardinals in Rome who were part of the homosexual network of socialist thinkers. That was seventy years ago! At present, researchers estimate that 40% to 80% of the bishops and clergy in the service of the Vatican live secret homosexual lifestyles. Once the network thrives, no number of rules, policies, or educational courses can root out the corruption that is embedded in the emotional disposition and addictive habit of sodomy. And, of course, the Masonic old-fashioned art of blackmail fortified the preservation of the network of iniquity.

By July 16, AD 1949: After no less than five encyclicals, between 1849 and 1937, condemning communism, Pope Pius XII released a decree against communism. The decree clarified and put a sharp edge to the Church's already stated opposition to communism. With four succinct points, it laid down the law: It is prohibited to either join or show favor to the communist party; it is prohibited to write, publish, distribute, or read publications that support communist doctrines or activities; Catholics who knowingly and freely commit such acts must be denied the sacraments. Furthermore, Christians who profess, defend, or promote materialistic communistic doctrines incur the penalty of automatic excommunication as apostates from the Christian faith, with the penalty reserved so that it may only be lifted by the Holy See.

AD 1959: The year opened with a Papal announcement of the upcoming Vatican II Council, aimed at making the Church more friendly and approachable to the world. Fundamentally, distancing itself from the historic role of a general council to combat and clarify the doctrinal threats of the age, this upcoming council would be a pastoral experiment. It focused on how the Church ought to appear before the world and approach its mission. If it had mirrored a traditional council, it would have strongly condemned modernism, masonry, communism, and the like. But such great threats to the Church barely found a place in the conciliar documents. These great heresies of the age barely received attention as important dangers to the faith.

Many "expert theologians" spearheaded the production of the documents that often ended up ambiguous, seemingly, purposefully, prone to heretical interpretations and implementations. Post-conciliar developments would latch on to this doctrinal frailty to further dissociate the Church from its magisterial roots. The council led to a confrontation period that put the Church in a position of trying to interpret the conciliar documents in a way consistent with Catholic magisterial history while managing a catastrophic Church decline. This confrontational period paved the way for progressive, modernist thinkers to advance liberal agendas with "doctrinal support" in the conciliar documents. During this confusing period of Church transition, Lucifer advanced his influence over the Church.

A few statistics might provide a glimpse of the free fall of the Church from the close of the council to the turn of the century. In thirty-five years, only in the United States, priests fell by thirteen thousand, seminarians fell by forty-five thousand, annual ordination fell by one thousand, Sunday Mass attendance fell by 50%, and Catholic parochial students fell by two million and five hundred thousand.

During the early preparation period for the Council of Vatican II, Pope John XXIII had surveys sent to all the bishops of the world. In response, the most frequent appeal was for the council to condemn communism again. During the Council's preparation period, the condemnations of communism were prepared in a schema, supported with ample enthusiasm.

But a strange, scandalous silence prevailed by the end of the Council. The condemnations were scrapped, and a feeble footnote undermined the real nature and threat of communism against the Church. Pope John XXIII, Pope Paul VI, and persuasive members of the Catholic hierarchy wanted the Russian Orthodox hierarchy to participate in the Council. Nothing was going to stand in the way of that. Socialist-leaning cardinals and bishops exercised their influence to weaken the Church's anti-communist stance in favor of conciliar politics.

Only a few months after his papal election, Pope John XXIII shockingly announced the General Council of Vatican II. The general consensus was that he'd serve for a few years as an interim or place-holder Pope. A busy preparation period ensued, with elaborate plans for the grand opening of the Council in AD 1962. The Pope and the organizing Cardinals and bishops meanwhile looked forward to the event with high hopes, believing in the positive renewal of the Church.

Six months following the announcement of Vatican II and waist-deep in organizing a historic renewal of the Catholic Church, the long-awaited public exposure of the third secret of Fatima had finally arrived. On August 17, AD 1959, Pope John XXIII and his closest collaborators sliced open the double envelopes.

Upon reading, an ashen hue washed over the Pope. He turned white as a ghost and fainted. This could never be published! It was a traumatic experience to read and difficult to process mentally. After recovering, the Pope was confused. At first, he wondered if the prophecy applied to him or not.

John XXIII said, "This does not concern my pontificate." He then had his personal secretary scribble a note on the envelope, "I leave it to others to comment or decide." He washed his hands of the responsibility to publish the dreadful thing! By February 8, AD 1960, the Vatican sent out an anonymous press release to an anxiously waiting Catholic world. It stated plainly that the third secret of Fatima would not be disclosed and "would probably remain, forever, under absolute seal." Nothing would obstruct the optimistic momentum of John XXIII's Council of Vatican II.

John XXIII judged that a public release of the message would undermine the upbeat preparations for Vatican II, stir doubts about papal authority, and likely provoke international turmoil. The message was then buried in the Vatican archive system. Furthermore, on October 11, AD, 1962, Pope John XXIII opened the Vatican II council with a speech that rejected the thoughts of "prophets of doom who are always forecasting disaster" in the world and the future of the Church. No doubt, this alluded to the third secret of Fatima. Sister Lucia's humble note was scorned in favor of a naive trust and confidence in hierarchical judgments.

After the Pope's inner circle became aware of the content of the third secret, future Popes and their key prelates would come to know the secret, too. Meanwhile, a second reading took place with Cardinal Bea (John XXIII's closest confident) and his secretary, Father Malachi Martin. Everyone had to vow to secrecy before hearing a word. Father Martin was a competent theologian, exorcist, and linguist. Later in life, Martin would admit that his life was never the same again once the content of the secret hit his ears. To this day, most of the general public has little idea of the secret's content.

On May 13, AD 1967, Sister Lucia was able to meet with Pope Paul

VI at Fatima. She asked him to release the content of the third secret to the Public. She simply wanted to follow the instructions of the Blessed Mother. Pope Paul VI pleasantly refused to comply.

As time passed, the following souls (not exclusively) are known to have read the third secret of Fatima: Pope John XXIII, Monsignor Paulo Jose Tavarez, Cardinal Ottaviani, Archbishop Loris Francesco Capovilla, Cardinal Bea, Father Malachi Martin, Pope Paul VI, two Portuguese translators, Pope John Paul II, Cardinal Mario Ciappi, Pope Benedict XVI, Cardinal Bertone, and presumably Pope Francis and his inner circle.

The mystic and miracle worker Saint Padre Pio knew the third secret of Fatima precisely because it was divinely revealed to him. Subsequently, the holy and famed exorcist of the Vatican, Father Gabriele Amorth, also knew the content of the third secret, as Padre Pio had shared the content with him. These two men had been close friends for twenty-six years. Father Amorth considered Padre Pio, his spiritual father.

Through some of these credible "readers," we can know with a decent degree of certitude the content of the twenty-five-line, single-page, hand-written letter by Lucia that conveyed the spoken words of the Blessed Mother. Although the readers had agreed to keep the content secret, most of them nonetheless slipped hints here and there throughout the years. After piecing the leaks together, the essential message emerges. Sister Lucia herself offered a useful framework for catching the essence of the message. She said that the third secret is in the last book of the Bible.

Relying on multiple complementary intimations, a core element of the third secret of Fatima is close to the following, in my opinion:

> If the sinful Church continues unabated, a spiritual chastisement will fall upon it in the form of a catastrophic loss of faith globally. Great spiritual suffering shall ensue. Led by an evil Pope under the control of Satan, the Great Apostasy will split the Church in two. This evil Pope will be a heretic, anti-Pope, schismatic, and apostate. A diabolical disorientation of cardinals, bishops, and priests will leave the Church drained of strength and sane guidance.

The divinely revealed faith shall evaporate from the greater-sized separating body. This body will morph into a false Church run by the devil, a false prophet, a wicked Pope. The remaining true Church shall shrink to an infinitesimally small remnant of humanity, vulnerable, persecuted, tested, and at times martyred.

The Pope himself will lead the false Church, just as a false shepherd or false prophet leads his followers to eternal damnation. Further, he shall betray the real Church to the civil powers of evil, the beast, or Antichrist. The true Church shall scatter and worship in hiding, like in the days of the Roman persecutions.

The Great Apostasy described is the same as revealed by Saint Paul in II Thessalonians 2:1-12. Additionally, it is the same as revealed in complementary passages in the book of Revelation, especially 13:1-18 and 12:1-18.

Frere Michel, a world-renowned expert on Fatima, made his own abridgment of the third secret of Fatima. He employed a similar methodology to the one just used. He pieced together the leaks and scraps of knowledgeable insiders, who offhandedly shared their "allowable perceptions." Frere Michel, after exhaustive studies, concisely summarized the third secret as follows:

It will be the time of the decisive battle between the Virgin and the Devil. A flood of diabolic confusion will spread throughout the world. Satan will penetrate to the highest levels of the Church. This will be the Great Apostasy announced for the last days, the false prophet who betrays the Church in favor of the beast according to the prophecy of the Apocalypse. In fact, Sister Lucia herself pointed out that the secret is revealed in the last book of holy scripture.

The Vatican exorcist, Father Gabriele Amorth, flatly summarizes the essence of the third secret of Fatima without wasting any words: "There would soon be a great apostasy in the Church from its apex. The devil will be introduced to the head of the Church by means of a Pope under the control of Satan."

June 29, AD 1963: On the feast day of Saints Peter and Paul, the Archangel Lucifer was enthroned in the chapel of Saint Paul near the papal palace in the Vatican. The purpose of the enthronement was to establish a far-reaching curse over the entire Catholic Church and seize control of the final papacy (soon to arrive) for Lucifer. With the blasphemous sacrilege of a woman laid upon the altar, the sacred sacrifice of the Mass was profaned. The defiled was adored. Leading a group of bishops, the presider ceremoniously placed the following decree upon the soiled altar cloth:

Whosoever shall, by means of this inner chapel, be designated and chosen as the final In-The-Line successor in the Petrine office, shall by his very oath of office commit himself and all he does command to be the willing instrument and collaborator with the Builders of Man's Home of Earth and throughout Man's Cosmos. He shall transform the ancient enmity into Friendship, Tolerance, and Assimilation....

The decree goes on to dedicate the last Pope to the Satanic orientation of every human activity and dimension. This formal enthronement took place on the eve of the coronation of the newly elevated Pope Paul VI. Further, the enthronement followed a precise "prophetic" calendar. The agents of the ceremony adhered to a long-standing demonic tradition. The age of the prince of evil would arrive when a Pope would take the name of the Apostle Paul. Cardinal Giovanne Montini's assumption of the name "Paul" signaled that the time of intensified evil had arrived.

A knowledgeable Vatican insider commented on a few aftereffects of this enthronement:

Suddenly it became unarguable that now during this papacy [of Paul VI], the Roman Catholic organization carried a permanent presence of clerics who worshipped Satan and liked it, of bishops and priests who sodomized boys and each other, of nuns who performed the 'Black Rites' of Wicca, and who lived in lesbian relationships. Sacrilegious actions and rites were not only performed on Christ's altars but had the connivance or at least the tacit permission of certain cardinals, archbishops, and bishops.

Many of these prominent members of the hierarchy occupied extremely high positions and ranks in the Church. The Vatican insider goes on to note that a systematic network between clerical homosexual groups and Satanist covens ensued globally. This network soon assumed extraordinary influence and power within the administrative, governmental, and liturgical dimensions of the Church.

January, AD 1964: Pope Paul VI appointed a Masonic archbishop to develop a new manner of Catholic worship globally. His name was Archbishop Annibale Bugnini, a member of the Masonic Lodge of Rome with the code name "Buan."

From the beginning of Vatican II, Pope John XXIII had entrusted Bugnini with the responsibility of leading the development of liturgical ideas. Once Pope Paul VI had approved the Constitution on the Liturgy, he appointed Bugnini to handle the implementation of the Constitution. Bugnini also held other prestigious positions that touched upon worship and the sacraments.

Accordingly, a minimalist approach was taken to modernize the ancient liturgy. With the help of six protestants, Bugnini streamlined the Mass. The rich oblationary, sacrificial, and sacerdotal theology was deemphasized. Instead, the communal meal became the emphasis. This led to replacing the altar with a table and no longer designing Churches that centered upon God and the sacrifice but upon the societal interaction of humans as the center of worship. The replacement of the traditional music and Latin de-mystified the experience of worship at Mass. Bugnini borrowed from Luther and Cramner to "protestantize" the Mass. He called his Mass the "Novus Ordo," a cryptic reference to the Masonic "New World Order."

After the damage was done and the liturgical implementation of Bugnini's new Mass spread globally, evidence was presented to Paul VI of Bugnini's undeniable Masonic membership. Shocked, the Pope grieved! In AD 1976, Pope Paul VI sent Archbishop Annibale Bugnini to Iran to serve as the nuncio. Of course, the name "Annibale" means "Gift of Baal." His exile to Iran then was a return to the land of Baal.

November 16, AD 1965: A short twenty-three days before the formal closing of Vatican II, forty-two conciliar bishops met in secret in the Catacomb of Saint Domitilla, Rome. These modernist bishops met to swear an oath and sign a pact. They no longer believed that the Catholic Church was the sole means of salvation established by Jesus Christ. In ages past, if discovered, these bishops would have been called heretics and rooted out of the body. With the intention of remaining in the Church and transforming it from within, these influential prelates vowed to make a new Church.

The mastermind of the pact was a radical, liberal bishop from Brazil: Bishop Helder Camara. He was a socialist, laden with virulent Marxist sympathies, living the heretical liberation theology mindset. Because of his Marxist tendencies, many called him the "Red Bishop." Because of his frequent visits to the slums and televised sermons, he had gained a reputation as a champion of the poor. Later, his sermons were gathered and published under the title *Revolution Through Peace.*

At that secret midnight gathering, the Catacombs Pact committed the signers to create "a poor Church for the poor." The signers would no longer use fancy clothing and traditional vestments. They would abandon their titles and exchange their ornate rings for the simplest rings they could find. The idea was to divest themselves from the ostentatious appearances of traditional Catholicism. They sought to become welcoming and approachable to the poor.

Yet, the pact went far beyond the symbolic. The overall idea of vesting down to bond with the poor stemmed from a deeper determination to replace the old with a new Church completely. The simplification of vestments, architecture, music, rings, titles, and more was only the attractive, compassionate packaging. Their sworn vows aimed at replacing the theology, morals, and liturgy of the Church. They intended to create a soft, subtle, palatable revolution inside the Catholic Church. The Pact was a clandestine declaration of revolution. Meeting in secret made sense.

The focus of the Church would be drawn away from traditional, supernatural beliefs and practices and replaced with a religion dedicated to man. The pious needs of the soul, sin and repentance, death and judgment, virtue, mystery, salvation, the sacraments and eternity, divine revelation, the ten commandments, and so much more would all be deemphasized: devested from the believer. The ancient mysteries of Christianity would be replaced with a striving to build a paradise on earth, just as the communists had outlined so long ago.

Here's a taste of the signed document:

> We will do our utmost that those responsible for our government and for our public services make, and put into practice, laws, structures, and social institutions required by justice and charity, equality and the harmonic and holistic development of all men and women, and by this means bring about the advent of another social order, worthy of the sons and daughters of mankind and God." (*Catacombs Pact*, paragraph 10)

This new society would not be based on the kingship of Christ but on the exultation and brotherhood of man. They envisioned a "New World Order" and used the terminology typical of Masonry. As such, they committed themselves to help erect a Church in lockstep with the principles of communism and masonry.

Bishop Camara's progressive way of thinking would spread to both Bishop Jorge Bergoglio (Pope Francis) and Claus Schwab of the World Economic Forum. These personages considered Bishop Camara, an admirable mentor and followed his vision regarding the ideal path of development regarding the Catholic Church. When Cardinal Bergoglio chose the name "Francis" for his pontificate, he signaled his agenda of walking the path once laid out by Bishop Camara. Notice Francis's first address to the crowd after his election. He said we must have "a poor Church for the poor." That's pure Catacombs Pact terminology. For anyone paying attention, Francis was really affirming his determination to follow the organizing principle established by Bishop Camara during Vatican II.

During the Amazon synod of 2019, Pope Francis finally made the Catacombs Pact public. He publicly spoke of it in glowing terms as a wonderful "development of Vatican II." Celebrating its anniversary, he welcomed its commemoration, reinforcing his personal commitment to enlist the Church's collaboration in helping to establish a new social order in the world. A knowledgeable bishop interviewed at that time summarized the reality succinctly: "Pope Francis is the Catacombs Pact!" Most people had no idea of the meaning of this statement.

So, that historic pact still lives today as a guiding post for where the Church is heading. The synods of 2023 and 2024 will be heavily influenced by that Pact —fermented in the intellect of Lucifer. These catastrophic synods will bring the long-maturing Pact to the fruition of the Great Apostasy. At the end of Francis's Synod of Synodality in 2023, he provided a copy of the Catacombs Pact for every participant. He happily passed out the game plan for abandoning traditional Catholicism.

June 29, AD 1972: On the feast day of Saint Peter and Paul, exactly nine years after the Satanic enthronement, Pope Paul VI spoke most uncharacteristically. He exhibited exasperation and buyer's remorse regarding the mushrooming destruction, distortion, and trashing of the once-cherished ancient liturgy of the Catholic Church. Perhaps he naively felt like the servants in Christ's parable who had asked in dismay, "Master, did you not sow good seed in your field? Where have the weeds come from?" Did Pope Paul VI know anything of the Satanic enthronement that transpired beneath his feet nine years earlier?

Although he lacked the theological mindset to defy the liturgical experiment gone wild, the Pope, nonetheless, honestly, publicly lamented:

> Through some crack, the smoke of Satan has entered the Church of God. There is doubt, uncertainty, problems, unrest, dissatisfaction, confrontation. The Church is no longer trusted. It was thought that, after the Council, sunny days would come for the history of the Church. Nevertheless, what came were days of clouds, of storms, or darkness, of searching, of uncertainty….

October 13th, 1977: On the 60th anniversary of the miracle of the Sun at Fatima, Portugal, Paul VI reflected again on the aftermath of Vatican II. Ten months before his death, he pondered out loud:

> The tale of the devil is functioning in the disintegration of a Catholic world. The darkness of Satan has entered and spread throughout the Catholic Church, even to its summit. Apostasy, the loss of faith, is spreading throughout the world and into the highest levels within the Church.

September 28, 1978: thirty-three days into his pontificate, Pope John Paul I died. Truly, he was assassinated by the Masons. Once his pontificate began, the new Pope encountered a Vatican Bank scandal that exposed prominent Italian Freemasons. Through the Vatican Bank, two cardinals and an archbishop were working with Freemasons and the Sicilian Mafia to launder 288 million dollars in heroin profits. Not willing to comply or silently play along, John Paul learned that the laundering operation involved two Masonic bankers, a Freemasonic cardinal, and a Masonic archbishop. The Pope became a threat.

Meanwhile, from a Masonic insider, the Pope got his hands on a just-released partial list of Masonic Cardinals and bishops. John Paul I wanted the entire list and pursued it. He was determined to uncover and remove every Masonic mole hidden in the hierarchical structure of the Catholic Church. A mere sixteen days later, under extremely mysterious circumstances, Pope John Paul I was found dead in the papal apartment. He had been poisoned. A Masonic cardinal took charge of covering up suspicions.

October 16, AD 1978: Cardinal Karol Wojtyla of Poland was elected the new Pope and took the name John Paul II. This Pope had learned how to operate beneath the foot of a communist regime. He was aware of the Roman chatter that both John XXIII and Paul VI may have been Masons at one time. Additionally, he came to know the surroundings of the death of Pope John Paul I at the hands of the Masons. He, accordingly, deliberately chose not to confront the Masons head-on; rather, he chose to give his life to the energetic proclamation of the Gospel far and wide. He made a deliberate choice not to confront the enemies of the Church openly but to evangelize radically. His vision was to conquer evil by the overwhelming proclamation of the Gospel.

Yet, Pope John Paul II knew how to read the signs of the times. He was not naive about a significant clash about to descend upon the world. Take note of the brief reflection he delivered in Philadelphia, U.S.A., as a cardinal in AD 1976:

> We are now standing in the face of the greatest historical confrontation humanity has ever experienced. I do not think that the wide circle of American society, or the whole wide circle of the Christian community realizes this fully. We are now facing the final confrontation between the Church and the anti-church, between the Gospel and the anti-gospel, between Christ and the Antichrist.

February 11, AD 2013: The famed Vatican exorcist, Father Gabriele Amorth, compelled Lucifer to divulge his plans against the Church:

> The Catholic Church is under attack…. That one [Jesus Christ] up there is about to return to earth. I don't know where or when, but I feel that day is very, very, very close. I concentrate all my energies to channel my billions of demons against the Apostolic See. Corruption is not enough. Greed for money is not enough, it is not enough to provoke scandals; a battle must be waged that has as its final result the destruction of the so-called Church of Rome…. We must come to occupy the throne of the Vicar of the one nailed to the cross. By hook or by crook. Whatever it takes…. By now, many cardinals, bishops, and priests are in total disagreement with the tradition of your Church. We want confusion, dissociation, division inside and outside the Petrine See, as you call it.

By the evening of the same day of this demonic interrogation, Pope Benedict XVI publicly announced his intention to resign from the papacy. This development represented a seismic shift in the spiritual realm of the Church. Pope Benedict XVI would unexpectedly resign. Lightening fell from heaven and struck Saint Peter's Basilica. The Catholic world was left dumbstruck. Satan snatched a victory that hour. The last Pope to resign from the Petrine office had taken place 598 years ago. It was a Satanic victory because Lucifer had his own man in mind for occupying the papal office.

February 28, AD 2013: Lucifer successfully manipulated the resignation of Pope Benedict XVI, the chief gatekeeper assigned by Christ, to preserve traditional Christianity. Confusion and deception are hallmarks of the demonic. To this day, confusion and deception best describe the whirlwind of the resignation. It seems nobody can forthrightly state why Pope Benedict XVI resigned.

The speculations of researchers vary. Some claim Benedict retired because of sickness. Some claim that he could not handle the three-hundred-page investigative report of Vatican Bank money laundering that also uncovered a vast homosexual network of cardinals, bishops, and priests. These researchers say Pope Benedict believed himself incapable of addressing such a pervasive problem. A younger Pope was needed for the task. Benedict lacked the temperament to operate with a heavy hand of discipline. Although such was part of his job.

Some say that Benedict was coerced to resign by the "Roman Circle," also known as the "Dome of Demons." This was an insider group of Church prelates who colluded with Satan. Benedict's striving to preserve the old Latin Mass and interpret Vatican II in a way that preserved the ancient doctrines of the Church were unacceptable to the forces of modernism. One example of the isolation and pressures put upon him was the theft of his deeply personal notes and their publication.

Some say that a counter-intelligence operation, known by the NSA, forced a resignation under pressure. If true, his position of being the true Pope until his death is possible. Some researchers believe that Bendict's inner circle may have encouraged the resignation due to a combination of factors, such as health and the inability to withstand the pressure of the modernists and the daunting task of rooting out the homosexual network embedded in the Church.

This inner group of friends and close advisors supposedly reassured Benedict that the votes were in hand to elect a new conservative cardinal (Angelo Scola) to tackle the task at hand. They equally judged that Cardinal Jorge Bergoglio would not rally enough votes to gain the papacy. They knew that Bergoglio from Argentina could damage the Church immensely. Or, perhaps, even this inner circle may have included an ecclesial mole who deceptively favored Bergoglio.

Canon lawyers point out that the manner of Benedict's resignation was strangely non-canonical and thereby ineffective. Benedict knew better. Accordingly, Benedict innovatively renounced the "ministry" of the papacy but not the "office" as required by canon law. No Pope had ever split these two roles into two, handed over one, and kept the other. This was both bizarre and tragically confusing. Then, the details of the mess further affirmed the ambiguity. Benedict created the new title of "Pope Emeritus" (with no precedent of historic usage) and retained the official appearance and ring of authority, besides the right to grant papal blessings. Yet, he would later state that Pope Francis was the true Pope.

Finally, some believe Pope Benedict stepped away from the papacy for a theological reason. He believed we are living in the time of the Great Apostasy. The prophesied great falling away of believers was both imminent and unstoppable. The momentum of the avalanche could not be avoided.

He, therefore, took it upon himself to initiate the end-times remnant Church, soon to be rejected by the institutional false Church of the apostasy. Doing so, Benedict knew he'd certainly be misunderstood. His affinity for the theology of Tyconius, who wrote a commentary on the book of the Apocalypse, seemed to support this view. Inseparable from this paradigm, the ultimate corruption and Satanic control of the larger part of the Catholic Church was inevitable. He, therefore, chose to give the remnant Church an example of stepping away from the institutional false Church when it will become necessary to remain faithful to Christ.

In earlier years, when Benedict XVI was known as Cardinal Ratzinger, the man already had a sense of where the Church was heading:

The Church will become small and will have to start afresh more or less from the beginning… And so it seems to me that the Church is facing very hard times. The real crisis has scarcely begun. We will have to count on terrific upheavals. But I am equally certain about what will remain at the end: not the Church of the political cult, which is dead already, but the Church of faith. She may well no longer be the dominant social power to the extent that she was until recently, but she will enjoy a fresh blossoming and be seen as man's home, where he will find life and hope beyond death.

March 13, AD 2013: On the second day of voting, by the fifth ballot, Cardinal Jorge Bergoglio won the papal election with an impressive ninety votes. Although publicly he feigned surprise, he knew his favorable odds and the magic of a powerful "Mafia." Indeed, he had given his support to the conspiracy that had rigged the election. Everything had been meticulously set in place long before the doors of the Sistine Chapel were wax-sealed for the election. Church law legislated an automatic excommunication for anyone who was a knowing party of the conspiracy. But no cardinal-conspirator bothered with that canonical technicality.

Bergoglio's victory far surpassed the personal achievement of a modestly known, modernist cardinal from South America. Rather, his election represented the revolutionary victory of a group called the "Sankt Gallen Mafia." This group had finally succeeded in placing a Pope on the chair of Saint Peter, who was hand-selected by Freemasonic interests. Adhering to the multi-generational plan of the *Alta Vendita*, it had taken 191 years to achieve. It was a genuine coup d'état orchestrated by Satan himself.

Rewind: aware of the Soviet-style, fake elective process characteristic of communist regimes, Pope John Paul II had decreed guidelines for the papal election procedure. He did so to contain the possibility of rigging a papal election. Understanding the determination of prelates to radically liberalize the Catholic Church and use unscrupulous methods to achieve their ends, Pope John Paul II promulgated an Apostolic Constitution. These guidelines strictly prohibited the secret manipulation of votes:

> Confirming the prescriptions of my predecessors, I likewise forbid anyone, even if he is a cardinal, during the Pope's lifetime and without having consulted him, to make plans concerning the election of his successor, or to promise votes, or to make decisions in this regard in private gatherings. (Pope John Paul II, *Universi Domini Gregis, 79*)

The many cardinals and bishops of the Sankt Gallen Mafia, who met annually in Sankt Gallen, Switzerland, to plan for a liberalized Catholic Church, brazenly defied this authoritative instruction issued by Pope John Paul II. The "Mafia" decided to play hardball. The way they felt, the time had come: nothing would stand in their way of seizing the papal throne and placing their own man in the chair.

For years, the "Mafia's" heated, annual conversations had targeted the removal of the conservative nexus of Pope John Paull II and Cardinal Joseph Ratzinger. Then, when Benedict XVI stood alone, the "Mafia" settled on Cardinal Jorge Bergoglio of Buenos Aires, Argentina. He knew the manipulative art of appearing conservative while underhandedly advancing modernism.

When Pope John Paul II died, the conservative blockade endured in one man standing alone. Cardinal Ratzinger eventually won enough papal votes to slow down the liberalization of the Church. Bergoglio's votes had been climbing, but Ratzinger beat Bergoglio. Once Pope Benedict XVI was removed, the opportune moment for the internal revolution had arrived.

Bergoglio would never have become Pope Francis without the illegalities of this "Mafia" in Switzerland. The group had also maintained a revolving door for guests who might benefit from the plan to subdue the Church. Such "visitors" historically included all kinds: communists, militant homosexuals, Masons, Illuminati, and friends of Lucifer. The lobbying and politicking for Bergoglian votes represented collusion with Satan. The wickedness of the plot is proven by the ultimate intention to dismantle and rebuild a new Church, regardless of laws. The once-hidden motives of Bergoglio's papacy are clear now. He is a demonically led destroyer of the Church.

Many cardinals know that Bergoglio was not validly placed on the throne of Saint Peter. There was not a universal acceptance of his election, although it seemed so publicly. But as Satan's reign advances, such cardinals are gripped in a paralyzing silence. Fear controlled them and still does. They mortally failed in their duty of protecting the Church from evil.

We now kneel at the foot of the Church crucified. Here, God calls us to pray, trust, resist evil, and stand steadfast. Our suffering has its place to cleanse, and this shall pass. The resurrection comes. Wait on God, his glory appears on the horizon.

Jesus promised Saint Peter, "And so I say to you, you are Peter, and upon this rock I will build my Church, and the gates of hell shall not prevail against it." (Matthew 16:18) Do we believe in Jesus or not? A renewed Church will rise again. The crucible of suffering and divine love will draw all the scattered churches back into the embrace of the one Church founded by Christ, renewed so gloriously that its splendor shall enlighten the whole world.

The False Prophet will have his reign of terror, yes, but the Lord has circumscribed the extent of evil. The false Pope shall only be able to make it appear that all has changed, but he cannot touch or change the magisterial teachings of the Church, rooted in ancient Christianity. He will crush the saints, but we shall rise again.

Take to heart the old, tested wisdom of Saint Vincent of Lerins to Christians surviving in a heretical environment: "Avoid the profane novelty of words, Saint Paul says. (Timothy 6:20) … For if novelty is to be avoided, antiquity is to be held tight; and if novelty is profane, antiquity is sacred."

In hindsight, it seems the resignation of Pope Benedict XVI and the rise of Pope Francis manifests a prophetic sign for our perilous times. By the time of his "removal," Benedict stood like a rock of orthodoxy. Yet, he wasn't always that way. During the years of Vatican II and some years thereafter, as a theological consultant, Ratzinger tended toward some strains of liberal theology. But by the dawn of the pontificate of Pope John Paul II in 1978, Cardinal Ratzinger had matured into a conservative thinker. In 1981, Pope John Paul II appointed him the Prefect of the Congregation for the Doctrine of the Faith. This was the old office of the Inquisition, tasked with the oversight of not letting the true faith lapse into error.

This position represented the right arm of the Pope on matters of faith and morals. The Prefect oversaw defending the magisterial teachings of the Catholic Church. He was like the gatekeeper of the true faith revealed by Christ, the watchdog of orthodoxy, the "restrainer" who protected the doctrines, morals, and laws of the Church. He spent his days clarifying Church teachings and pushing back against modernist heresies.

Cardinal Ratzinger was elected the Pope in AD 2005, assuming the name Pope Benedict XVI. Although he had accepted the developments of Vatican II in general, he nonetheless exerted great labor holding back the raging river of modernism rushing against the Church. Moral, doctrinal, and liturgical innovations threatened to transform the Catholic Church into something entirely removed from its traditional and magisterial roots. Benedict stood in the way, fighting to promote an interpretation of Vatican II consistent with the ancient Church. He tried to preserve the custom of the traditional Mass, precisely to retain the doctrines and praxis of ancient Christianity.

But he was one man, worn down by weariness. After thirty-two years of defending the Church, a wolf in sheep's clothing, a false prophet, Cardinal Bergoglio waited in the wings and panted for the chair of Saint Peter. Benedict, sadly, finally resigned. His resignation in AD 2013 suggests a type of "removal" from office. Further, his death on December 31, 2022, sealed the removal of his restraining moral presence within the walls of the Vatican. With Benedict's restraining influence cut loose, the new Pope Francis could transform the Church as he wished, but only enough as God's permissive will would allow.

Pope Francis would use the Council of Vatican II as the primary pressure point of change. He would lead the Great Apostasy by demanding the Church's absolute conformity to the radical, liberal, modernist interpretation of the Council, henceforth pushed as the official and only valid interpretation of the conciliar documents. The Church would split into two, but not an even split. Most believers would remain in the false Church of the "Catacomb Pact." A surviving remnant would flee underground.

Perhaps Saint Paul's teaching regarding the Great Apostasy and the Antichrist may shed light on the state of the Catholic Church today.

In II Thessalonians 2:6, the grammatical structure of the Greek shows that the "restrainer" is either an entity or a person, depending on the perspective of consideration. The way the sentence is written, the "restrainer" is both. As such, the "restrainer" is a "law-sustaining-power" and a person besides. Traditionally, the "restrainer" was often viewed as either the Roman Empire or the Roman emperor. While this notion provides a helpful way forward, it is nonetheless a non-magisterial interpretation, leaving wiggle room for theological speculation. Accordingly, the "restrainer" could be a person and that same person's official position or office that functions as a gatekeeper of the law. The "restrainer," as both Empire and Emperor, fits this viewpoint.

The Old Testament's "Giver of the Law," Moses, demonstrates an ancient type of "restrainer." As a person and a divinely assigned authority, he holds back whatever evil might befall a potentially lawless nation. Moses laid down the law, orally promulgated it, wrote it as an unfailing way of life, and legislated the discipline and enforcement of it for the preservation of the *Ekklesia*. He and his authoritative "office" of the law testified to the world of a special God who chose his own special people. Moses offers us an early, veiled archetype of Saint Paul's "restrainer." How so? Imagine, after the rescue through the Red Sea, if Moses had been removed from establishing and overseeing the law. Lawlessness would have destroyed the chosen people. A "restrainer" to prevent the corruption of the chosen people was necessary.

Moreover, the Great Apostasy and lawlessness of the Antichrist manifest anarchy, chaos, and rebellion of a moral and doctrinal kind. The lawlessness of the Antichrist is about forcing moral depravity and imposing ways of thought and belief in opposition to Christ's revelation. The authority and person of the "restrainer" then would be the protector of Christ's moral laws and doctrinal truths.

After pondering recent Church history, reflecting on the archetype of Moses, and probing the ancient supposition of a Roman Emperor holding back lawlessness, I believe that the "restrainer" is the Roman Pontiff of the Roman Catholic Church, inseparably linked with his divinely appointed papal office to uphold the law and proclaim the truth. More specifically, the "restrainer" would have been Pope Benedict XVI.

Several considerations suggest this possible conclusion: 1. It's highly probable that the "restrainer" and the Great Apostasy refer to the Church founded by Jesus Christ, which is the Catholic Church. 2. The Pope represents divinely delegated authority. Yet, he's also the inheritor of Roman jurisprudence, which still imprints its legal modality in the governing apparatus of the papal office. This papal characteristic reflects the ancient

Fathers' sense of the "restrainer" as a Roman emperor. 3. The lifetime mission and placement of Pope Benedict XVI reflect the role of a "restrainer," holding the enemies of the Church at bay. 4. Recent Church history also shows an unprecedented era of Church lawlessness caused by Benedict's absence and the assumption of power by Pope Francis. 5. Truly, the resignation of Benedict reflects a coerced historic event best described as a "removal" with calamitous consequences for the Church. 6. Pope Benedict XVI's removal caused the rise of a heretical Pope who is now attempting to crush magisterial believers and erect a false Church disconnected from the ancient Church of Jesus Christ. 7. This false Church is fashioned according to the ideals, values, ways of thinking, and beliefs of the Antichrist. With the removal of the "restrainer," we are now entering into the Great Apostasy. The appearance of the Antichrist will soon arrive as lawlessness peaks.

In summary, the state of the Catholic Church is complex. Notwithstanding its indestructible nature guaranteed by the prophecy of Jesus Christ, it survives wounded, suffering from an accelerated state of corruption. The sacred sacraments, magisterial teachings, and holy souls endure, although under attack. The Church teeters on the tip of the Great Apostasy. The underlying historical facts of its corruption and satanic infiltration are certain. At the same time, my personal interpretation of the facts and scriptural speculations are welcome to varied viewpoints.

The Catholic Bible: Threshold of the Church

The study of ancient Bible context has swept us against the aged and scuffed doors of the Catholic institution. It's essential then to make further critical distinctions. We have already underlined the continuity between the primitive and modern Catholic institution. The continuous line of apostolic succession of Popes and bishops traced to the Apostles supports this unbroken endurance. Further, we explained that the founding of the Church is demonstrable by a careful reading of the entire Gospels and Acts and is not only reliant on Matthew 16:17-19.

We then distinguished the multiple influences of the Church's development (the good, bad, and ugly) throughout the centuries. Finally, we stressed the demonic powers aimed at unrelentingly destroying the Church from the beginning. Truly, the greater the good and the more salvific an entity, respectively, the more determinedly Satan and his minions pursue the destruction or neutralization of that holy fount of salvation.

Observe the state of the Jewish religion during the time of Christ. It contained the few holy, the sea of lukewarm, and the wicked bureaucracy that manipulated the crucifixion of Christ. This threefold grouping mirrors the present state of the Catholic Church. Finally, today's partly dysfunctional Church shoulders the cross and staggers on the path of her passion and crucifixion. The blindside of the resurrection awaits, covered by a mysterious veil at present.

Why so much fuss about understanding the Church better? Some may begrudgingly acknowledge the ancient Catholic Church as the parent of Scripture but prefer to race ahead beyond the implications of history. However, if the Catholic Church is the true Church founded by God, and if this same Church still exists today, and if Christ founded only one Church, and if the Church established by Christ was meant for the salvation of all souls, including mine, where does that leave me? This is the importance of the question.

Once known, in good conscience, I have little choice but to embrace the truth, whatever it may be, wherever it may lead. No doubt, each person walks at his own pace as he seeks to grasp the truth. Sharp, unbiased minds perceive truth quickly; bleeding souls, nursing traumas, discover paradigm-breaking truths only at a snail's pace. Yet, the blinding light of God's grace can cut through any ignorance instantaneously.

The Bible and the Catholic Church go together, just as a parent and child go together. They live together. They love each other. They complement each other. They serve each other. They suffer with each other. They dwell in the same home and rejoice together. If I choose one, the choice of the other is implied.

But some may say that a child may be virtuous and a parent evil; better to welcome the child and cut off the parent. Believing strongly in the supremacy of private inspiration, this is the worn presumption of the Protestant revolution. Abandon the parent; claim the child. But Jesus promised his presence in the Church he founded until the end of time: "The gates of hell shall not prevail against it." (Matthew 16:18) Scripture endures; the Church endures, still holding the scriptures it wrote, canonized, and transmitted to the future. The revelation of Christ is meant to be received in the context of this pairing of scripture and the Church. Both enrich us. Both enrich each other. Both preserve each other.

If God inspired the thousands of Christian denominations, why would He come to earth to establish one Church that would absolutely corrupt? If so, why promise that his Church would withstand the powers of hell when it wouldn't? Would God break such a promise? Isn't God's divine providence capable of founding a Church that could withstand the wear and tear of time, besides the onslaught of the devil?

And if the Church almost immediately, utterly failed, why wait over a thousand years to correct the corruption with individually inspired Protestants? Why inspire different Protestant founders with doctrines that contradict each other? Does that really fix anything? Doesn't it just create more uncertainty about God? In truth, the vast assortment of Christian denominations results in turning Christianity into a smorgasbord of ideas, encouraging participants to scoop up beliefs according to personal tastes. Can God make a mistake and contradict himself? Does Protestantism ultimately rest upon a God who contradicts himself —observable by the contradictory inspirations of thousands of denominations? Can diametrically opposing doctrines both be inspired by God?

These are only a few questions that deserve the mind's pursuit. It makes more common sense, and Biblical sense besides, to stand firm upon the one Church founded by Jesus that still exists today. This one Church did suffer corruption throughout the ages (Paul's letters introduce this reality), but not to the point of self-dissolution by demonic powers. Furthermore, the proliferation of denominations represents a historic breaking-off or gradual defragmentation of the Catholic Church itself.

History repeats itself. This same kind of doctrinal defragmentation happened during the first centuries of the Church, as various heresies rose and ripped away believers from the one true Catholic Church. Accordingly, Protestantism is not a sign of Church renewal but Church corruption. At the same time, this is not to mean that Protestants are void of the mystery of God's love at work in their midst. God is certainly not restricted from nurturing supernatural wonders out of protests. He does it all the time, institutionally and personally.)

If our overall study of the ancient context of the Bible has resulted in a fresh view of the Catholic Church for some readers, I would like to offer some advice. I'd like to share a few insights on a way forward for devoted Christian Bible readers. Yet, my advice applies equally to infrequent Catholic Bible readers too. Regardless, if your Bible is either dog-eared or draped in cobwebs, my advice starts with an encouragement not to fear the beckoning of Jesus.

Stand before the foreboding doors of the Catholic Church and consider the parents of your Bible. Whisper to Jesus: "My dear friend, what do you want of me?" Take his hand and gently push. Crack the door. Take a small step forward. Do not be afraid to peer inside.

This glimpse will be less daunting than perhaps imagined. Start with the foundation you are familiar with: the Bible. Open the Bible and read. Read, knowing that the primary authors of this book were the Father, Son, and Holy Spirit. But there's a nuance. Read, knowing too that, apart from the question of the authorship of Hebrews, the secondary human authors of the New Testament were Catholic bishops.

Historical research and traditions have confirmed this. Let this sink into your mind. You will never read the New Testament the same again. (Note: Earlier, we explained the history of the term "Catholic." By the end of the first century, the new term was applied to the already existing Church founded by Christ.)

Peter, of course, was the first Bishop of Antioch and later the principal Bishop of Rome. Peter and Paul shared recognition as dual founders of Christianity in the city of Rome. Paul had consecrated Timothy a bishop, which indicates his position as a bishop. It has always been held from ancient practice that only a bishop can consecrate another person a bishop. Linus, Cletus, and Clement served as bishops in Rome, too, and worked alongside both Peter and Paul. It was Peter who had consecrated Linus, Cletus, and Clement bishops.

Precisely as Apostles: Matthew, John, James, and Jude were also Catholic bishops. They certainly had the power to consecrate other bishops, as tradition substantiates. Following his missionary work in Judaea and Persia, Matthew was the Bishop of Ethiopia. The Apostle John, after returning from exile on the island of Patmos and writing the Apocalypse, traveled throughout Asia Minor (modern-day Turkey), ordaining and consecrating numerous bishops for the spiritual needs of the dramatically expanding Church. James was the first bishop of Jerusalem. The Apostle Jude had preached the Gospel in Samaria, Judea, Idumaea, Syria, Mesopotamia, and Libya, settling as the Bishop of Armenia.

According to Orthodox tradition, Luke, the most extensive writer of the New Testament, became the Bishop of Thebes in Boeotia (modern-day Turkey). Mark was the founding Catholic Bishop of Alexandria, Egypt.

Accordingly, the New Testament is a Catholic production. It was written by literary-capable Catholic bishops inspired by the Holy Spirit for the early needs of the Church. The primary need was to teach fresh converts. The Bible was especially used within the context of the Catholic Mass. Yet, God certainly had much more in mind. The Catholic Bible is a divine instrument through which the Holy Spirit speaks to the reader. It is a gift of the Catholic Church for the world, including you, until the end of time.

It will not take long, led by the Spirit, to view the interpretation of scripture through Catholic eyes. As Catholic bishops had placed the Bible in your hands, desiring your salvation, their successors remained engaged in helping the reader understand the written word. These successor bishops remained the official teachers of the Church.

Suppose you want to learn as much as you can about something. Let's say you want to understand the sport of baseball. Seeking sound information on the matter, you go to the official baseball rule book, consult experienced coaches and players, and try your hand at the sport. Now, you are in a genuine learning environment regarding the issue. Strong emotions shape ideas. This can be a positive or negative persuasion in the learning process. So, you sensibly put away the books that viciously attack the sport of baseball.

Something similar happens when a person wants to interpret the Bible correctly. Rather than read biased, modern commentaries, it's more productive to excavate the unfiltered, historic, ancient letters, documents, or commentaries that touch upon this or that passage in scripture. Read the Bible and ask for the help of the Holy Spirit. But also ask for help from the successor bishops of the Bible. Practically speaking, such private consultation boils down to learning what Apostolic Fathers taught, how early Christians lived, and what early Church councils clarified.

A few tools may help along the journey. The Ignatius Study Bible offers much Catholic insight regarding scripture. The official Catechism of the Catholic Church (CCC) does the same. Much better, clear, old, question & answer, catechisms exist. The testimonies of Christian ministers who had become Catholic are particularly enlightening. Such truth-seekers had their own rough beginnings as they struggled with the inner world of prejudice, but God's grace happily enlightened them. Saul once knew a lot of theology, but it didn't properly piece together until he was shaken and blinded by his humbling encounter with Jesus Christ on the road to persecuting the Catholics.

CONCLUSION

Welcome to the Authentic Bible and Church

The purpose of this book is to reconnect Catholics and Christians with the ancient scriptures –birthed by the Catholic Church. This study confirms the early liturgical usage of the Alexandrian Septuagint and the New Testament writings by the Apostolic Church. It also explains the pertinent historical context that surrounds the production and canonization of the ancient seventy-three-book Bible.

There are inherent weaknesses and strengths regarding how the material is presented. As academic standards go, the weakness is that it is not a genuine scholarly advancement. Copious references, footnotes, exhaustive proofs, and a professor's highbrow pedigree are noticeably absent.

However, the strength of the presentation paradoxically rests upon the weakness. The book's simple approach fits the easy-reading needs of the average "blue-collar" believer. It grabs hold of complex content, simplifies it, and orientates the reader to an ancient paradigm that once defined Biblical usage. The book then replants the guideposts for using the Bible, led by the wisdom of the Church that produced it. It is a book that belongs in the hands of devout believers, less so in the hands of atheistic scholars.

The first book review, from a voracious reader and veteran Christian pastor, nailed the book's methodology. Pastor Williams wrote to me: "You have a depth of theological and historical perspective written in ways that can engage a non-academic reader. You draw the reader into deeper understandings than are commonly offered." As such, the book offers the ancient understanding of the Bible to the third millennial reader floating in space, woefully detached from the safe anchorage of genuine history.

Chapter by chapter, the progression of ideas led to an inevitable conclusion. If the reader would embrace the Bible, with its full ancient context, he must welcome the Bible as a member of the Church that created it. Simply put, embracing the Bible implies reading the official Catholic version of the Bible and hearing the scriptures read and explained at the official liturgical celebrations of the Catholic Church. The reader could get no closer to the original scriptures than by walking this path.

Sadly, this is why chapter sixteen became necessary. If the story of the Bible concludes with the implication of joining the Catholic Church, evil must be explained. There must be an upfront and honest presentation of the present-day state of the Catholic Church. Accordingly, the book fairly wraps up with an explanation of the nature of Church corruption. In short, the true Church founded by Jesus would always be a primary demonic target throughout history.

My confidence is that Jesus Christ is present as you read each line. May the Holy Spirit make you pause, pray, and ponder as he urges. May you rediscover the Bible in a brand-new light from the perspective of Catholic Bishops who toiled to give us the power of the oral Gospel etched on papyrus ages past.

APPENDIX

Jesus Christ's Divinity in the New Testament

God incarnated on the earth two thousand years ago. The greatest event in human history! The creator entered his creation —to rescue us from sin. Throughout the ages, the identity of Jesus Christ faded. Finally, encyclopedic scholars categorize him together with Muhammad, Budda, and Hindu gurus. They think he's just a human being, like any other.

Vain "theologians" tickle the ears of the ignorant with faithless theories about Jesus. They speculate: He's a prophet, religious teacher, monk, magician, revolutionary, angel, future time traveler, or far-advanced evolved alien. It's all nonsense and tragically sad.

Our demented world plunges into deeper chaos by the day. It has no chance of surviving unless we return to the divine person of Jesus Christ. He is the foundation not only of salvation but of sanity. It's critical to inform the conscience with this ageless truth.

There are numerous ways to prove the divinity of Jesus Christ. For our purposes, it will suffice to simply call to mind the many assertions of Christ's divinity in the New Testament.

References to Jesus Christ as God's own Son abound in scripture. Of course, genuine sonship, neither in an analogical, rhetorical, or poetical sense, affirms a being who shares the same nature as the Father. As such, if a father is human, so the son is human. If the Father is God, so the Son is God:

At the announcement of his incarnation, with no earthly father, Jesus is called the Son of God:

'Behold, you will conceive in your womb and bear a son, and you shall name him Jesus. He will be great and will be called Son of the Most High, and the Lord God will give him the throne of David his father, and he will rule over the house of Jacob forever, and of his kingdom there will be no end.' But Mary said to the angel, 'How can this be, since I have no relations with a man?' And the angel said to her in reply, 'The holy Spirit will come upon you, and the power of the Most High will overshadow you. Therefore, the child to be born will be called holy, the Son of God.' (Luke 1:31-35)

Demons confessed with submissiveness that Jesus Christ was the Son of God: "And wherever the unclean spirits saw him, they fell down before him and cried out, 'You are the Son of God.'" (Mark 3:11) Demons cried out: "What have you to do with us, Son of God?" (Matthew 8:29)

John the Baptist identified Jesus as "the Son of God." (John 1:34) After walking on water and bidding Peter to do the same, the Apostles venerated Jesus: "After they got into the boat, the wind died down. Those who were in the boat did him homage, saying, 'Truly, you are the Son of God.'" (Matthew 14:32-33) The wonder of the Apostles is also evident when Jesus rebuked a violent storm on the sea and immediate calm descended: "The men were amazed and said, 'What sort of a man is this, whom even the winds and sea obey?" (Matthew 8:27)

Twice, at Jesus' baptism and transfiguration, a voice from heaven audibly announced for all to hear, "This is my beloved Son, with whom I am well pleased." (Matthew 3:16-17; 17:5)

Jesus Christ, the Son of God, is exalted above the angels: "Let all the angels of God worship him." (Hebrews 1:6) John attributes Jesus' glory to His divine Sonship:

In the beginning was the Word, and the Word was with God, and the Word was God….And the Word became flesh and dwelt among us, full of grace and truth; we have beheld his glory, glory as of the only Son from the Father. (John 1:1,4)

Soon after Saul's conversion, he boldly proclaimed in the synagogues that Jesus is "the Son of God." (Acts 9:20) Paul quickly learned this core belief of Christianity and almost immediately began to preach it with power and eloquence. The Jews soon conspired to kill him!

The New Testament also abounds with assertions of the Son of God's pre-existence before incardinating on earth. It repeats that God the Father "sent his only Son to save us." (John 3:16; Romans 8:3; Galatians 4:4)

John quotes Jesus, who explains this "sending." "No one has gone up to heaven except the one who has come down from heaven…." (John 3:13) "I came down from heaven not to do my own will but the will of the one who sent me." (John 6:38) "What if you were to see the Son of Man ascending to where he was before?" (John 6:62) "I came from the Father and have come into the world. Now I am leaving the world and going back to the Father." (John 16:28) The Son of God clearly existed with his Father in heaven before assuming human flesh on earth and receiving the name of Jesus.

Jesus reveals the mystery of the Son's eternal existence with further details: "I saw Satan fall like lightning from heaven." (Luke 10:18) Remember, the creation of the angels and Lucifer's rebellion took place before Adam and Eve. The Son of God saw it all.

Speaking to the Pharisees, Jesus reveals another detail: "Amen. Amen, I say to you, before Abraham came to be, I AM.' So, they picked up stones to throw at him." (John 8:58-59) Abraham was born two thousand years before Jesus was born. Jesus both assigns the sacred name of God to himself and claims his own pre-existence before Abraham. The Jews understood the meaning of Jesus' packed statement. They immediately began his execution for the sin of blasphemy because Jesus declared himself to be God.

Way back then, claiming to be God was a sin punishable by death. Jesus stood before Pilate, and the Jews hollered for a crucifixion. Seeking to resist their appeal, "Pilate said to them, 'Take him yourselves and crucify him. I find no guilt in him.' The Jews answered, 'We have a law, and according to that law, he ought to die because he made himself the Son of God." (John 19:6-7)

The night before the crucifixion, anticipating his victorious death and resurrection, Jesus shared a telling prayer: "And now, Father, glorify me in your own presence with the glory that I had with you before the world existed." (John 17:5)

After years of reflection and the grace of clarity, Paul further spells out the early belief in the divinity of Jesus Christ:

For in him were created all things in heaven and on earth, the visible and the invisible, whether thrones or dominions or principalities or powers; all things were created through him and for him. He is before all things, and in him all things hold together. (Colossians 1:15-17)

Jesus clarifies that the monotheistic God of the Jews is actually their divine Father. He goes on to reveal himself as this same Father's only begotten Son. He then teaches about his relationship with the Father: "The one who sent me is with me." (John 8:29) "The Father is in me, and I am in the Father." (John 10:38) "Whoever has seen me has seen the Father." (John 14:11) "The Father and I are one." (John 10:30) This proclamation provoked the Jews to stone Jesus to death "…for blasphemy. You, a man, are making yourself God." (John 10:33)

Further testifying to the divinity of Christ, the New Testament readily accepts the worship of Jesus as proper and praiseworthy. Remember the man born blind? "'I do believe Lord,' and he worshiped him." (John 9:38) "Those who were in the boat did him homage." (Matthew 14:33)

Jesus understood very well that God alone may be worshipped. Recall the conversation between Satan and Jesus:

Then the devil took him up to a very high mountain, and showed him all the kingdoms of the world in their magnificence, and said to him, 'All these I shall give to you if you will prostrate yourself and worship me.' At this, Jesus said to him, 'Get away, Satan! It is written: 'The Lord, your God, shall you worship, and him alone shall you serve.' Then the devil left him, and, behold, angels came and ministered to him. (Matthew 4:8-11)

Yet, Jesus never objected to others worshipping him. He welcomed it as proper. "When they saw him, they worshipped…." (Matthew 28:17) "They approached, embraced his feet, and did him homage." (Matthew 28:9) "As he blessed them, he parted from them and was taken up to heaven. They did him homage…." (Luke 24:51-52) Relating his revelation, John describes the worship of Jesus Christ as proper of all creatures. (Rev. 4:9-11; 5:12-14; 7:11-17)

Jesus explains that whatever is due to God the Father is equally due to God the Son: "…all may honor the Son just as they honor the Father. Whoever does not honor the Son does not honor the Father who sent him." (John 5:22-23)

Although the many miracles of Jesus indicate his divinity, the ultimate miracle of his resurrection affirms it beyond doubt. Christ's raising of three persons foreshadows his own resurrection. He raised the widow's son in Nain. (Luke 7:15) He raised the twelve-year-old daughter of Jairus. (Mark 5:42) And he raised his friend, Lazarus, who had been in the tomb already for four days. (John 11:44) John explains Jesus' power to resurrect anyone he wishes. "As the Father raises the dead and gives them life, so also the Son gives life to whom he will...." (John 5:21-22) The Son's power to resurrect anyone —also applies to himself.

During his ministry, Jesus revealed that he would die and resurrect. Sometimes, the references were veiled with metaphors. The scribes and Pharisees asked for a sign of his identity and mission. "An evil and unfaithful generation seeks a sign, but no sign will be given it except the sign of Jonah the prophet. Just as Jonah was in the belly of the whale three days and three nights, so will the Son of man be in the heart of the earth three days and three nights." (Matthew 12:39-40)

Christ also used another metaphor to hint at his resurrection: "Destroy this temple, and in three days I will raise it up." (John 2:19) John had to add a precious detail: "He was speaking about the temple of his body." (John 2:21)

But at times, too, Jesus spoke clearly to his dearest friends: "Behold, we are going up to Jerusalem, and the Son of Man will be handed over to the chief priests and the scribes, and they will condemn him to death. And hand him over to the Gentiles to be mocked and scourged and crucified, and he will be raised on the third day." (Matthew 20:18-19)

At last, Jesus clearly states that he raises himself from the dead. Only God has the power over death. Most eloquently, Jesus is claiming divinity:

I am the good shepherd, and I know mine and mine know me, just as the Father knows me and I know the Father; and I will lay down my life for the sheep.... This is why the Father loves me, because I lay down my life in order to take it up again. No one takes it from me, but I lay it down on my own. I have power to lay it down, and power to take it up again. This command I have received from my Father." (John 10:14-15; 17-18)

Made in the USA
Columbia, SC
19 November 2024

46429401R00135